CRIME AND LAW ENFORCEMENT ISSUES

CRIMINAL JUSTICE, LAW ENFORCEMENT AND CORRECTIONS

Additional books in this series can be found on Nova's website under the Series tab.

Additional E-books in this series can be found on Nova's website under the E-books tab.

CRIME AND LAW ENFORCEMENT ISSUES

JAMES E. HIRSCH
EDITOR

Nova Science Publishers, Inc.
New York

Copyright © 2011 by Nova Science Publishers, Inc.

For permission to use material from this book please contact us:
Telephone 631-231-7269; Fax 631-231-8175
Web Site: http://www.novapublishers.com

NOTICE TO THE READER

The Publisher has taken reasonable care in the preparation of this book, but makes no expressed or implied warranty of any kind and assumes no responsibility for any errors or omissions. No liability is assumed for incidental or consequential damages in connection with or arising out of information contained in this book. The Publisher shall not be liable for any special, consequential, or exemplary damages resulting, in whole or in part, from the readers' use of, or reliance upon, this material. Any parts of this book based on government reports are so indicated and copyright is claimed for those parts to the extent applicable to compilations of such works.

Independent verification should be sought for any data, advice or recommendations contained in this book. In addition, no responsibility is assumed by the publisher for any injury and/or damage to persons or property arising from any methods, products, instructions, ideas or otherwise contained in this publication.

This publication is designed to provide accurate and authoritative information with regard to the subject matter covered herein. It is sold with the clear understanding that the Publisher is not engaged in rendering legal or any other professional services. If legal or any other expert assistance is required, the services of a competent person should be sought. FROM A DECLARATION OF PARTICIPANTS JOINTLY ADOPTED BY A COMMITTEE OF THE AMERICAN BAR ASSOCIATION AND A COMMITTEE OF PUBLISHERS.

Additional color graphics may be available in the e-book version of this book.

LIBRARY OF CONGRESS CATALOGING-IN-PUBLICATION DATA

Crime and law enforcement issues / editors, James E. Hirsch.
    p. cm. -- (Criminal justice, law enforcement and corrections)
  Includes bibliographical references and index.
  ISBN 978-1-61122-877-9 (hardcover : alk. paper)
  1. Criminal justice, Administration of--United States. 2. Law
enforcement--United States. I. Hirsch, James E.
  HV9950.C7268 2011
  364.973--dc22

2010044711

Published by Nova Science Publishers, Inc. † *New York*

CONTENTS

PREFACE

This book presents and discusses information in the study of criminal justice and law enforcement. Topics discussed include capital punishment; juvenile justice; the use of DNA in cold cases; statutes of limitation in federal criminal cases; the illicit drug market in Taiwan and leadership in police organizations.

Chapter 1 - In 1995, the National Institute of Justice (NIJ) began research that would attempt to identify how often DNA had exonerated wrongfully convicted defendants. After extensive study, NIJ published the report Convicted by Juries, Exonerated by Science: Case Studies in the Use of DNA Evidence to Establish Innocence After Trial, which presents case studies of 28 inmates for whom DNA analysis was exculpatory.

Chapter 2 - With the passage of P.L. 103-322, the Violent Crime Control and Law Enforcement Act of 1994, the federal death penalty became available as a possible punishment for a substantial number of new and existing civilian offenses. On April 24, 1996, the Antiterrorism and Effective Death Penalty Act of 1996 made further modifications and additions to the list of federal capital crimes. On June 25, 2002, P.L. 107-197, the Terrorist Bombings Convention Implementation Act of 2002, added another capital crime to the United States Code. The Intelligence Reform and Terrorism Prevention Act of 2004, P.L. 108-458, enacted December 17, 2004, included provisions which impacted or expanded some of the existing death penalty provisions. This report lists the current federal capital offenses and summarizes the procedures for federal civilian death penalty cases.

Chapter 3 - As more attention is being focused on juvenile offenders, some question whether the justice system is dealing with this population appropriately. Since the late 1960s, the juvenile justice system has undergone significant modifications resulting from U.S. Supreme Court decisions, changes in federal and state law, and the growing belief that juveniles were increasingly involved in more serious and violent crimes. Consequently, at both the federal and states levels, the juvenile justice system has shifted from a mostly rehabilitative system to a more punitive one, with serious ramifications for juvenile offenders. Despite this shift, juveniles are generally not afforded the panoply of rights afforded to adult criminal defendants. The U.S. Constitution requires that juveniles receive many of the features of an adult criminal trial, including notice of charges, right to counsel, privilege against self-incrimination, right to confrontation and cross-examination, proof beyond a reasonable doubt, and double jeopardy. However, in *McKeiver v. Pennsylvania*, the Court held that juveniles do not have a fundamental right to a jury trial during adjudicatory proceedings.

The Sixth Amendment explicitly guarantees the right to an impartial jury trial in criminal prosecutions. In *Duncan v. Louisiana*, the U.S. Supreme Court held that this right is fundamental and guaranteed by the Due Process Clause of the Fourteenth Amendment. However, the Court has since limited its holding in *Duncan* to adult defendants by stating that the right to a jury trial is not constitutionally required for juveniles in juvenile court proceedings. Some argue that because the Court has determined that jury trials are not constitutionally required for juvenile adjudications, courts should not treat or consider juvenile adjudications in subsequent criminal proceedings. In addition, some argue that the use of non-jury juvenile adjudications in subsequent criminal proceedings violates due process guarantees, because juvenile justice and adult criminal proceedings are fundamentally different.

Has the juvenile justice system changed in such a manner that the Supreme Court should revisit the question of jury trials in juvenile adjudications? Are the procedural safeguards in the juvenile justice system sufficient to ensure their reliable use for sentence enhancement purposes in adult criminal proceedings? To help address these questions, this report provides a brief background on the purpose of the juvenile system and discusses procedural due process protections provided by the Court for juveniles during adjudicatory hearings. It also discusses the Court's emphasis on the jury's role in criminal proceedings and will be updated as events warrant.

Chapter 4 - A statute of limitations dictates the time period within which a legal proceeding must begin. The purpose of a statute of limitations in a criminal case is to ensure the prompt prosecution of criminal charges and thereby spare the accused of the burden of having to defend against stale charges after memories may have faded or evidence is lost.

There is no statute of limitations for federal crimes punishable by death, nor for certain federal crimes of terrorism, nor, since passage of the Adam Walsh Child Protection and Safety Act (P.L. 109-248, H.R. 4472, 2006), for certain federal sex offenses. Prosecution for most other federal crimes must begin within five years of the commitment of the offense. There are exceptions. Some types of crimes are subject to a longer period of limitation; some circumstances suspend or extend the otherwise applicable period of limitation.

Arson, art theft, certain crimes against financial institutions and various immigration offenses all carry statutes of limitation longer than the five year standard. Regardless of the applicable statute of limitations, the period may be extended or the running of the period suspended or tolled under a number of circumstances such as when the accused is a fugitive or when the case involves charges of child abuse, bankruptcy, wartime fraud against the government, or DNA evidence.

Ordinarily, the statute of limitations begins to run as soon as the crime has been completed. Although the federal crime of conspiracy is complete when one of the plotters commits an affirmative act in its name, the period for conspiracies begins with the last affirmative act committed in furtherance of the scheme. Other so-called continuing offenses include various possession crimes and some that impose continuing obligations to register or report.

Limitation-related constitutional challenges arise most often under the Constitution's ex post facto and due process clauses. The federal courts have long held that a statute of limitations may be enlarged retroactively as long as the previously applicable period of limitation has not expired. The Supreme Court recently confirmed that view; the ex post facto proscription precludes legislative revival of an expired period of limitation. Due process condemns pre-indictment delays even when permitted by the statute of limitations if the prosecution wrongfully caused the delay and the accused's defense suffered actual, substantial harm as a consequence.

Chapter 5 - Definition: "Drug crime organization" in this analysis refers to criminal organizations that are engaged in trafficking, transporting, producing and distributing large quantities of drugs in Taiwan. Individual drug dealers and drug users are excluded from this analysis.

Chapter 6 - Posttraumatic life change was investigated in a sample of nonrecent sexual assault survivors. An average of 16 years postassault, most survivors identified positive changes that had resulted from the assault, particularly in the domains of self (e.g., increased assertiveness), spirituality (e.g., spiritual well-being), and empathy (e.g., concern for others' suffering). Negative changes in beliefs about the fairness and safety of the world also were common, however. Controlling for recent life stressors and personality, positive changes were associated with fewer symptoms of depression, anxiety and Post Traumatic Stress Disorder (PTSD) and greater life satisfaction. Self-reported positive changes generally were related to personality, social support, coping, and control appraisals in hypothesized directions. Coping and control appraisals (particularly control over the recovery process) mediated the relations among personality and social support and positive life change.

Chapter 7 - Many police organizations across the United States use traditional written assessments to promote individuals to first line supervisor positions. Written assessments are cost effective. Recent research has shown assessments have shown problems with validity. One specific issue is with attempting to predict a candidate's leadership abilities or behavior. Other research uncovers issues relating to the lack of leadership training for aspiring first line supervisors. First line supervisors have been traditionally viewed as managers rather than leaders. The process has deterred many from applying for promotion within the ranks. This meta-analysis offers insight to the improvement of police promotional process may improve the selection of the right candidate and overall organizational leadership, but also aid in succession planning as well.

Chapter 8 - The primary goal of this study was to identify characteristics of licensed drinking establishments that predict alcohol sales to obviously intoxicated barroom patrons. Of particular interest was the relationship between "secondary servers" of alcohol and irresponsible alcohol service. Relying on a structured observation guide listing a large number of variables believed to be related to irresponsible alcohol service, trained observers spent a total of 444 hours collecting data in 25 licensed drinking establishments in Hoboken, New Jersey. Observations took place at two separate time periods, 7:30pm – 10:30pm and 11:00pm – 2:00am, on Thursday, Friday, and Saturday nights. Ordinary least squares (OLS) regression analyses revealed "number of secondary servers" as the strongest predictor of alcohol service to obviously intoxicated patrons in Hoboken barrooms. Another significant predictor of alcohol service to intoxicated patrons in this study was the presence of "aversive environmental stimuli" within licensed premises, such as excessive heat, smoke, and crowding. Several prevention strategies aimed at reducing irresponsible alcohol service in bars and associated problems with alcohol-related harm are proposed.

Chapter 9 - Many police organizations across the United States promote leadership training to those individuals that are first line supervisor positions. Many departments, however, do not have a true command structure in place. This in turn introduces the basic patrol officer to many leadership situations. Recent research has shown those not of rank do not receive leadership training. One specific issue is with increasing the patrol officers leadership abilities or behavior for situations that face often. Other research uncovers issues relating to the lack of leadership training for not only aspiring first line supervisors but basic patrol as well. First line supervisors have been traditionally viewed as managers rather than leaders. This meta-analysis offers insight to the improvement of police leadership training beginning with the basic police academy curriculum. By doing so, it may improve the overall organizational leadership, but also aid in succession planning as well.

Versions of these chapters were also published in *Journal of Current Issues in Crime, Law and Law Enforcement,* Volume 1, Numbers 1-4, and Volume 2, Numbers 1-4, published by Nova Science Publishers, Inc. They were submitted for appropriate modifications in an effort to encourage wider dissemination of research.

In: Crime and Law Enforcement Issues   ISBN 978-1-61122-877-9
Editor: James E. Hirsch   © 2011 Nova Science Publishers, Inc.

Chapter 1

USING DNA TO SOLVE COLD CASES[*]

Shirley S. Abrahamson, John Ashcroft, Deborah J. Daniels and Sarah V. Hart

U.S. Department of Justice; Office of Justice Programs,
810 Seventh Street N.W.; Washington, DC 20531

NATIONAL COMMISSION ON THE FUTURE OF DNA EVIDENCE

In 1995, the National Institute of Justice (NIJ) began research that would attempt to identify how often DNA had exonerated wrongfully convicted defendants. After extensive study, NIJ published the report Convicted by Juries, Exonerated by Science: Case Studies in the Use of DNA Evidence to Establish Innocence After Trial, which presents case studies of 28 inmates for whom DNA analysis was exculpatory.

On learning of the breadth and scope of the issues related to forensic DNA, the Attorney General asked NIJ to establish the National Commission on the Future of DNA Evidence as a means to examine the most effective use of DNA in the criminal justice system. The Commission was appointed by the NIJ Director and represented the broad spectrum of the criminal justice system. Chaired by the Honorable Shirley S. Abrahamson, Chief Justice of the Wisconsin Supreme Court, the Commission consisted of representatives from the prosecution, the defense bar, law enforcement, the scientific community, the medical examiner community, academia, and victims' rights organizations.

---

[*] Excerpted from http://www.ncjrs.gov/pdffiles1/nij/194197.pdf.

The Commission's charge was to submit recommendations to the Attorney General that will help ensure the best use of DNA as a crimefighting tool and foster its use throughout the entire criminal justice system. Other focal areas for the Commission's consideration included crime scene investigation and evidence collection, laboratory funding, legal issues, and research and development. The Commission's working groups, consisting of commissioners and other experts, researched and examined various topics and reported back to the Commission.

The working groups' reports were submitted to the full Commission for approval, amendment, or further discussion and provided the Commission with background for its recommendations to the Attorney General.

By nature of its representative composition and its use of numerous working groups, the Commission received valuable input from all areas of the criminal justice system. The broad scope of that input enabled the Commission to develop recommendations that both maximize the investigative value of the technology and address the issues raised by its application.

COMMISSION MEMBERS

Chair
The Honorable Shirley S. Abrahamson
Chief Justice
Wisconsin Supreme Court

Members
Dwight E. Adams
Director
Federal Bureau of Investigation
    Laboratory

Jan S. Bashinski
Chief
Bureau of Forensic Services
California Department of Justice
Sacramento, California

George W. Clarke
Deputy District Attorney

San Diego, California

James F. Crow
Professor
Department of Genetics
University of Wisconsin

Lloyd N. Cutler
Wilmer, Cutler and Pickering
Washington, D.C.

Joseph H. Davis
Former Director
Miami-Dade   Medical   Examiner
    Department
Paul B. Ferrara
Director
Division of Forensic Sciences
Commonwealth of Virginia

Norman Gahn
Assistant District Attorney
Milwaukee County, Wisconsin

Terrance W. Gainer
Executive Assistant Chief
Metropolitan Police Department
Washington, D.C.

Terry G. Hillard
Superintendent of Police
Chicago Police Department
Chicago, Illinois

Aaron D. Kennard
Sheriff
Salt Lake County, Utah

Philip Reilly
Interleukin Genetics
Waltham, Massachusetts

Ronald S. Reinstein
Associate Presiding Judge
Superior Court of Arizona
Maricopa County, Arizona

Darrell L. Sanders
Chief
Frankfort Police Department
Frankfort, Illinois

Barry C. Scheck
Professor

Cardozo Law School
New York, New York

Michael Smith
Professor
University of Wisconsin Law School

Jeffrey E. Thoma
Public Defender
Mendocino County, California

Kathryn M. Turman
Director
Office for Victim Assistance
Federal Bureau of Investigation

William Webster
Milbank, Tweed, Hadley and McCloy
Washington, D.C.

James R. Wooley
Baker and Hostetler
Cleveland, Ohio

Commission staff
Christopher H. Asplen
Executive Director

Lisa Forman
Deputy Director

Robin W. Jones
Executive Assistant

Crime Scene Investigation Working Group

The Crime Scene Investigation Working Group is a multidisciplinary group of criminal justice professionals from across the United States who represent both urban and rural jurisdictions. Working group members and contributors were recommended and selected for their experience in the area of criminal investigation and evidence collection from the standpoints of law enforcement, prosecution, defense, the forensic laboratory, and victim assistance.

DNA has proven to be a powerful tool in the fight against crime. DNA evidence can identify suspects, convict the guilty, and exonerate the innocent. Throughout the Nation, criminal justice professionals are discovering that advancements in DNA technology are breathing new life into old, cold, or unsolved criminal cases. Evidence that was previously unsuitable for DNA testing because a biological sample was too small or degraded may now yield a DNA profile. Development of the Combined DNA Index System (CODIS) at the State and national levels enables law enforcement to aid investigations by effectively and efficiently identifying suspects and linking serial crimes to each other. The National Commission on the Future of DNA Evidence made clear, however, that we must dedicate more resources to empower law enforcement to use this technology quickly and effectively.

Using DNA to Solve Cold Cases is intended for use by law enforcement and other criminal justice professionals who have the responsibility for reviewing and investigating unsolved cases. This report will provide basic information to assist agencies in the complex process of case review with a specific emphasis on using DNA evidence to solve previously unsolvable crimes. Although DNA is not the only forensic tool that can be valuable to unsolved case investigations, advancements in DNA technology and the success of DNA database systems have inspired law enforcement agencies throughout the country to reevaluate cold cases for DNA evidence. As law enforcement professionals progress through investigations, however, they should keep in mind the array of other technology advancements, such as improved ballistics and fingerprint databases, which may substantially advance a case beyond its original level.

Chair
Terrance W. Gainer

Executive Assistant Chief
Metropolitan Police Department

Washington, D.C.

Members

Susan Ballou
Office of Law Enforcement Standards
National Institute of Standards and
Technology
Gaithersburg, Maryland

Jan S. Bashinski
Chief
Bureau of Forensic Services
California Department of Justice
Sacramento, California

Sue Brown
INOVA Fairfax Hospital
SANE Program
Falls Church, Virginia

Lee Colwell
Director
Criminal Justice Institute
University of Arkansas System
Little Rock, Arkansas

Thomas J. Cronin
Chief
City of Coeur d'Alene Police
   Department
Coeur d'Alene, Idaho

Terry G. Hillard
Superintendent of Police

Chicago Police Department
Chicago, Illinois

Mark Johnsey
Master Sergeant (Ret.)
Division of Forensic Services
Illinois State Police Department
Springfield, Illinois

Christopher Plourd
Attorney at Law
San Diego, California

Darrell L. Sanders
Chief
Frankfort Police Department
Frankfort, Illinois

Clay Strange
Assistant District Attorney
Travis County District Attorney's
   Office
Austin, Texas

Contributors

Cheryl May
Assistant Director
Forensic Sciences Education Center
Little Rock, Arkansas

William McIntyre
Detective Sergeant (Ret.)
Atlantic County Prosecutor's Office
Homicide Unit
Hammonton, New Jersey

INTRODUCTION

In 1990, a series of brutal attacks on elderly victims occurred in Goldsboro, North Carolina, by an unknown individual dubbed the "Night Stalker." During one such attack in March, an elderly woman was brutally raped and almost murdered. Her daughter's early arrival home was the only thing that saved the woman's life. The suspect fled, leaving behind materials intended to burn the residence and the victim in an attempt to conceal the crime. In July 1990, another elderly woman was brutally raped and murdered in her home. Three months later, a third elderly woman was raped and stabbed to death. Her husband was also murdered. Their house was burned in an attempt to cover up the crime, but fire/rescue personnel pulled the bodies from the house before it was engulfed in flames.

When DNA analysis was conducted on biological evidence collected from vaginal swabs from each victim, authorities concluded that the same perpetrator had committed all three crimes. However, there was no suspect.

For 10 years, both the Goldsboro Police Department and the crime laboratory refused to forget about these cases. With funding from the National Institute of Justice, the crime laboratory retested the biological evidence in all three cases with newer DNA technology and entered the DNA profiles into North Carolina's DNA database. This would allow the DNA profile developed from the crime scene evidence to be compared to thousands of convicted offender profiles already in the database.

In April 2001, a "cold hit" was made to the perpetrator's convicted offender DNA profile in the database. The perpetrator had been convicted of shooting into an occupied dwelling, an offense that requires inclusion in the North Carolina DNA database. The suspect was brought into custody for questioning and was served with a search warrant to obtain a sample of his blood. That sample was analyzed and compared to the crime scene evidence, thereby confirming the DNA database match. When confronted with the DNA evidence, the suspect confessed to all three crimes.

Mark Nelson, special agent in charge of the North Carolina State Crime Laboratory, said, "Even though these terrible crimes occurred more than 10 years ago, we never gave up hope of solving them one day."

Every law enforcement department throughout the country has unsolved cases that could be solved through recent advancements in DNA technology. Today, investigators who understand which evidence may yield a DNA profile can identify a suspect in ways previously seen only on television. Evidence invisible to the naked eye can be the key to solving a residential burglary, sexual assault, or murder. The saliva on the stamp of a stalker's threatening letter, the perspiration on a rapist's mask, or the skin cells shed on the ligature of a strangled child may hold the key to solving a crime.

In Austin, Texas, for example, an investigator knowledgeable about DNA technology was able to solve the rape of a local college student. Having read about the potential for obtaining DNA evidence from the ligature used to strangle a victim, the investigator requested DNA testing on the phone cord used to choke the victim in his case. He realized that in the course of choking someone, enough force and friction is applied to the rope or cord that the perpetrator's skins cells may rub off his hands and be left on the ligature.

The investigator's request paid off in an unanticipated way. In spite of the attacker's attempt to avoid identification through DNA evidence by wearing both a condom and rubber gloves, a reliable DNA profile was developed from the evidence. During the struggle, the attacker was forced to use one hand to hold the victim down, leaving only one hand to pull the phone cord tight. The attacker had to grab the remaining end of the cord with his mouth, thereby depositing his saliva on the cord. Although the developed profile came from saliva rather than skin, DNA not only solved the case in Austin, but also linked the perpetrator to a similar sexual assault in Waco.

Without the investigator's understanding of DNA technology and where DNA might be found, the case may have gone unsolved. The successful review and investigation of unsolved cases require the same basic elements as the investigation of new cases: cooperation among law enforcement, the crime laboratory, and the prosecutor's office. Investigators should be aware of technological advances in DNA testing that may yield profiles where previous testing was not performed or was unsuccessful. The crime laboratory can be essential to the preliminary review of unsolved cases, for example, by providing investigators with laboratory reports from previous testing and consultation regarding the investigative value of new DNA analysis techniques and DNA database search capabilities. Additionally, the prosecutor's office should be involved as soon as a case is reopened so that legal issues are addressed appropriately. It is also extremely important that case reconstruction considers the victim or victim's family and the importance of finality to closing a case.

Although DNA is not the only forensic tool available for the investigation of unsolved cases, advancements in DNA testing and the success of DNA database systems have inspired law enforcement agencies throughout the country to reevaluate cases previously thought unsolvable. The purpose of this report is to provide law enforcement with a practical resource for the review of old, cold, or unsolved cases that may be solved through DNA technology and

DNA databases. "The Long and Short of DNA" and "How Can DNA Databases Aid Investigations?" will educate the reader about the science and technology of DNA testing and DNA databases. "Practical Considerations" provides important background information on legal and practical considerations regarding the application of DNA technology to old, cold, or unsolved cases. Finally, a step-by-step process is provided to help investigators select cases that would most likely be solved with DNA evidence. As investigators advance through this process, they should also keep in mind the array of other technology advancements, such as improved ballistics and fingerprint databases, that may benefit their investigation.

Advancements in DNA Technology

Advancements in DNA analysis, together with computer technology and the Combined DNA Index System (CODIS),[1] have created a powerful crimefighting tool for law enforcement. CODIS is a computer network that connects forensic DNA laboratories at the local, State, and national levels.

DNA database systems that use CODIS contain two main criminal indexes and a missing persons index. When a DNA profile is developed from crime scene evidence and entered into the forensic (crime scene) index of CODIS, the database software searches thousands of convicted offender DNA profiles (contained in the offender index) of individuals convicted of offenses such as rape and murder. Similar to the Automated Fingerprint Identification System (AFIS), CODIS can aid investigations by efficiently comparing a DNA profile generated from biological evidence left at a crime scene against convicted offender DNA profiles and forensic evidence from other cases contained in CODIS. CODIS can also aid investigations by searching the missing persons index, which contains DNA profiles of unidentified remains and DNA profiles of relatives of those who are missing. Because of the recidivistic nature of violent offenders, the power of a DNA database system is evident not only in the success of solving crimes previously thought unsolvable, but perhaps more importantly, through the prevention of crime.

When properly documented, collected, and stored, biological evidence can be analyzed to produce a reliable DNA profile years, even decades, after it is collected. Just as evidence collected from a crime that occurred yesterday can be analyzed for DNA, today evidence from an old rape kit, bloody shirt, or stained bedclothes may contain a valuable DNA profile. These new analysis techniques, in combination with an evolving database system, make a powerful argument for the reevaluation of unsolved crimes for potential DNA evidence.

Knowledgeable law enforcement officers are taking advantage of powerful DNA analysis techniques by investigating crime scenes with a keener eye toward biological evidence. The same new approach being applied to crime scene processing and current case investigation can be applied to older unsolved cases. Law enforcement agencies across the country are establishing cold-case squads to systematically review old cases for DNA and other new leads. This report will serve as a resource to assist law enforcement with maximizing the potential of DNA evidence in unsolved cases by covering the basics of DNA analysis and its application to forensic casework. The report will also demonstrate how DNA database systems, advancing technology, and cooperative efforts can enhance unsolved case investigative techniques.

New Laws

Advancements in DNA technology have led to significant changes in many States' statutes, which may affect the manner in which unsolved cases are investigated, filed, and prosecuted. Advancements in the technology have been so significant that laws are being created, amended, and even repealed to take advantage of its ability to identify and convict the guilty and exonerate the innocent. Laws regarding DNA admissibility in court, its use in postconviction appeals, the creation and expansion of databases, and the extension or elimination of statutes of limitation are examples of the quickly evolving impact of DNA on the criminal justice system. Given the legal changes occurring throughout the country, constant contact and consultation with the local prosecutor is critical not only for the investigation of older cases but for all cases in which DNA may be relevant evidence.

Statutes of Limitation

Statutes of limitation may be one of the most difficult issues to overcome when examining older cases. Statutes of limitation establish time limits under which criminal charges can be filed for a particular offense. These statutes are rooted in the protection of individuals from the use of evidence that becomes less reliable over time. For example, witnesses' memories fade as time goes by.

However, although some evidence, such as eyewitness accounts, can lose credibility over time, DNA evidence has the power to determine truth 10, 15, even 20 years after an offense is committed. States are beginning to realize that the reliability of DNA technology may necessitate the reevaluation of statutes of limitation in the filing of cases.

Database Expansion

The use of DNA evidence and convicted offender DNA databases has expanded significantly since the first U.S. DNA database was created in 1989.

Although State and local DNA databases established in the early 1990s contained only DNA profiles from convicted murderers and sex offenders, the undeniable success of DNA databases has resulted in a national trend toward database expansion. All States require at least some convicted offenders to provide a DNA sample to be collected for DNA profiling and, in 2000, the Federal Government began requiring certain offenders convicted of Federal or military crimes to also provide a DNA sample for the criminal DNA database.

Recognizing that the effectiveness of the DNA database relies on the volume of data contained in both the forensic index (crime scene samples) and the convicted offender index of CODIS, many States are changing their database statutes to include less violent criminals. Many States are enacting legislation to require all convicted felons to submit a DNA profile to the State database. The tendency for States to include all convicted felons in their databases dramatically increases the number of convicted offender DNA profiles against which forensic DNA evidence can be compared, thus making the database system a more powerful tool for law enforcement.

New Legal Approaches

DNA technology and DNA databases have encouraged the development of new approaches to old cases. One such approach is the filing of charges by "John Doe" warrant. These warrants are based on the unique DNA profile obtained from the analysis of unsolved crime scene evidence. Although John Doe warrants are traditionally filed based on the physical description or alias of an unnamed suspect, investigators and prosecutors are now filing charges using the suspect's DNA profile as the identifier. This innovative approach has allowed charges to be filed that toll and permit old cases to be prosecuted when the person matching the John Doe DNA profile is identified. John Doe DNA warrants are one way to permit cases to remain active, allowing them the chance to be solved through the DNA database in the future.

THE LONG AND SHORT OF DNA

DNA is the fundamental building block for an individual's entire genetic makeup. It is a component of virtually every cell in the human body, and a person's DNA is the same in every cell. That is, the DNA in a person's blood is the same as the DNA in his skin cells, saliva, and other biological material.

DNA analysis is a powerful tool because each person's DNA is unique (with the exception of identical twins). Therefore, DNA evidence collected from a crime scene can implicate or eliminate a suspect, similar to the use of fingerprints. It also can analyze unidentified remains through comparisons with DNA from relatives. Additionally, when evidence from one crime scene is compared with evidence from another using CODIS, those crime scenes can be linked to the same perpetrator locally, statewide, and nationally.

DNA is also a powerful tool because when biological evidence from crime scenes is collected and stored properly, forensically valuable DNA can be found on evidence that may be decades old. Therefore, old cases that were previously thought unsolvable may contain valuable DNA evidence capable of identifying the perpetrator.

Similar to Fingerprints

DNA is often compared with fingerprints in the way matches are determined.

When using either DNA or fingerprints to identify a suspect, the evidence collected from the crime scene is compared with a "known" standard. If identifying features are the same, the DNA or fingerprint can be determined to be a match. However, if identifying features of the DNA profile or fingerprint are different from the known standard, it can be determined that it did not come from that known individual.

DNA Technology Advancements

Recent advancements in DNA technology have improved law enforcement's ability to use DNA to solve old cases. Original forensic applications of DNA analysis were developed using a technology called restriction fragment length polymorphism (RFLP). Although very old cases (more than 10 years) may not have had RFLP analysis done, this kind of DNA testing may have been attempted on more recent unsolved cases. However, because RFLP analysis required a relatively large quantity of DNA, testing may not have been successful. Similarly, biological evidence deemed insufficient in size for testing may not have been previously submitted for testing. Also, if a biological sample was degraded by environmental factors such as dirt or mold, RFLP analysis may have been unsuccessful at yielding a result. Newer technologies could now be successful in obtaining results.

Newer DNA analysis techniques enable laboratories to develop profiles from biological evidence invisible to the naked eye, such as skin cells left on ligatures or weapons. Unsolved cases should be evaluated by investigating both traditional and nontraditional sources of DNA. Valuable DNA evidence might be available that previously went undetected in the original investigation.

If biological evidence is available for testing or retesting in unsolved case investigations, it is important that law enforcement and the crime laboratory work together to review evidence. Logistical issues regarding access to and the cost of DNA analysis will be a factor, as well as issues that relate to the discriminating power of each technology and that might affect the outcome of the results. Laboratory personnel can also provide a valuable perspective on which evidence might yield valuable and probative DNA results. Finally, if previously tested biological evidence produced a DNA profile but excluded the original suspect, revisiting those "exclusion" cases in the context of comparing them with DNA databases might prove to be very valuable to solving old cases.

PCR Analysis

PCR (polymerase chain reaction) enhances DNA analysis and has enabled laboratories to develop DNA profiles from extremely small samples of biological evidence. The PCR technique replicates exact copies of DNA contained in a biological evidence sample without affecting the original, much like a copy machine. RFLP analysis requires a biological sample about the size of a quarter, but PCR can be used to reproduce millions of copies of the DNA contained in a few skin cells. Since PCR analysis requires only a minute quantity of DNA, it can enable the laboratory to analyze highly degraded evidence for DNA. On the other hand, because the sensitive PCR technique replicates any and all of the DNA contained in an evidence sample, greater attention to contamination issues is necessary when identifying, collecting, and preserving DNA evidence. These factors may be particularly important in the evaluation of unsolved cases in which evidence might have been improperly collected or stored.

STR Analysis

Short tandem repeat (STR) technology is a forensic analysis that evaluates specific regions (loci) that are found on nuclear DNA. The variable (polymorphic) nature of the STR regions that are analyzed for forensic testing intensifies the discrimination between one DNA profile and another. For example, the likelihood that any two individuals (except identical twins) will have the same 13-loci DNA profile can be as high as 1 in 1 billion or greater.

The Federal Bureau of Investigation (FBI) has chosen 13 specific STR loci to serve as the standard for CODIS. The purpose of establishing a core set of STR loci is to ensure that all forensic laboratories can establish uniform DNA databases and, more importantly, share valuable forensic information. If the forensic or convicted offender CODIS index is to be used in the investigative stages of unsolved cases, DNA profiles must be generated by using STR technology and the specific 13 core STR loci selected by the FBI.

Mitochondrial DNA Analysis

Mitochondrial DNA (mtDNA) analysis allows forensic laboratories to develop DNA profiles from evidence that may not be suitable for RFLP or STR analysis. While RFLP and PCR techniques analyze DNA extracted from the nucleus of a cell, mtDNA technology analyzes DNA found in a different part of the cell, the mitochondrion (see exhibit 1). Old remains and evidence lacking nucleated cells--such as hair shafts, bones, and teeth--that are unamenable to STR and RFLP testing may yield results if mtDNA analysis is performed. For this reason, mtDNA testing can be very valuable to the investigation of an unsolved case. For example, a cold case log may show that biological evidence in the form of blood, semen, and hair was collected in a particular case, but that all were improperly stored for a long period of time. Although PCR analysis sometimes enables the crime laboratory to generate a DNA profile from very degraded evidence, it is possible that the blood and semen would be so highly degraded that nuclear DNA analysis would not yield a DNA profile. However, the hair shaft could be subjected to mtDNA analysis and thus be the key to solving the case. Finally, it is important to note that all maternal relatives (for example, a person's mother or maternal grandmother) have identical mtDNA.

This enables unidentified remains to be analyzed and compared to the mtDNA profile of any maternal relative for the purpose of aiding missing persons or unidentified remains investigations. Although mtDNA analysis can be very valuable to the investigation of criminal cases, laboratory personnel should always be involved in the process.

Y-Chromosome Analysis

Several genetic markers have been identified on the Y chromosome that can be used in forensic applications. Y-chromosome markers target only the male fraction of a biological sample. Therefore, this technique can be very valuable if the laboratory detects complex mixtures (multiple male contributors) within a biological evidence sample. Because the Y chromosome is transmitted directly from a father to all of his sons, it can also be used to trace family relationships among males. Advancements in Y-chromosome testing may eventually eliminate the need for laboratories to extract and separate semen and vaginal cells (for example, from a vaginal swab of a rape kit) prior to analysis.

Cooperative efforts with the crime laboratory are essential to deciding which analysis methods will be most valuable in a particular case. It is important to note, however, that while RFLP and mtDNA testing may be valuable to the investigation of an old case, current DNA databases are being populated with DNA profiles that are generated using STR analysis. RFLP and mtDNA profiles are not compatible with the convicted offender or forensic indexes of CODIS.[2]

How Can DNA Databases Aid Investigations?

The development and expansion of databases that contain DNA profiles at the local, State, and national levels have greatly enhanced law enforcement's ability to solve cold cases with DNA. Convicted offender databases store hundreds of thousands of potential suspect DNA profiles, against which DNA profiles developed from crime scene evidence can be compared.

Given the recidivistic nature of many crimes, such as sexual assault and burglary, a likelihood exists that the individual who committed the crime being investigated was convicted of a similar crime and already has his or her DNA profile in a DNA database that can be searched by CODIS. Moreover, CODIS also permits the cross-comparison of DNA profiles developed from biological evidence found at crime scenes. Even if a perpetrator is not identified through the database, crimes may be linked to each other, thereby aiding an investigation, which may eventually lead to the identification of a suspect.

What is CODIS?

CODIS is a computer software program that operates local, State, and national databases of DNA profiles from convicted offenders, unsolved crime scene evidence, and missing persons. Every State in the Nation has a statutory provision for the establishment of a DNA database that allows for the collection of DNA profiles from offenders convicted of particular crimes. CODIS software enables State, local, and national law enforcement crime laboratories to compare DNA profiles electronically, thereby linking serial crimes to each other and identifying suspects by matching DNA profiles from crime scenes with profiles from convicted offenders. The success of CODIS is demonstrated by the thousands of matches that have linked serial cases to each other and cases that have been solved by matching crime scene evidence to known convicted offenders.

The missing persons index consists of the unidentified persons index and the reference index. The unidentified persons index contains DNA profiles from recovered remains, such as bone, teeth, or hair. The reference index contains DNA profiles from related individuals of missing persons so that they can be periodically compared to the unidentified persons index. All samples for this index are typed using mtDNA and STR DNA analysis (if possible) to maximize the power of advancing technology.

How Does CODIS Work?

CODIS uses two indexes to generate investigative leads in crimes for which biological evidence is recovered from a crime scene. The convicted offender index contains DNA profiles of individuals convicted of certain crimes ranging from certain misdemeanors to sexual assault and murder. Each State has different "qualifying offenses" for which persons convicted of them must submit a biological sample for inclusion in the DNA database. The forensic index contains DNA profiles obtained from crime scene evidence, such as semen, saliva, or blood. CODIS uses computer software to automatically search across these indexes for a potential match.

A match made between profiles in the forensic index can link crime scenes to each other, possibly identifying serial offenders. Based on these "forensic hits," police in multiple jurisdictions or States can coordinate their respective investigations and share leads they have developed independent of each other.

Matches made between the forensic and convicted offender indexes can provide investigators with the identity of a suspect(s). It is important to note that if an "offender hit" is obtained, that information typically is used as probable cause to obtain a new DNA sample from that suspect so the match can be confirmed by the crime laboratory before an arrest is made.

LDIS, SDIS, and NDIS

CODIS is implemented as a distributed database with three hierarchical levels (or tiers)--local, State, and national. All three levels contain forensic and convicted offender indexes and a population file (used to generate statistics).

The hierarchical design provides State and local laboratories with the flexibility to configure CODIS to meet their specific legislative and technical needs.

A description of the three CODIS tiers follows (see exhibit 2).

- Local. Typically, the Local DNA Index System (LDIS) installed at crime laboratories is operated by police departments or sheriffs' offices. DNA profiles originated at the local level can be transmitted to the State and national levels.
- State. Each State has a designated laboratory that operates the State DNA Index System (SDIS). SDIS allows local laboratories within that

State to compare DNA profiles. SDIS also is the communication path between the local and national tiers. SDIS is typically operated by the agency responsible for implementing and monitoring compliance with the State's convicted offender statute.

- National. The National DNA Index System (NDIS) is the highest level of the CODIS hierarchy and enables qualified State laboratories that are actively participating in CODIS to compare DNA profiles. NDIS is maintained by the FBI under the authority of the DNA Identification Act of 1994.

Limitations of Using the DNA Database

The more data contained in the forensic and offender indexes of CODIS, the more powerful a tool it becomes for law enforcement, especially in its application to unsolved case investigation. However, because many jurisdictions are in the process of developing and populating their DNA databases, convicted offender and forensic casework backlogs have been created over time and continue to grow for several reasons. First, as States recognize the crime-solving potential of DNA databases, they continue to expand the scope of their convicted offender legislation, which increases the number of samples to be collected and analyzed by the DNA laboratory. As a result, more than 1 million uncollected convicted offender DNA profiles are "owed" to the system.

An equally important but more difficult problem to quantify is that of unprocessed casework that contains biological evidence. This casework backlog may include nonsuspect or unsolved cases that could be analyzed and solved as a result of advancements in DNA technology.

Convicted Offender Backlogs

Although all 50 States have passed DNA database legislation, many States have backlogs of convicted offender samples that have been collected but have not yet been analyzed. Although Federal funding has played an important role in reducing existing backlogs, the crimefighting potential of DNA has prompted many States to revise their statutes to require nonviolent convicted offenders to provide a DNA sample for analysis and upload into CODIS. The trend toward expanding convicted offender DNA statutes to include nonviolent offenders has significantly increased the number of DNA samples requiring collection and analysis. Although the success of using the DNA database as a crime-solving and crime-prevention tool can easily be demonstrated once convicted offender backlogs are reduced, it should be recognized that new backlogs are instantly created by the passage of expanded DNA legislation laws. Convicted offender backlogs are an ongoing logistical issue that can compound the complexity of investigating cold cases by using the DNA database.

Forensic Casework Backlogs

Addressing issues that affect the efficient and effective use of DNA databases in the United States is complicated further by the existence of casework backlogs. This refers to biological evidence in perhaps tens of thousands of criminal cases, including violent and nonviolent crimes, that has not been tested or retested for DNA.

Unprocessed rape kits are a clear example of this kind of backlog. Despite the established fact that rape typically yields biological evidence, as of October 1999, at least 180,000 rape kits remained on shelves across the country, unprocessed, because no suspects have been identified. The DNA evidence from these and other criminal cases often is not analyzed and entered into the DNA database because forensic laboratories have to prioritize their work and cases scheduled for trial take precedence over cases in which no suspect is known. In most jurisdictions, nonsuspect criminal cases that contain biological evidence are not being analyzed and entered into the DNA database. In many jurisdictions, DNA from crime scenes is still primarily used to prosecute offenders, not to investigate crimes. The convicted offender backlog and limited resources for casework going to trial preclude State forensic laboratories from analyzing all biological evidence for DNA, which in turn prevents law enforcement from being able to realize the full crime-solving potential of CODIS.

The backlog of forensic cases has practical consequences for most law enforcement agencies in the United States. Laboratory capacity limitations result in the ability to process crime scene samples from only the most serious of offenses. More and more, however, agencies such as those in the United Kingdom are discovering the value of DNA technology in solving property crimes. Blood left on a broken apartment window or saliva found on a discarded beer bottle can be used to identify burglars, and the skin cells rubbed off onto the steering wheel of a stolen vehicle can solve car thefts. However, as long as forensic laboratories remain able to process only the most serious cases, the full potential of DNA technology to solve crime will remain untapped.

PRACTICAL CONSIDERATIONS

A broad range of considerations must be made long before any DNA testing is actually attempted in older, unsolved cases. These include:

- Legal considerations, such as the application or expiration of statutes of limitation.
- Technological considerations, such as the nature and condition of the evidence as originally collected, stored, and in some instances, subjected to other forensic tests.
- Practical considerations, such as the availability of witnesses in the event DNA testing would identify a suspect and lead to an arrest and a trial.
- Resource issues, such as the time and money available for investigation and forensic analysis.

The nature and scope of these issues require that any approach to reexamining old cases for potential DNA evidence be collaborative, whether by an individual investigator or by a specialized unit developed specifically for cold case review. Local prosecutors can provide valuable insight into legal issues that might prevent or help a future prosecution. Victim/witness units or advocates can provide valuable assistance with locating, educating, and encouraging witnesses. Consultation with representatives from the crime laboratory is critical to ensuring that potential DNA evidence can be successfully analyzed.

Evidence Considerations

When collecting unsolved case evidence from storage facilities, the case investigator should be ready to handle all types of packaging disasters. Evidence may be stored in heavy-duty plastic bags, stapled shut as the past form of "sealing." Multiple items may be sealed in one plastic bag, or even unpackaged in large, open, cardboard boxes. Unprotected microscope slides from medical facilities might also be found as a result of investigating old cases.

No attempt should be made on the part of the investigator to separate and repackage evidence. The condition and position that the evidence has been stored in could provide valuable clues to the forensic scientist for testability of evidence. Only when evidence is found unpackaged should the investigator properly package and label the item(s) to minimize the possibility for contamination from that point forward. It is important that any evidence items are handled minimally and only by individuals wearing disposable gloves. As always, it is also very important that all actions taken as a result of opening, evaluating, packaging, or repackaging evidence are documented thoroughly in the case folder.

Degraded Evidence

Prior to the frequent use of DNA technology, biological evidence may have been collected and stored in ways that were not necessarily the best methods for preserving samples for future DNA testing. For example, evidence containing biological fluids that were originally collected for ABO Blood Typing analysis or other serology methods may have been packaged or stored in ways that can limit DNA testing. Some methods of collection and storage may promote the growth of bacteria and mold on the evidence. Bacteria can seriously damage or degrade DNA contained in biological material and inhibit the ability to develop a DNA profile; however, evidence can still sometimes yield DNA results. For example, PCR technology can allow the laboratory to develop profiles from some moldy biological samples, whereas other evidence may fail to yield a usable DNA profile, even when no mold is visible. Therefore, close consultation with the laboratory is important to determine the type of DNA testing most likely to yield results on the available evidence.

Contamination Issues

Because of the particularly sensitive nature of DNA technology, the potential contamination of evidence should be carefully considered. Technologies used to analyze evidence prior to the forensic application of DNA were not always sensitive to contaminants. Evidence in older cases may have been collected in ways that lacked appropriate contamination or cross-contamination safeguards, which can make the DNA results less useful or even misleading. In these cases, clarifying results by identifying the contributor of an additional profile can determine whether the DNA results may now be used. When a mixture is detected, a careful reconstruction of the evidence collection, storage, and analysis process must be undertaken. It may be determined that DNA profiles will be required from on-scene officers, evidence technicians, or laboratory scientists who had access to the evidence for comparison with evidence results.

In these instances, proper chain-of-custody reconstruction is critical. It is also important to avoid contamination when handling biological evidence during the course of the current review. If evidence that may contain biological material is already sealed, do not reopen it before sending it to the laboratory. (See Evidence Handling Recommendations)

Legal Considerations

Numerous legal issues might arise when examining older cases for potential DNA evidence. These issues are most likely jurisdictionally specific and may differ from State to State. Although most jurisdictions maintain no statute of limitation for filing charges in a homicide case, States can vary widely in the time allowed for filing charges in other cases, such as rape and other sexual assault crimes. Furthermore, in recognition of DNA technology's ability to solve old cases, many States are extending or even eliminating statutes of limitation for certain crimes.

Chain of Custody

When a case remains unsolved for a long period of time, evidence is usually handled by an increased number of individuals. Many unsolved cases to be reviewed for DNA evidence may have been previously reinvestigated or handled by several different investigators as a result of new leads or periodic, systematic reviews. Furthermore, as cases age, the likelihood increases that evidence may be moved to new or remote storage locations as evidence from newer cases fills police department shelves.

Many cases may also have had evidence submitted to the laboratory for various forms of forensic testing. Evidence in older cases may have been submitted for standard serological testing, but can now be tested for DNA with much greater success. Hair previously submitted for standard microscopic hair analysis may now be submitted for mtDNA testing. As with all criminal investigations, chain-of-custody issues are critical to maintaining the integrity of the evidence.

In all cases, the ultimate ability to use DNA evidence will depend on the ability to prove that the chain of custody was maintained.

Statutes of Limitation

One of the first issues to address when reviewing an unsolved case is whether the statutes of limitation on a case have run out. Several considerations arise when addressing a statute of limitation issue. Good communication between law enforcement and local prosecutors is critical when examining these legal questions.

Changes in statutes. Advances in DNA technology and the creation of DNA databases are leading many criminal justice professionals to rethink time limits placed on the filing of criminal charges. Because biological evidence can yield reliable DNA analysis results years after the commission of a crime, many State legislatures have begun to extend, and in some cases eliminate, the statutes of limitation for some crimes and in certain circumstances. Many States have extended the length of time for which a complaint can be filed, other States have eliminated statutes of limitation for certain crimes, and some legislation is retroactive.

Exceptions to statutes. Exceptions often exist under existing and new statutes. Under such exceptions, time can be added to the statute of limitation, giving police the legal authority to arrest even if it appears as though the statute has run out. For example, many jurisdictions have exceptions for a suspect's flight from jurisdiction. In a case for which there is a 5-year statute of limitation, if the government can prove that the suspect has been absent from the jurisdiction for 2 years, the State can still file against the suspect for up to 7 years after the commission of the crime. Exceptions also exist for cases in which child victims are assaulted by a family member, which can be valuable in the context of a current investigation.

Victim and Witness Considerations

Another important consideration to be made early in the process is the willingness of victims and witnesses to proceed. Although many victims may continuously monitor the progress of their investigations, some choose to detach from the process over time. Reinvestigating a case may cause renewed psychological trauma to the victim and victim's family. It should not be assumed that victims and witnesses, even if they were eager to pursue the case when it occurred, are still interested in pursuing the case. A phone call from an investigator years later may not be a welcome event. Whenever possible, enlist the aid of victim service providers. If a new officer is handling the investigation, enlisting the assistance of the original investigator to make the first contact with the victim may also be helpful.

The older a case is, the more difficult it may be to locate witnesses. However, early identification of victim and witness availability may ultimately save significant resources. Consultation with prosecutors is mandatory when considering whether a witness would be necessary at trial.

Identifying, Analyzing, and Prioritizing Cases

Whether the process of reviewing unsolved cases is initiated by a single officer or by a specialized unit, it must ultimately be a team effort. At all stages of the process, investigators should avail themselves of the scientific advice of the laboratory and the legal expertise of the local prosecutor's office. Close consultation with the laboratory can ensure that evidence integrity is maintained and that limited laboratory resources are allocated effectively. Similarly, prosecutors can help identify issues that might occur at trial if a suspect is identified and arrested upon successful DNA testing. Good communication between police, laboratories, and prosecutors can help identify and convict serious offenders and save valuable time and resources.

IDENTIFY POTENTIAL CASES FOR REVIEW

An initial step in the DNA review of unsolved cases is to identify cases that might be amenable to DNA testing. While the cases considered for this kind of review will vary from jurisdiction to jurisdiction, it is important to define minimum requirements that will likely benefit from this approach.

Issues such as statutes of limitation and solvability factors should be thoroughly examined in cooperation with a prosecutor and the forensic laboratory to establish guidelines for case selection. It also will be important to identify the ultimate goals of the program so that the selection criteria can be tailored to meet those specific goals.

Cases that could benefit from a review for potential DNA evidence can be identified from numerous sources. In some instances a single police officer or investigator may remember an unsolved case from years ago. In some departments a formalized cold-case unit may systematically review cases for the potential of DNA testing. Other cases may be identified by coordinated, interdepartmental efforts, victims or witnesses who have heard about the potential of DNA evidence, and laboratories taking inventory of their storage facilities. If a department is pursuing a systematic review of cases, either by one or two officers or by a formal unit, there are many sources that can be consulted for valuable investigative information, such as

- Autopsy, laboratory, prosecutor, and local agency logbooks.
- Retired investigators.
- Computer databases.

Identify Statute of Limitation Issues

Statute of limitation issues might affect the ultimate ability to prosecute a case. Cases should be preliminarily reviewed by investigators in conjunction with the prosecutor's office to identify which prosecutions would be barred by the statutes of limitation. If the goal of the unsolved case review program is to obtain convictions and statutes of limitation have expired on a particular case, a department may wish to save its resources for cases likely to yield convictions.

However, if the goal of the program is to solve and close unsolved cases regardless of whether a conviction could be obtained, a jurisdiction may decide to review all cases that qualify under its guidelines. This is an important consideration in the context of investigating serial offenders whose criminal acts might span the course of years or decades.

Define Categories of Cases--Solvability Factors

Because the number of cases that qualify for reinvestigation might be very large, it may be beneficial for a jurisdiction to define cases according to several solvability factors. Solvability factors include facts and circumstances of a case that influence the likelihood that it might be solved through advancements in DNA technology. For example, a high probability exists that analysis of nonsuspect rape kits will yield valuable DNA results. Profiles generated as a result of DNA analysis can now be entered into CODIS, which can solve a case by matching to a convicted offender, or aid investigations by linking serial rapes to each other. Additionally, if an unsolved murder case contains biological evidence foreign to the victim that did not produce viable results from ABO blood typing or RFLP DNA analysis, evidence could be reanalyzed with the more discriminating and powerful STR technology. It is also important to recognize and sort out cases that might not be as likely to be solved with DNA technology. An example might be an unsolved drive-by homicide because the perpetrator most likely would not have left biological evidence at this kind of crime scene.

Case Review-Establish Priorities

Once solvability factors and statute of limitation issues are addressed, it is important to continue the process by identifying the cases to be reviewed first. To preserve investigative resources when considering a larger number of unsolved cases for review, jurisdictions may prioritize according to the likelihood that cases will be solved or the likelihood that investigations will be aided. In establishing this priority, the following criteria can be considered:

- How many qualifying cases are there?
- Where are the case files located?
- Are case summaries available?
- How many cases will be assigned to an investigator?

To establish an investigative hierarchy, qualifying cases should be reviewed by experienced, proficient investigators. A checklist can be used throughout the review process so that managers can decide which cases will be worked first. A checklist can also provide review process consistency throughout the agency. (See Sample Checklist at the end of this report.) The following categories may serve as a model for a hierarchy in prioritizing cases:

- There is a known suspect and physical evidence appears to have been preserved in a manner consistent with successful DNA testing and use of CODIS.
- There is no known suspect but physical evidence has been preserved in a manner consistent with successful DNA testing and use of CODIS.
- There is no known suspect and evidence was collected and preserved in a manner that may make it difficult to obtain a DNA profile.

Locating Case Files, Obtaining Evidence Logs, and Other Documentation

Locating the case file and original evidence for the investigation may be a challenging endeavor. Changes in personnel, procedure, and facilities and the passage of time may complicate the process. When searching for a case file or evidence, an investigator may need to look in numerous places. Potential locations include, but are not limited to, the following:
- Police department property rooms (case files, evidence logs, whole evidence).
- Property warehouses (case files, evidence logs, whole evidence).
- Public crime laboratories (previously tested/submitted evidence, lab reports).
- Private laboratories (previously tested evidence, lab reports).
- Hospital/medical facilities (rape kits, medical reports, slides).
- Coroner/medical examiners' offices (autopsy reports).
- Courthouse property rooms.
- Prosecutors' offices (previous trial or suspect investigation).
- Retired investigators' files (case notes and details not contained in file).
- Other investigating agency offices (investigative leads--serial offender).

Forensic Testing Reports and Previously Tested Evidence

Because advancements in DNA technology enable laboratories to successfully analyze old evidence that might have been improperly stored or subjected to previous forensic analysis, it will be very valuable to locate any and all forensic reports that were produced as a result of previous analysis and/or testing. ABO blood typing, microscopic hair analysis, RFLP DNA analysis, or fingerprint analysis (among others) might have been performed in the course of the original investigation. The original case file should indicate whether and which types of forensic analysis were attempted. These reports also serve to memorialize proper chain of custody. Cooperation with the crime laboratory is crucial to locate and interpret existing forensic reports and to determine whether evidence would be amenable to reanalysis with new DNA techniques.

Many combinations of options are available to investigators and laboratory personnel if biological evidence was available and previously tested. Exhibit 3 may serve to help investigators as they work with the laboratory to discuss options throughout the course of the investigation.

Locate Biological Evidence

When reviewing the case file for potential DNA evidence, it is important to know what kinds of evidence may yield a DNA profile. Given the power and sensitivity of newer DNA testing techniques, DNA can be collected from virtually anywhere. Only a few cells can be sufficient to obtain useful DNA information to help solve a case. Exhibit 4 identifies some common items of evidence that may have been collected previously but not analyzed for the presence of DNA evidence. Remember, if a stain is not visible it does not mean that there are not enough cells for DNA typing. Further, DNA does more than just identify the source of the sample; it can place a known individual at a crime scene, in a home, or in a room where the suspect claimed not to have been. It can refute a claim of self-defense and put a weapon in the suspect's hand. It can also provide irrefutable evidence that can change a suspect's story from an alibi to one of consent.

Evaluate for Probative DNA Evidence

On completion of reviewing the case file, reports, and evidence in consultation with the laboratory, it will be necessary to identify which evidentiary items will be amenable to DNA analysis. Consultation with the laboratory will be essential to determine the likelihood of obtaining results from DNA analysis, and consultation with a prosecutor is very important to determine which evidence will be probative to the case. Building the new investigation on cooperative efforts between the laboratory and prosecutor can save valuable resources, develop leads, and identify previously overlooked evidence that may yield a DNA profile.

Continue Investigative Protocol

If DNA analysis is to be conducted, it may be important to obtain reference samples from prior suspects, and it might be necessary to be creative when obtaining these samples. While a biological sample in the form of blood or saliva can be obtained voluntarily through a consent form, a standard reference sample might already exist if previous forensic analysis, such as serological testing, was performed during the course of the original investigation.

Additionally, elimination samples from anyone who had lawful access to the crime scene, such as family members, may be required if the laboratory determines that there is more than one DNA profile present in the evidence sample. Early identification of the location and status of persons who might be requested to submit an elimination sample could save valuable time and resources if the laboratory needs such information. Consultation with the laboratory is essential to properly coordinating this process.

Follow Agency Procedures for Submitting the DNA Profile to CODIS

On successful laboratory analysis resulting in a DNA profile developed from crime scene evidence, existing and/or new suspect DNA profiles should be compared with the evidence profile. If the laboratory determines a match between a suspect and the evidence, the prosecutor's office should be consulted on how to proceed. However, if a match is not found, agency procedures should be followed, in accordance with the crime laboratory, to submit the crime scene evidence DNA profile into CODIS.

Because CODIS contains hundreds of thousands of convicted offender DNA profiles, it is possible that the person who committed the unsolved crime being investigated was convicted of a qualifying offense that required submission of a DNA profile to the database. If that person has not previously been convicted of a qualifying offense, especially in light of expanding database law, it is possible that they will be convicted in the future. Further, because the forensic index of CODIS contains thousands of crime scene evidence profiles, the investigation could be aided if a match is made to another forensic DNA profile already in the database. Finally, an investigator should not assume that a new DNA profile generated from unsolved case evidence and submitted to the laboratory for entry into CODIS will be compared with every possible convicted offender or crime scene index profile. The investigator may need to proactively request that his CODIS administrator search the new profile against the local, State, and national DNA databases.

Prepare a John Doe Warrant

CODIS is a powerful crime-solving and crime-prevention tool, but many cases will not be solved as a result of entering a DNA profile into the forensic index of the database. Additionally, many cases will have statute of limitation issues that might prevent the prosecution of the case if a match is not determined in a timely manner. Therefore, if no offender match occurs in cases in which statutes of limitation are an issue, consideration may be given, in consultation with the prosecutor, to preparing a John Doe warrant. These types of warrants can identify the perpetrator according to his or her DNA profile. The 13-loci profile generated by the crime laboratory should be clearly printed on the face of the warrant. The John Doe warrant is not novel; however, the unconventional method of describing an individual by his or her DNA profile may allow for prosecution of a case if a DNA match is determined in the course of future investigations or as a result of the CODIS system being populated with more convicted offender and forensic DNA profiles.

Notes

1. CODIS uses two indexes--the forensic index and the offender index— to generate investigative leads in crimes where biological evidence is recovered from crime scenes. The forensic index contains DNA profiles of biological crime scene evidence and the offender index

contains DNA profiles of individuals convicted of a qualifying offense.

2. CODIS has a missing persons index that exclusively contains mtDNA profiles; the convicted offender and forensic indexes of CODIS exclusively contain STR DNA profiles.

The successful review and investigation of unsolved cases require cooperation among law enforcement, the crime laboratory, and the prosecutor's office.

The power of a DNA database system is evident not only in the success of solving crimes previously thought unsolvable, but through the prevention of crime.

The reliability of DNA technology may necessitate the reevaluation of statutes of limitation.

If biological evidence is available for testing or retesting in unsolved case investigations, it is important that law enforcement and the crime laboratory work together to review evidence.

If the convicted offender or forensic index of CODIS is to be used in the investigative stages of an unsolved case, DNA profiles must be generated using STR analysis.

Success Story

A "forensic hit" occurred in the National DNA Index System (NDIS) that linked a dead Florida man's DNA profile to eight serial unsolved rapes in Washington, D.C. and three offenses in Florida.

In 1999, Leon Dundas was killed in a drug deal. Investigators remembered Dundas refusing to give a blood sample in connection with a rape investigation in 1998. They were able to obtain Dundas' blood sample through the medical examiner's office and forwarded it to the DNA lab at the Florida Department of Law Enforcement. Dundas' DNA profile was compared with the national forensic index and a match was made between Dundas and DNA evidence from a rape victim in Washington, D.C.

The FBI then entered DNA evidence from additional unsolved rapes committed in Washington. Dundas' DNA matched seven additional rapes in Washington and three more in Jacksonville, Florida. Police in Washington said that without DNA, they would have never identified Dundas, who had no prior recorded history of violent crime.

The offender index contains DNA profiles of individuals convicted of certain crimes. The forensic index contains DNA profiles obtained from crime scene evidence.

Local prosecutors can provide valuable insight into legal issues. Victim/witness units or advocates can help locate, educate, and encourage witnesses. Consultation with representatives from the crime laboratory is critical.

Evidence Handling Recommendations

- Wear gloves. Change them between handling each item of evidence.
- Use disposable instruments or clean instruments thoroughly before and after handling each evidence sample.
- Avoid touching the area where you believe DNA may exist.
- Avoid touching your face, nose, and mouth when examining and repackaging evidence.
- Put dry evidence into new paper bags or envelopes; do not use plastic bags.
- Do not use staples.
- If repackaging of evidence is necessary, consult with laboratory personnel.

Statute of Limitation Recommendations

- Know the original statute of limitation.
- Determine whether the law has changed regarding time limits for filing. If so, is the law retroactive?
- Determine whether there are exceptions to the statute.
- Consult with the prosecutor.

It should not be assumed that victims and witnesses are still interested in pursuing the case. Whenever possible, enlist the aid of victim service providers.

Good communication between police, laboratories, and prosecutors can help identify and convict serious offenders and save valuable time and resources.

DNA Can Do More . . .

. . . than identify a suspect. It can also--

- Place a known individual at a crime scene.
- Refute a claim of self-defense.
- Put a weapon in a suspect's hand.
- Change a suspect's story from an alibi to one of consent.

Sample Checklist

- Identify potential cases.
  - Identify any statute of limitation issues (consult with prosecutors).
  - Define case categories according to solvability factors.
- Prioritize cases (consider solvability factors).
- Locate and review the case file; obtain evidence logs and other documentation such as laboratory and autopsy reports.
- Locate previous forensic testing reports and location of previously tested evidence.
  For example--
  - Blood previously ABO typed.
  - Hair analyzed microscopically.
  - Fingerprint evidence.
- Locate crime scene evidence containing biological material.
- Evaluate the case and evidence for potential probative DNA. Be sure to--
  - Consider all evidentiary possibilities.
  - Take appropriate precautions against contamination.
- In consultation with the laboratory and prosecutors, submit appropriate (probative) evidence to the laboratory for testing.

- Continue investigative protocol. If needed, obtain reference samples from suspects--
  - Voluntarily using a consent form.
  - By using a previously obtained sample (e.g., if a reference sample was used for standard serological testing).
- Identify witness issues
  - Legal availability.
  - Willingness to proceed.

-     Location.
- If a profile does not match suspect profiles, follow agency procedures for submitting the evidence profile to CODIS.
- If no offender match occurs in cases in which statutes of limitation are an issue, prepare a John Doe warrant.

About the National Institute of Justice

NIJ is the research, development, and evaluation agency of the U.S. Department of Justice and is solely dedicated to researching crime control and justice issues. NIJ provides objective, independent, nonpartisan, evidence-based knowledge and tools to meet the challenges of crime and justice, particularly at the State and local levels. NIJ's principal authorities are derived from the Omnibus Crime Control and Safe Streets Act of 1968, as amended (42 U.S.C. Sections 3721-3722).

NIJ's Mission

In partnership with others, NIJ's mission is to prevent and reduce crime, improve law enforcement and the administration of justice, and promote public safety. By applying the disciplines of the social and physical sciences, NIJ--

- Researches the nature and impact of crime and delinquency.
- Develops applied technologies, standards, and tools for criminal justice practitioners.
- Evaluates existing programs and responses to crime.
- Tests innovative concepts and program models in the field.
- Assists policymakers, program partners, and justice agencies.
- Disseminates knowledge to many audiences.

NIJ's Strategic Direction and Program Areas

NIJ is committed to five challenges as part of its strategic plan: 1) rethinking justice and the processes that create just communities; 2) understanding the nexus between social conditions and crime; 3) breaking the cycle of crime by testing research-based interventions; 4) creating the tools and technologies that meet the needs of practitioners; and 5) expanding horizons through interdisciplinary and international perspectives. In addressing these strategic challenges, the Institute is involved in the following program areas: crime control and prevention, drugs and crime, justice systems and offender behavior, violence and victimization, communications and information technologies, critical incident response, investigative and forensic sciences (including DNA), less-than-lethal technologies, officer protection, education and training technologies, testing and standards, technology assistance to law enforcement and corrections agencies, field testing of promising programs, and international crime control. NIJ communicates its findings through conferences and print and electronic media.

NIJ's Structure

The NIJ Director is appointed by the President and confirmed by the Senate. The NIJ Director establishes the Institute's objectives, guided by the priorities of the Office of Justice Programs, the U.S. Department of Justice, and the needs of the field. NIJ actively solicits the views of criminal justice and other professionals and researchers to inform its search for the knowledge and tools to guide policy and practice.

NIJ has three operating units. The Office of Research and Evaluation manages social science research and evaluation and crime mapping research. The Office of Science and Technology manages technology research and development, standards development, and technology assistance to State and local law enforcement and corrections agencies. The Office of Development and Communications manages field tests of model programs, international research, and knowledge dissemination programs. NIJ is a component of the Office of Justice Programs, which also includes the Bureau of Justice Assistance, the Bureau of Justice Statistics, the Office of Juvenile Justice and Delinquency Prevention, and the Office for Victims of Crime.

To find out more about the National Institute of Justice, please contact:

National Criminal Justice Reference Service
P.O. Box 6000
Rockville, MD 20849-6000
800-851-3420
e-mail: askncjrs@ncjrs.org

In: Crime and Law Enforcement Issues   ISBN 978-1-61122-877-9
Editor: James E. Hirsch   © 2011 Nova Science Publishers, Inc.

Chapter 2

CAPITAL PUNISHMENT: AN OVERVIEW OF FEDERAL DEATH PENALTY STATUTES

Elizabeth B. Bazan

ABSTRACT

With the passage of P.L. 103-322, the Violent Crime Control and Law Enforcement Act of 1994, the federal death penalty became available as a possible punishment for a substantial number of new and existing civilian offenses. On April 24, 1996, the Antiterrorism and Effective Death Penalty Act of 1996 made further modifications and additions to the list of federal capital crimes. On June 25, 2002, P.L. 107-197, the Terrorist Bombings Convention Implementation Act of 2002, added another capital crime to the United States Code. The Intelligence Reform and Terrorism Prevention Act of 2004, P.L. 108-458, enacted December 17, 2004, included provisions which impacted or expanded some of the existing death penalty provisions. This report lists the current federal capital offenses and summarizes the procedures for federal civilian death penalty cases.

INTRODUCTION

With the passage of P.L. 103-322, the Violent Crime Control and Law Enforcement Act of 1994, the federal death penalty became available as a possible punishment for a substantial number of new and existing civilian offenses. Further changes to the list of federal capital punishment statutes resulted from the passage of the Antiterrorism and Effective Death Penalty Act of 1996, P.L. 104-132, on April 24, 1996. On June 25, 2002, the Terrorist Bombings Convention Implementation Act of 2002, P.L. 107-197, added another capital crime to the United States Code. Some of the existing death penalty provisions were expanded, directly or indirectly, by the enactment on December 17, 2004, of the Intelligence Reform and Terrorism Prevention Act of 2004, P.L. 108-458. This report lists the current federal death penalty offenses and summarizes the procedures for civilian death penalty cases [1].

CAPITAL OFFENSES

In Furman v. Georgia, 408 U.S. 238 (1972), the Supreme Court held unconstitutional a capital sentencing scheme which gave the sentencing decision-maker unbridled discretion in determining whether to impose a death sentence in a given case. Prior to the passage of the Violent Crime Control and Law Enforcement Act of 1994, P.L. 103-322, all but two [2] of the existing federal civilian death penalty provisions suffered from constitutional frailties like those of the Georgia statute at issue in Furman. The Act revived the death penalty for several previously unenforceable capital offenses, added capital punishment to the penalties available for a few other existing federal offenses and created a number of new capital offenses. The Antiterrorism and Effective Death Penalty Act of 1996, P.L. 104-132, expanded and modified the list of federal capital punishment offenses. Two other statutes further expanded the reach of the federal death penalty, the Terrorist Bombings Convention Implementation Act of 2002, P.L. 107-197, and the Intelligence Reform and Terrorism Prevention Act of 2004, P.L. 108-458. In the wake of these Acts, the death penalty is an available sentencing option for the following offenses:

- 7 U.S.C. § 2146(b)–first degree murder of any person while engaged in or on account of the performance of his or her official duties with respect to the transportation, sale, or handling of certain animals under 7 U.S.C. ch. 54, §§ 2131 et seq. This provision cross-references 18 U.S.C. §§ 1111 (murder) and 1114 (protection of officers and employees of the United States) for applicable punishment.
- 8 U.S.C. § 1324(a)–murder, with death resulting from smuggling aliens into the United States.

- 15 U.S.C. § 1825(a)(2)(C)–killing of an official while engaged in or on account of performance of his or her official duties under 15 U.S.C. § 1821 *et seq.*, which deals with protection of horses in horse shows, exhibitions, sales or auctions.
- 18 U.S.C. §§ 32 and 34–willful destruction of aircraft within the special aircraft jurisdiction of the United States; of any civil aircraft used, operated, or employed in interstate, overseas or foreign air commerce; or of aircraft facilities, where death results [3]. Sections 32 and 34 also cover performing an act of violence or incapacitation against any individual on such aircraft which is likely to endanger the safety of the aircraft, where death results. Where a U.S. national is on board the civil aircraft involved or would have been on board, where an offender is a U.S. national, or where an offender is found in the U.S. after commission of such an offense, these provisions would also cover: engaging in a willful act of violence against an individual while on board a civil aircraft registered in a country other than the United States, which act is likely to endanger the aircraft in flight, where death results; willfully destroying a civil aircraft registered in a country other than the U.S. or damaging it so as to make it incapable of flight or endangering its safety in flight, where death results; or willfully placing a device or substance on such an aircraft likely to destroy that aircraft, to render it incapable of flight, or to endanger its safety while in flight, where death results.
- 18 U.S.C. §§ 33 and 34–willful destruction of motor vehicles engaged in interstate or foreign commerce, or their facilities, where death results [4]
- 18 U.S.C. § 36–murder committed in furtherance of or to escape detection of a major drug offense by firing a weapon into a group of two or more people(drive-by shooting) [5]
- 18 U.S.C. § 37–murder, with death resulting from a violation of the proscription against the use of violence at international airports. U.S. jurisdiction under this provision covers instances where the prohibited activity takes place in the United States or where it takes place outside the United States and the offender is later found in the United States, or where an offender or a victim is a U.S. national. It does not cover instances where the relevant conduct was committed in the United States during or in connection with a labor dispute and the conduct is a felony under pertinent State law [6]

- 18 U.S.C. § 115(b)(3)–first degree murder of a member of the immediate family of a United States official, a United States judge, a Federal law enforcement officer, or an official whose killing would be a crime under 18 U.S.C. § 1114, with intent to impede, intimidate, or interfere with such official, judge, or law enforcement officer while engaged in the performance of official duties, or with intent to retaliate against such official, judge, or law enforcement officer on account of the performance of official duties.
- 18 U.S.C. §§ 229 and 229A(a)(2)–knowingly developing, producing, acquiring, transferring directly or indirectly, receiving, stockpiling, retaining, owning, possessing, using, or threatening to use any chemical weapon; or knowingly assisting or inducing any person to do any of the above; or knowingly attempting or conspiring to do any of the above, where death results. The offenses are defined in 18 U.S.C. § 229 and do not cover retention, ownership, possession, transfer, or receipt of a chemical weapon by a department, agency, or other entity of the United States, pending destruction of the weapon. Also exempt from coverage of these offenses are persons, including members of the U.S. Armed Forces, authorized by law or by an appropriate officer of the United States to retain, own, possess, transfer or receive the chemical weapon pending destruction of the weapon. Similarly exempt is any otherwise nonculpable person, in an emergency situation, if the person is attempting to destroy or seize the weapon. This covers conduct committed within the United States; committed by a U.S. national outside the United States; committed against a U.S. national while the national is outside the United States; or committed against property owned, leased, or used by the United States or any federal agency or department, whether within or outside the United States.
- 18 U.S.C. § 241–murder, with death resulting from a conspiracy to violate civil rights. Also appears to provide for possible capital punishment where acts constituting a conspiracy against rights under this section involve kidnapping or attempted kidnapping, aggravated sexual abuse or attempted aggravated sexual abuse, or attempted killing, regardless of whether death results from the commission of the offense. *But see*, 18 U.S.C. § 3591(a)(2). [7]
- 18 U.S.C. § 242–murder, with death resulting from a deprivation of civil rights under color of law. Also appears to make capital punishment available for acts constituting a deprivation of rights

under color of law involving kidnapping or attempted kidnapping, aggravated sexual abuse or attempted aggravated sexual abuse, or attempted killing, regardless of whether a death occurs during the commission of the offense. *But see*, 18 U.S.C. §3591(a)(2) [8]

- 18 U.S.C. § 245(b)–murder, with death resulting from a deprivation of federally protected rights. Also appears to make death penalty available for deprivation of federally protected rights if such acts include kidnapping or an attempt to kidnap, aggravated sexual abuse or attempted aggravated sexual abuse, or attempted killing, regardless of whether a death occurs during the commission of the offense. *But see*, 18 U.S.C. § 3591(a)(2) [9]

- 18 U.S.C. § 247–murder, with death resulting from intentionally damaging religious property or intentionally obstructing the free exercise of religion.

- Also appears to make capital punishment available for acts which constitute intentionally damaging religious property or intentionally obstructing free exercise of religion involving kidnapping or attempted kidnapping, aggravated sexual abuse or attempted aggravated sexual abuse, or attempted killing. *But see*, 18 U.S.C. § 3591(a)(2) [10]

- 18 U.S.C. § 351–assassination of Members of Congress, the Cabinet, or the Supreme Court, or major Presidential or Vice Presidential candidates.

- 18 U.S.C. § 794(a), 18 U.S.C. § 3591(a)(1)–espionage resulting in the identification and consequent death of an agent of the United States, or involving nuclear weaponry, military spacecraft or satellites, early warning systems or other means of defense or retaliation against large-scale attack, war plans, communications intelligence or cryptographic information, or any other major weapons system or major element of defense strategy [11]

- 18 U.S.C. § 794(b), 18 U.S.C. § 3591(a)(1)–espionage in time of war with intent that information be communicated to the enemy. Covers collection, recording, publishing, or communicating, or attempting to elicit any information with respect to movement, numbers, description, condition, or disposition of Armed Forces, ships, aircraft, or war materials of the United States; plans, conduct, or supposed plans or conduct of naval or military operations; any works or measures undertaken to fortify or defend any place; or any other information relating to the public defense, which might be useful to the enemy [12]

- 18 U.S.C. § 844(d)–interstate transportation or receipt of explosives with the knowledge or intent that they are to be used to kill another, where death results directly or proximately to any person, "including any public safety officer performing duties."

- 18 U.S.C. § 844(f)(3)–malicious damage or destruction or attempted damage or destruction of any building, vehicle, or other personal or real property in whole or in part owned or possessed by, or leased to, the United States or any department or agency thereof through use of fire or explosives, where the conduct directly or proximately caused the death of any person, "including any public safety officer performing duties."

- 18 U.S.C. § 844(i)–malicious damage or destruction or attempted damage or destruction, through the use of fire or explosives, of real or personal property used in interstate or foreign commerce or used in any activity affecting such commerce, where death results directly or proximately to any person, "including any public safety officer performing duties."

- 18 U.S.C. § 924(c) and (j)(1)–gun murders during federal crimes of violence or drug trafficking crimes.

- 18 U.S.C. § 930–first degree murder involving use of firearm or other dangerous weapon during attack on a federal facility.

- 18 U.S.C. § 1091–genocide committed in the United States or by a United States national

- 18 U.S.C. § 1111–first degree murder within the special maritime or territorial jurisdiction of the United States [13]

- 18 U.S.C. § 1114–first degree murder of federal officers or employees, including members of the uniformed services, while such officer or employee is engaged in or on account of the performance of official duties, or of any person assisting such officer or employee in the performance of such duties or on account of that assistance.

- 18 U.S.C. § 1116(a)–first degree murder of foreign officials, official guests, or internationally protected persons. Authorizes United States jurisdiction over the offense if the victim is an internationally protected person outside the United States where the victim is a representative, officer, employee, or agent of the United States; where an offender is a U.S. national; or where an offender is afterwards found in the United States.

- 18 U.S.C. § 1118–murder by a federal prisoner serving life sentence at the time of the offense.
- 18 U.S.C. § 1119–first degree murder of U.S. national outside the United States but within the jurisdiction of a foreign country.
- 18 U.S.C. § 1120–first degree murder by escaped federal prisoner who was confined under a life sentence.
- 18 U.S.C. § 1121–murder of state or local official, officer, or employee, or other person aiding federal criminal investigations, or of state correctional officer while the victim is engaged in the performance of official duties, because of the performance of such duties, or because of the victim's status as a public servant.
- 18 U.S.C. § 1201–violation of federal kidnapping laws where death results. Except in the case of kidnapping of a minor by his or her parent, this section covers kidnapping when the victim is transported in interstate or foreign commerce; when the act is committed within the special maritime or territorial jurisdiction of the United States or within the special aircraft jurisdiction of the United States; when the victim is a foreign official, internationally protected person, or official guest; or when the victim is a federal officer or employee covered by 18 U.S.C. § 1114 who is kidnapped while engaged in or on account of performance of official duties. Where the victim is an internationally protected person outside the United States, U.S. jurisdiction is authorized if the victim is a representative, officer, employee, or agent of the United States; if an offender is a U.S. national; or if an offender is afterwards found in the United States.
- 18 U.S.C. § 1203–hostage taking where death results.
- 18 U.S.C. § 1503–first degree murder of court officer or juror in federal judicial proceedings.
- 18 U.S.C. § 1512–murder, with death resulting from tampering with a federal witness, victim or informant.
- 18 U.S.C. § 1513–first degree murder, with death resulting from retaliation against a federal witness, victim or informant.
- 18 U.S.C. § 1716–mailing or depositing for mailing nonmailable injurious articles where death results.
- 18 U.S.C. § 1751(a), (b)–assassination/first degree murder of the President, President-elect; Vice President; or, if there is no Vice President, the officer next in order of succession to the Presidency; of the Vice President-elect; of another person acting as President under the Constitution and laws of the United States; or of certain

employees of the Executive Office of the President or of the Office of the Vice President. Also covers kidnapping of any of these officials or employees, where death results.

- 18 U.S.C. § 1958–murder, with death resulting from the use of facilities of interstate commerce in the commission of a murder for hire.
- 18 U.S.C. § 1959(a)(1)–murder, as consideration for receipt of, or as consideration for a promise or agreement to pay, anything of pecuniary value from an enterprise engaged in racketeering activity; or murder for the purpose of gaining entrance to or maintaining or increasing position in an enterprise engaged in racketeering activity [14]
- 18 U.S.C. § 1992–murder, with death resulting from wrecking trains or related structures, facilities or appurtenances, employed in interstate commerce.
- 18 U.S.C. § 2113(e)–murder, with the death resulting from: robbery or attempted robbery of a federally insured bank or savings and loan association or credit union; knowing receipt of stolen goods from such a robbery; avoiding or attempting to avoid apprehension for such an offense; or escaping or attempting to escape from arrest or confinement from such an offense.
- 18 U.S.C. § 2119(3)–murder, with death resulting from carjacking or attempted carjacking, of a car transported in interstate commerce.
- 18 U.S.C. § 2245–murder, with death resulting from a federal sexual abuse offense [15]
- 18 U.S.C. § 2251–murder, with death resulting from violation of federal laws against sexual exploitation of children.
- 18 U.S.C. § 2280–violence against maritime navigation where death results: committed against or on board a ship flying the United States flag; committed in the United States where the activity is not prohibited by pertinent state criminal law; committed by a United States national or a stateless person who habitually resides in the United States; committed against a United States national; committed to coerce the United States; or committed by one later found within the United States.
- 18 U.S.C. § 2281–murder, with death resulting from violence committed aboard a fixed ocean platform within the United States or by a United States national or against a United States national, committed to coerce the United States, or committed by one later

found within the United States. 18 U.S.C. § 2332(a)(1)–murder of a
United States national overseas.

- 18 U.S.C. § 2332a–where death results, use, attempted use, or
conspiracy to use, weapons of mass destruction (1) against a United
States national outside the United States; (2) against any person or
property within the United States, where either (A) the mail or any
facility of interstate or foreign commerce is used in furtherance of the
offense, (B) such property is used in interstate or foreign commerce or
in an activity that affects interstate or foreign commerce, (C) any
perpetrator travels in or causes another to travel in interstate or foreign
commerce in furtherance of the offense, or (D) the offense or the
results of the offense affect interstate or foreign commerce or, in the
case of a threat, attempt or conspiracy, would have affected interstate
or foreign commerce; [16] (3) against any property owned, leased or
used by the federal government; or(4) against any property within the
United States that is owned, leased, or used by a foreign government.
18 U.S.C. § 2332a(a). Subsection 2332a(b), added by P.L. 104-132
and amended by P.L. 108-458, makes the death penalty also available
with respect to any U.S. national who, without lawful authority, uses
or threatens, attempts, or conspires to use a weapon of mass
destruction outside of the United States, where death results. P.L. 104-
132 modified the definition of "weapon of mass destruction," to
include any destructive device as defined in 18 U.S.C. § 921; any
weapon that is designed or intended to cause death or serious bodily
injury through the release, dissemination, or impact of toxic or
poisonous chemicals, or their precursors; any weapon involving a
disease organism; or any weapon that is designed to release radiation
or radioactivity at a level dangerous to human life. However, before
passage of Section 6802(b) of P.L. 108-458, both 18 U.S.C. §§
2332a(a) and(b) excluded chemical weapons as defined under 18
U.S.C. § 229F from the"weapons of mass destruction" included in the
elements of these offenses. Section 6802(b) eliminated that exclusion
so that the offenses defined in 18 U.S.C. §§ 2332a(a) and (b) now can
involve such chemical weapons [17]

- 18 U.S.C. § 2332b–acts of terrorism transcending national boundaries,
where death results. Specifically prohibits killing, kidnapping,
maiming, committing an assault resulting in serious bodily injury or
committing an assault with a dangerous weapon within the United
States. Also prohibits creating a substantial risk of serious bodily

injury to another by destroying or damaging any structure, conveyance, or other real or personal property within the United States, or attempting or conspiring to do so, where the conduct transcends national boundaries and meets set jurisdictional criteria. Those criteria include: the offender used the mails or any facility of interstate or foreign commerce; the offense obstructed, delayed or affected interstate or foreign commerce, or the offense would have done so if consummated; the victim or intended victim is the U.S. government, a member of the uniformed services, or any official, officer, employee, or agent of the any of the three branches of the U.S. government or of any department or agency of the United States; the structure, conveyance or other real or personal property is, in whole or in part, owned, possessed, or leased by the United States or a department or agency thereof; the offense is committed in the territorial sea of the United States, including the airspace above, the seabed and subsoil below, and artificial islands and fixed structures erected thereon; or the offense is committed within the special maritime or territorial jurisdiction of the United States. The death penalty is available for any such offense involving a killing or resulting in death to any person from conduct prohibited by this section.

- 18 U.S.C. § 2332f–unlawfully delivering, placing, discharging, or detonating an explosive or other lethal device in, into, or against a place of public use, a government facility, a public transportation system, or an infrastructure facilities, with intent to cause death or serious bodily injury or to cause extensive destruction, where such destruction causes or is likely to cause major economic loss, where death results [18]

- 18 U.S.C. § 2340A–torture or attempted torture committed outside the United States by a person acting under color of law, where death results. United States jurisdiction under this provision covers offenses where the alleged offender is a U.S. national or where the alleged offender is present in the United States, regardless of the nationality of the victim or alleged offender

- 18 U.S.C. § 2381, 18 U.S.C. § 2391(a)(1); U.S. Constitution, Article 3, Sec. 3, cl. 1–treason by a person owing allegiance to the United States. Involves either levying war against the United States or adhering to enemies of the United States, giving aid and comfort to them either within the United States or elsewhere. Constitution provides that no person shall be convicted of treason except on the testimony of two witnesses to the same overt act or on confession in open court [19]

- 18 U.S.C. § 2441–War crimes committed by or against a member of the Armed Forces of the United States or a national of the United States as defined in section 101 of the Immigration and Nationality Act, 8 U.S.C. §1101, [20] where death results.
- 21 U.S.C. § 461–killing of a person engaged in or on account of his or her official duties under 21 U.S.C. § 451 *et seq.*, with respect to inspection of poultry or poultry products
- 21 U.S.C. § 675–killing of a person engaged in or on account of his or her official duties with respect to meat inspection under 21 U.S.C. § 601 *et seq.*
- 21 U.S.C. § 848(c)(1), 18 U.S.C. § 3591(b)(1)–drug kingpin violation committed as part of a continuing enterprise under conditions set forth in 21 U.S.C. § 848(b), involving twice the amount of controlled substances specified in 21 U.S.C. § 848(b)(2)(A) or twice the gross receipts specified in21 U.S.C. § 848(b)(2)(B) [21]
- 21 U.S.C. § 848(c)(1), 18 U.S.C. § 3591(b)(2)–attempted murder by a drug kingpin endeavoring to obstruct justice [22]
- 21 U.S.C. § 848(e)(1)–intentional killing in the course of a violation of the drug kingpin statute.
- 21 U.S.C. § 848(e)(1)–murder of a law enforcement officer in furtherance of a controlled substances offense.
- 21 U.S.C. § 1041–killing of a person engaged in or on account of his or her official duties under 21 U.S.C. § 1031 *et seq.*, with respect to inspection of eggs and egg products.
- 49 U.S.C. §§ 46502(a)(2)(B) and (b)(1)(B)–air piracy, where death of another person results from the commission or the attempt. Subsection46502(a)(2)(B) applies to aircraft piracy committed within the special aircraft jurisdiction of the United States. Subsection 46502(b)(1)(B) applies to an offense committed on an aircraft in flight outside the special aircraft jurisdiction of the United States and later found in the United States, where the takeoff or landing of the aircraft involved was located outside the territory of the aircraft's country of registration

CAPITAL SENTENCING PROCEDURES

Under 18 U.S.C. § 3432, a capital defendant must be provided a copy of the indictment and a list of veniremen and prosecution witnesses, stating the place of abode of each, at least three full days before trial begins. P.L. 103-322 amended this provision to permit the list of veniremen and witnesses to be withheld from a capital defendant if the court finds by a preponderance of the evidence that providing the list may jeopardize the life or safety of any person.

P.L. 103-322 also amended 18 U.S.C. § 3005 to provide that the trial court in a capital case shall, upon defendant's request, promptly assign two counsel, at least one of whom shall be learned in the law applicable to capital cases. Counsel shall have free access to the accused at all reasonable hours. In assigning such counsel, the court must consider the recommendations of the Federal Public Defender organization, if one exists in the district. Otherwise, the recommendation of the Administrative Office of the United States Courts must be taken into account.

Sentencing procedures for federal civilian capital cases are codified at 18 U.S.C. §§ 3591-3598. [23] The government must give a capital defendant timely notice before trial or before a guilty plea is accepted that the prosecution intends to seek a death sentence and must specify the aggravating factor or factors upon which it intends to rely for this purpose [24]. This notice must be filed with the court [25]. The new statutory procedures specify mitigating and aggravating factors to be considered in determining whether a death sentence is warranted in a given case [26]. In addition to the specified mitigating factors, [27] other factors in the defendant's background, record, or character or any other mitigating circumstances may be considered. In addition to the specified aggravating factors, [28] the jury, or if there is no jury, the court, may consider whether any other aggravating factor for which notice has been given exists [29]

In a capital case, a separate sentencing hearing must be held before a jury or, if there is no jury, before the court [30]. The government must prove aggravating factors beyond a reasonable doubt, while the defendant must prove mitigating factors by a preponderance of the information [31]. Where the hearing is before a jury, aggravating factors must be found unanimously. Special findings as to mitigating factors may be made by one or more members of the jury [32]. If no aggravating factors are found, the court must impose a sentence other than death [33].

The jury must be instructed that its capital sentencing decision must not involve any consideration of the race, color, religious beliefs, national origin, or gender of the defendant or of any victim. Each juror must certify that these considerations were not involved in his or her individual decision and that the juror would have made the same sentencing recommendation regardless of the race, color, religious beliefs, national origin, or sex of the defendant or of any victim [34].

No one may be sentenced to death for an offense committed while under the age of 18 [35]. Nor can a death sentence be carried out upon a pregnant woman, [36] a person who is mentally retarded, or who, because of a mental disability, lacks the capacity to understand the death penalty and the reason it was imposed [37]. Finally, a death penalty may not be imposed under these death penalty provisions upon a person subject to the criminal jurisdiction of an Indian tribal government for an offense which occurred within Indian country and for which federal jurisdiction is based "solely upon Indian country," unless the tribe's governing body has elected to have the new capital sentencing procedures in 18 U.S.C. ch. 228, §§ 3591-3598, applicable to the land and persons subject to its criminal jurisdiction [38].

The law provides for mandatory review of a death sentence upon timely notice filed. The court of appeals will reverse and remand for resentencing upon a finding that the sentence was the product of prejudice or passion, that the evidence does not support the finding of the existence of an aggravating factor, or that legal error requiring reversal exists [39].

Once appeals are exhausted, an execution is to be conducted according to the laws of the state in which the sentence is imposed. If the laws of that state do not provide for implementation of a death sentence, the court will designate another state which does have such laws, and the execution will be carried out in the manner prescribed by the latter state's laws [40]. State or local facilities may be used for execution. The United States marshal charged with supervising the implementation of the death sentence may also use the services of state or local officials or of a person such officials employ for that purpose. However, neither federal nor state employees may be required to participate in a capital prosecution or execution [41].

REFERENCES

[1] While a discussion of the death penalty provisions applicable to military personnel is beyond the scope of this paper, there are a number of these statutory provisions in the Uniform Code of Military Justice, including: 10 U.S.C. §§ 885 (desertion in time of war); 890 (assaulting or willfully

disobeying a superior commissioned officer in time of war); 894 (mutiny, sedition, attempted mutiny, or failure to suppress or report a mutiny or sedition); 899 (misbehavior before the enemy); 900 (subordinate compelling surrender); 901 (improper use of countersign in time of war); 902 (forcing a safeguard); 904 (aiding the enemy); 906 (spying in time of war); 910 (improper hazarding of a vessel); 913 (misbehavior of a sentinel in time of war); and 918 (premeditated murder or murder in the course of burglary, sodomy, rape, robbery, or aggravated arson). A military death penalty statute creating a capital offense for the commission of espionage in violation of the Uniform Code of Military Justice, enacted in the 99th Congress, is codified at 10 U.S.C. § 906a. The sentencing procedures set forth for the court-martial in this section specify aggravating and mitigating factors to be considered, require special findings regarding the existence of these factors, and direct that an accused may have broad latitude in presenting mitigating or extenuating evidence. This statute evidently was intended to conform to minimum constitutional standards, but the Supreme Court has not yet passed upon its constitutional validity.

10 U.S.C. § 920(a) also provides for capital punishment as a possible punishment for rape. Under Rule 1004(c)(9) of the Rules for Court-Martial in the *Manual for Courts-Martial*, the death penalty is only available as a sentencing option in a rape case under 10 U.S.C. § 920 if "(A) The victim was under the age of 12; or (B) The accused maimed or attempted to kill the victim." In Coker v. Georgia, 433 U.S. 584 (1984), the United States Supreme Court held the death penalty disproportionate, under the Eighth Amendment's prohibition of cruel and unusual punishment, to the rape of an adult woman by an escaped felon who had been serving sentences for murder, rape, kidnapping, and aggravated assault at the time of his escape, where the victim survived. (For more discussion of the *Coker* decision, see fn. 7, *infra*.) In United States v. Matthews, 16 M.J. 354 (C.M.A. 1983), *on remand,* 17 M.J. 978 (C.M.R. 1984) (substituting confinement for life at hard labor for death penalty), *review denied*, 18 M.J. 401 (C.M.A. 1984), the United States Court of Military Appeals observed that:

Congress obviously intended that in cases where an accused servicemember is convicted of premeditated murder, certain types of felony murder, or rape, the court-martial members should have the option to adjudge a death sentence. See Articles 118 and 120 [10 U.S.C. § 918 and 920]. Probably this intent cannot be constitutionally effectuated in a case where the rape of an adult female is involved, Coker v. Georgia, 433 U.S. 584 . . . (1977) – at least, where there is no purpose unique to the military mission that would be served by allowing the death penalty for this offense. . . .

16 M.J. at 380. *See*, United States v. Rojas, 15 M.J. 902, 927 n. 9 (N.M.C.M.R. 1983, *remanded on other grounds*, 17 M.J. 154 (C.M.A. 1984); United States v. Clark, 18 M.J. 775, 776 (N.M.C.M.R. 1984) ("Current appellate decisional authority indicates that the offense of rape, as alleged against the appellant, is not an offense for which the death penalty can be adjudged. . . . A sentence of death for the crime of rape of an adult woman is prohibited by the Eighth Amendment to the U.S. Constitution. Coker v. Georgia, 433 U.S. 584, . . . (1977). Therefore, the capital aspect of punishment purportedly authorized under Article 120 has been effectively invalidated."); United States v. Christie, 1995 CCA LEXIS 220 (A.F. Ct. Crim. App. August 28, 1995); United States v. Clark, 18 M.J. 775, 776 (N-M. Ct. Crim. App. 1984); United States v. McReynolds, 9 M.J. 881, 882 (A.F.C.M.R. 1980). *See also,* United States v. Curtis, 32 M.J. 252, 266 (C.M.A. 1991), and United States v. Straight, 42 M.J. 244, 247 (C.A.A.F 1995), interpreting Rule 1004(c)(9) as having been drafted in an effort to comply with *Coker.*

Prior to enactment of 10 U.S.C. § 906a, President Reagan issued an executive order which changed the sentencing procedures in the Manual of Courts-Martial in an apparent attempt to conform them to minimum constitutional standards. E.O. 12473, issued April 13, 1984. In Loving v. United States, 517 U.S.748 (1996), *writ of mandamus denied*, 47 M.J. 438 (C.A.A.F. 1998), *cert. denied*, 525 U.S. 1040 (1998), the Supreme Court addressed a constitutional challenge on Eighth Amendment and separation of powers grounds to the aggravating factors applicable to military death penalty cases promulgated by executive order and included in Rule for Courts-Martial (RCM) 1004, as amended. Loving contended that fundamental policy determinations with respect to aggravating factors in death penalty cases must be made by Congress through statutory enactments, rather than by the President. The Court, assuming that Furman v. Georgia, 408 U.S. 238 (1972), and subsequent cases applied to the crime and sentence before it, found that the aggravating factors included in RCM 1004 were necessary, from a constitutional perspective, to adequately narrow the class of persons eligible to receive the death penalty under the statute under which Loving was convicted and sentenced. Further, the Court rejected

Loving's contention that the President's promulgation of these aggravating factors by executive order violated separation of powers principles. The Court found that the Congress had the power to delegate the authority to prescribe aggravating factors in military capital murder cases to the President, and had in fact made a valid delegation of that authority in 10 U.S.C. §§ 818, 836(a) and 856. The Court also found a connection between the delegated authority and the President's constitutional duties as Commander in Chief. The capital sentencing procedures governing civilian capital cases first added by P.L. 103-322, Title VI, Sec. 60002(a), codified at 18 U.S.C. §§ 3591-3598, as amended, do not apply to "prosecutions under the Uniform Code of Military Justice (10 U.S.C. § 801)." P.L. 103-322, Title VI, Sec. 60004, 18 U.S.C. § 3591 note.

[2]   In 1974, the Congress enacted a death penalty statute for air piracy where death resulted from the commission of the offense, and responded to the concerns reflected in *Furman* by including procedures designed to tailor the sentencing discretion of the judge or jury in determining the appropriate sentence to impose in the case before them. The substantive provisions were codified at 49 U.S.C. §§ 1472(i) and (n) (49 U.S.C. § 46502 in the revised Title 49 of the United States Code), while the procedures for a separate sentencing hearing, specifying aggravating and mitigating factors to be considered in the sentencing determination, and requiring a special verdict finding the existence or non-existence of each of the factors, were codified at then existing 49 U.S.C. App. § 1473(c)/49 U.S.C. § 46503. The constitutional sufficiency of these procedures was not tested. They might have given rise to a question as to whether they satisfied the constitutional minimum in light of the Supreme Court's decision in Lockett v. Ohio, 438 U.S. 586, 604 (1978), which held invalid Ohio's death penalty statute because it failed to permit consideration, in a capital case, of any aspects of the defendant's character or record or the circumstances of the offense as a mitigating factor. The federal air piracy sentencing provisions in former 49 U.S.C. App. § 1473(c)/49 U.S.C. § 46503 appeared to limit the mitigating factors which may be considered in a capital case, and therefore might have been subject to attack. The death penalty sentencing procedures for aircraft piracy in former 49 U.S.C. App. 1473(c)/49 U.S.C. § 46503 were repealed by Sec. 60003(b)(2), 108 Stat. 1970, of P.L. 103-322. In a capital aircraft piracy case under current law, the general death penalty sentencing provisions in 18 U.S.C. § 3591 *et seq.* would apply. For a

discussion of capital sentencing provisions, see the discussion of capital sentencing procedures starting at page 13, *infra*.

In the Anti-Drug Abuse Act of 1988, P.L. 100-690, the death penalty was made available for certain controlled substances offenses where intentional death resulted from the offense. 21 U.S.C. §§ 848(e) and (g)-(r). The measure, as amended, includes sentencing procedures which provide for a separate sentencing hearing; specifies aggravating and mitigating factors, detailing the means of proof and requiring special findings concerning them; and supplies instruction for the imposition, appeal, and execution of a death sentence. The availability of counsel as well as investigative, expert and other services for indigent defendants is also addressed. The composition of the jury is specified, and the jury is required to return to the court a certificate signed by each juror indicating that discrimination played no part in his or her sentencing decision. Thus far, these capital sentencing provisions have withstood constitutional challenge.

[3]   The offense is set forth generally in 18 U.S.C. § 32, while the penalty for commission of the offense where death results is drawn from 18 U.S.C. § 34. The latter section makes the death penalty available for offenses prohibited by 18 U.S.C. ch. 2 (§§ 31-38), which result in the death of any person.

[4]   The offense is set forth generally in 18 U.S.C. § 33, while the penalty for commission of the offense where death results is specified in 18 U.S.C. § 34.

[5]   *See also*, 18 U.S.C. § 34, which makes capital punishment available for any offense prohibited by 18 U.S.C. ch. 2 (§§ 31-38) where death results.

[6]   *See also*, 18 U.S.C. § 34, which makes the death penalty available for any offense prohibited by 18 U.S.C. ch. 2 (§§ 31-38) where death results.

[7]   Under the Supreme Court's reasoning in Coker v. Georgia, 433 U.S. 584 (1977), and its progeny, a death penalty imposed under such circumstances, where the commission of the offense did not result in a death, might give rise to a question as to whether the punishment imposed was disproportionate to the crime committed. *Coker* involved the rape of an adult woman by an escaped felon who had been serving sentences for murder, rape, kidnapping, and aggravated assault at the time of his escape, where the victim survived. The Court, while acknowledging the seriousness of the crime, found the death penalty

disproportionate to the offense. This case has given rise to questions as to whether the death penalty would be found appropriate, under Eighth Amendment cruel and unusual standards, for any offense where a death did not result. *See, e.g., Coker*, 433 U.S., at 621 (Burger, C.J., dissenting). Indeed, Chief Justice Burger also raised a question as to whether the death penalty might also be open to challenge under the plurality's reasoning for crimes such as "treason," "airplane hijacking, kidnapping, and mass terrorist activity," which, although dangerous and constituting a serious threat to public safety, did not necessarily result in immediate death. *Id.* Similar reasoning might give rise to a question as to the constitutionality of a death penalty for espionage where death did not result from the commission of the offense.

Except with respect to espionage and treason as addressed in 18 U.S.C. § 3591(a)(1), and certain controlled substances offenses referred to in 18 U.S.C. § 3591(b), the *Coker* issue raised by provision of a death penalty for offenses not involving death may be minimized by the impact of 18 U.S.C. § 3591(a)(2), which provides that a death sentence may be imposed upon a defendant found guilty of (2) any other offense for which a sentence of death is provided, if the defendant, as determined beyond a reasonable doubt at the hearing under section 3593-- intentionally killed the victim; intentionally inflicted serious bodily injury that resulted in the death of the victim; (C) intentionally participated in an act, contemplating that the life of a person would be taken or intending that lethal force would be used in connection with a person other than one of the participants in the offense, and the victim died as a direct result of that act; or (D) intentionally and specifically engaged in an act of violence, knowing that the act created a grave risk of death to a person, other than one of the participants in the offense, such that participation in the act constituted a reckless disregard for human life and the victim died as a direct result of the act, ... Under Subsection 3591(a)(1), the death penalty is made available in cases where the defendant has been found guilty of an offense described in 18 U.S.C. § 794 (espionage) or § 2381 (treason), without explicitly restricting the availability of capital punishment to those cases in which death results. Subsection 3591(b) makes the death penalty available for a defendant who has been found guilty of (1) an offense referred to in section 408(c)(1) of the Controlled Substances Act (21 U.S.C. 848(c)(1)), committed as part of a continuing criminal enterprise offense under the conditions described in subsection (b) of that section which involved not less than twice the quantity of controlled substance described in subsection (b)(2)(A) or twice the gross receipts described in subsection (b)(2)(B); or (2) an offense referred to in section 408(c)(1) of the Controlled Substances Act (21 U.S.C. 848(c)(1)), committed as part of a continuing criminal enterprise offense under that section, where the defendant is a principal administrator, organizer, or leader of such an enterprise, and the defendant, in order to obstruct the investigation or prosecution of the enterprise or an offense involved in the enterprise, attempts to kill or knowingly directs, advises, authorizes, or assists another to attempt to kill any public officer, juror, witness, or member of the family or household of such person, ...

[8]   As discussed in greater depth at fn. 7, above, it is questionable whether the death penalty may be constitutionally applied in cases where the offense committed does not result in death, in light of the Supreme Court's 1977 decision in Coker v. Georgia, *supra*. Note that operation of 18 U.S.C. § 3591(a)(2) would appear to limit the availability of the death penalty where death did not result from commission of an offense under 18 U.S.C. § 242, despite language in the offense statute that appears to provide for possible capital punishment.

[9]   It is questionable whether the death penalty can constitutionally be applied in cases where the offense does not result in death, in light of the Supreme Court's decision in Coker v. Georgia, *supra,* as discussed in greater depth at fn. 7, above. Note that operation of 18 U.S.C. § 3591(a)(2) would seem to limit the availability of the death penalty for offenses under 18 U.S.C. § 245(b) which do not result in death, even though the language of the offense provision appears to provide for possible capital punishment.

[10]   As discussed in greater depth at fn. 7, *supra*, it is uncertain whether the death penalty may be applied to offenses which do not result in death in light of the Supreme Court's decision in Coker v. Georgia, *supra*. Note that operation of 18 U.S.C. § 3591(a)(2) would appear to limit the availability of the death penalty for offenses under 18 U.S.C. § 247 which do not result in death, even though the language of the offense provision appears to provide for possible capital punishment.

[11]   It is uncertain whether the death penalty may be applied to offenses which do not result in death, in light of the Supreme Court's analysis in Coker v. Georgia, *supra*, which is discussed in greater depth at fn. 7, *supra*. The issue would be whether, under the Eighth Amendment's cruel and unusual standard, the penalty would be deemed disproportionate to

the crime. *But see*, U.S. v. Regan, 221 F. Supp. 2d 661 (E.D. Va. 2002) (denying defendant's motion to strike government's Notice of Intention to Seek the Death Penalty in a case where the defendant was charged with attempted espionage and there was no allegation of death resulting from the commission of the offense. Defendant premised his motion not on *Coker*, but on an Eighth Amendment comparative proportionality argument. Statutory aggravating factors were that, in commission of the offense the defendant knowingly created a grave risk of substantial danger to the national security; and that, in commission of the offense the defendant knowingly created a grave risk of death to another person.).

[12] In light of the Court's reasoning in Coker v. Georgia, *supra*, as discussed at fn. 7, *supra*, a death sentence imposed for this offense may be subject to an Eighth Amendment challenge on the grounds that the punishment is disproportionate to the crime. Such a challenge would appear to have less force if the commission of the offense caused someone's death; such a result may be likely considering the nature of the information which may be involved in such war-time disclosures and the potential impact of such disclosures.

[13] 49 U.S.C. § 46506(1) extends federal criminal jurisdiction to certain offenses committed aboard an aircraft in flight. One of the offenses referenced by this subsection is 18 U.S.C. § 1111.

[14] Section 6802(e) of P.L. 108-458, the Intelligence Reform and Terrorism Prevention Act of 2004, expands the list of offenses considered "racketeering activity" as defined in 18 U.S.C. § 1961 to include any act which is indictable under 18 U.S.C. §§ 175-178 (relating to biological weapons), sections 229-229F (relating to chemical weapons), and section 831(relating to nuclear weapons). Under 18 U.S.C. § 1959(b), "racketeering activity" as used in § 1959 has the meaning set forth in § 1961, so the effect of the expansion of the definition of "racketeering activity" is, in part, to indirectly expand the possible circumstances in which the death penalty may be available under 18 U.S.C. § 1959.

[15] 49 U.S.C. § 46506(1) extends federal criminal jurisdiction to certain offenses committed aboard an aircraft in flight, including 18 U.S.C. ch. 109A, dealing with sexual abuse. Among the provisions of Chapter 109A is 18 U.S.C. § 2245, added by P.L. 103-322.

[16] Section 6802(a) of P.L. 108-458 amended subsection (2) of 18 U.S.C. §2332a(a), expanding the range of potential targets or victims covered by the offense. Section 6802(a) of P.L. 108-458 also added subsection

(4), again broadening the range of factual situations covered by the offense. In addition, it amended 18 U.S.C. § 2332a(c) to add a new definition of "property,"including all real and personal property. Section 6802(b) of P.L. 108-458 expanded the scope of "weapons of mass destruction" covered by the offense provisions in both 18 U.S.C. §§ 2332a(a) and (b) to include chemical weapons as defined in 18 U.S.C. § 229F. By expanding the victims, targets, and circumstances covered by the offense provisions in 18 U.S.C. §§ 2332a(a) and (b), Section 6802 of P.L. 108-458 expanded the circumstances in which the death penalty might be available where death resulted from the commission of the offenses involved.

[17]   18 U.S.C. § 229F defines the term "chemical weapon to mean, together or separately: a toxic chemical and its precursors, except where intended for a purpose not prohibited under 18 U.S.C., chapter 11B, as long as the type and quantity is consistent with such a purpose; a munition or device, specifically designed to cause death or other harm through toxic properties of such toxic chemicals, which would be released as a result of the employment of such a munition or device; and/or any equipment specifically designed for use directly in connection with the employment of such munitions or devices.

[18]   This provision was added on June 25, 2002, as part of the Terrorist Bombings Convention Implementation Act of 2002, P.L. 107-197, Section 102(a), 116 Stat. 721. For applicable criminal penalties, the section cross references to 18 U.S.C. § 2332c. Federal jurisdiction over the offenses in 18 U.S.C. § 2332f is based on the existence of the following specified circumstances: If the offense is committed in the United States, (1) the offense must be committed against another nation or political subdivision thereof or a governmental facility of such nation or political subdivision, including its embassy, other diplomatic or consular premises; (2) the offense must be committed in an attempt to compel another nation or political subdivision thereof or the United States to act or to abstain from acting; (3) the offense must be committed on board a vessel flying the flag of another nation, on board an aircraft registered under the laws of another nation, or on board an aircraft operated by the government of another nation or political subdivision thereof; (4) a perpetrator is found outside the United States; (5) a perpetrator is a national of another nation or a stateless person; or (6) a victim is a national of another nation or a stateless person. If the offense takes place outside the United States, (1) a perpetrator must be a U.S.

national; (2) a victim must be a U.S. national; (3) a perpetrator must be found in the United States; (4) the offense must be committed in an attempt to compel the U.S. to do or abstain from doing any act; (5) the offense must be committed against a governmental facility of the United States or a political subdivision thereof, including a U.S. embassy or other diplomatic or consular premises; (6) the offense must be committed on board a vessel flying the U.S. flag or registered under U.S. law at the time the offense was committed; or (7) the offense must be committed on board an aircraft operated by the United States. Federal jurisdiction does not apply to the activities of armed forces during an armed conflict under the laws of war; to activities undertaken by military forces of a state in exercise of their official duties; or to offenses committed within the United States, where both the alleged offender and the victim(s) are U.S. citizens and the alleged offender is found within the U.S.; or where jurisdiction is predicated solely on the nationality of the victims or the alleged offender and the offense has no substantial effect on interstate or foreign commerce.

[19] If no death results from the commission of this offense, then, under the reasoning of the Court in Coker v. Georgia, *supra*, a death sentence imposed for this crime may be open to constitutional challenge. See discussion in fn. 7, *supra*.

[20] 22 U.S.C. § 1101(a)(22) defines "national of the United States" to mean "(A) a citizen of the United States, or (B) a person who, though not a citizen of the United States, owes permanent allegiance to the United States."

[21] As noted in fn. 7, *supra*, it is questionable, in light of the Supreme Court's decision in Coker v. Georgia, *supra*, whether the death penalty may be constitutionally applied to cases where a death does not result from the commission of the offense.

[22] The imposition of a death sentence for this offense might also give rise to an Eighth Amendment proportionality challenge under Coker v. Georgia, *supra*, *see* fn. 7, *supra*.

[23] These capital sentencing procedures were added by P.L. 103-322, Title VI, Sept. 13, 1994, 108 Stat. 1960 ; and have been amended by P.L. 103-322 Title XXXIII, § 330021(1), Sept. 13, 1994, 108 Stat. 1960, 2150; P.L. 104-132, Title VII, § 728, April 13, 1996,110 Stat. 1302; P.L. 104-294, Title VI, §§ 601(b)(7), 604(b)(35), Oct. 11, 1996, 110 Stat. 3499, 3508; P.L. 105-6, § 2(c), March. 19, 1997, 111 Stat. 12; and P.L. 107-

273, Div. B., Title IV, §§ 4002(e)(2) and 4002(e)(8), Nov. 2, 2002, 116 Stat. 1810.

[24]   18 U.S.C. § 3593(a).

[25]   *Id.*

[26]   18 U.S.C. § 3592.

[27]   Under 18 U.S.C. § 3592(a), specified mitigating factors may include: a defendant's impaired capacity; the fact that the defendant acted under unusual and substantial duress; the defendant's minor participation in the capital offense; the fact that equally culpable defendant(s) will not be punished by death; the fact that the defendant has no prior criminal record; the defendant's severe mental or emotional disturbance when committing the offense; and the victim's consent to the conduct which resulted in his or her death.

[28]   18 U.S.C. § 3592(b) sets out aggravating factors applicable to treason or espionage capital offenses, including a defendant's prior espionage or treason offense for which he or she could have been sentenced to life imprisonment or death, the fact that the defendant knowingly created a grave risk of substantial danger to national security in the commission of the offense at bar, or the fact that the defendant knowingly created a grave risk of death to another person in commission of the offense.

18 U.S.C. § 3592(c) sets forth sixteen aggravating factors for homicide. Among these are: the fact that the death or injury resulting in death occurred during commission, attempted commission or flight from commission of one of a series of specified felonies; the defendant's prior conviction for a state or federal felony involving a firearm, other than a capital offense under 18 U.S.C. §924(c) and (j); the defendant's prior conviction for a federal or state offense which resulted in death, for which life imprisonment or a death sentence was authorized by statute; the defendant's prior conviction of two or more federal or state felonies, committed on separate occasions, involving infliction or attempted infliction of serious bodily injury or death; knowing creation of grave risk of death to one or more persons other than the victim of the offense during the commission of the offense or escape from apprehension for the offense; commission of the offense in an especially heinous, cruel, or depraved manner; procurement of commission of the offense by payment or promise of payment; commission of the offense for pecuniary gain; commission of the offense after substantial planning and premeditation to cause another's death or to commit an act of terrorism; the defendant's prior conviction of two or more federal or state drug

trafficking felonies; the victim's particular vulnerability due to old age, youth or infirmity; the defendant's previous conviction of serious drug felonies under title II or III of the Comprehensive Drug Abuse Prevention and Control Act of 1970, for which sentences of at least five years of imprisonment could be imposed, or previous conviction for engaging in a continuing criminal enterprise; the defendant's commission of the offense during the course of engaging in a continuing criminal enterprise where the offense involved distribution of drugs to persons under 21; the fact that the offense was committed against certain high public officials or federal public servants (including judges, law enforcement officers, or employees of a U.S. penal or correctional institution while engaged in official duties or because of their official duties or their status as public servants); where the offense involves sexual abuse under 18 U.S.C. § 2241 *et seq.*, or sexual abuse of children under 18 U.S.C. § 2251 *et seq.*, the fact that the defendant was previously convicted of sexual assault or child molestation; or the fact that the defendant intentionally killed or attempted to kill more than one person in a single criminal episode.

Aggravating factors for drug offense death penalties are set forth in 18 U.S.C. § 3592(d). These eight factors include: previous conviction of a state or federal offense involving the death of a person for which the death penalty or life imprisonment was authorized; previous conviction of two or more federal or state felonies committed on different occasions involving importation, manufacture or distribution of a controlled substance or involving the infliction of or attempted infliction of serious bodily injury or death; previous conviction of a state or federal offense involving manufacture, distribution, importation or possession of a controlled substance for which a sentence of imprisonment for five years or more was authorized; the defendant's use of a firearm in the commission of the offense or in furtherance of a continuing criminal enterprise, or the defendant's having knowingly directed, advised, authorized or assisted another to use a firearm to threaten, intimidate, assault or injure a person; the defendant directly distributed controlled substances to a person under age 21 during the commission of the offense or during a continuing criminal enterprise of which the offense was a part; the defendant directly used minors in drug trafficking during the offense or during a continuing criminal enterprise of which the offense was a part; or the defendant directly distributed controlled substances near schools during the offense or during a continuing criminal enterprise of which the offense was a part; or the offense involved the importation, manufacture, or distribution of a controlled substance mixed with a potentially lethal adulterant, where the defendant was aware of the presence of the adulterant.

[29] The statutory provisions permitting the prosecutor to propose and the jury to consider nonstatutory aggravating factors, 18 U.S.C. §§ 3592(c) and 3593(a), have withstood constitutional challenges alleging that it constituted an impermissible delegation of legislative powers to the Executive Branch. *See, e.g.,* United States v. Allen, 247 F.3d 741 (8th Cir. 2001), *vacated and remanded for reconsideration in light of Ring v. Arizona, 536 U.S. 584 (2002),* 536 U.S. 953 (2002), *cert. denied* ___ U.S. ___, 123 S. Ct. 2273 (2003), *rehearing denied,* ___ U.S. ___, 124 S. Ct. 19 (2003), *on remand* 357 F.3d 745(8th Cir. 2004) (death sentence vacated and remanded for imposition of life sentence); *motion for rehearing en banc granted and judgment vacated,* 2004 U.S. App. LEXIS 9190 (May 11, 2004); United States v. Sampson, 275 F. Supp. 2d 49 (D. Mass. 2003). They have also passed muster under Eighth Amendment analysis, United States v. Sampson, *supra*; United States v. Frank, 8 F. Supp. 2d. 253 (S.D.N.Y. 1998) (finding that Federal Death Penalty Act did not violate the constitutional prohibition against cruel and unusual punishment by permitting nonstatutory aggravating factors); U.S. v. Llera Plaza, 179 F. Supp. 2d 444 (E.D. Pa. 2001) (holding nonstatutory aggravating factors did not permit wholly arbitrary and capricious death sentences in violation of Eighth and Fourteenth Amendments); U.S. v. Nguyen, 928 F. Supp. 1525 (D. Kan. 1996) (holding that consideration of nonstatutory aggravating factors did not result in arbitrary and capricious sentencing in violation of the Eighth Amendment); U.S. v. Sampson, *supra* (risk of execution of innocent individuals did not mean that Federal Death Penalty Act was unconstitutional under Eighth Amendment). The Federal Death penalty Act has also withstood challenges based upon the ex post facto clause, Art. I, Sec. 9, cl. 3, of the U.S. Constitution, *see,* U.S. v. Allen, *supra*; U.S. v. Frank, *supra*; U.S. v. Nguyen, *supra*; U.S. v. McVeigh, 944 F. Supp. 1478 (D. Colo. 1996); U.S. v. Chanthadara, 928 F. Supp. 1055 (D. Kan. 1996). Some cases have considered the effect of Ring v. Arizona, *supra,* upon the sufficiency of an indictment in federal death penalty cases, *see,* U.S. v. Jackson, 327 F.3d 273 (4th Cir. 2003), *cert. denied,* 540 U.S. 1019 (2003) (holding that an aggravating factor necessary to the imposition of the death penalty must be alleged in the indictment);

U.S. v. Higgs, 353 F. 3d 281 (4th Cir. 2003), *cert. denied*, ___ U.S. ___, 125 S. Ct. 627 (2004) (finding that since only one aggravating factor need be found by the jury for the death penalty to be imposed under the Federal Death Penalty Act, if one statutory factor is alleged in the indictment and that aggravating factor is found by the petit jury, the indictment is not defective because it did not include all aggravating factors that the jury might consider in determining whether to impose the death penalty); U.S. v. Regan, 221 F. Supp. 2d 672 (E.D. Va. 2002). In U.S. v. Quinones, 317 F.3d 86 (2d Cir. 2003), the court denied a motion for rehearing on an unsuccessful challenge to the Federal Death Penalty Act on the basis that the death penalty was unconstitutional per se because DNA tests had indicated that innocent people have been sentenced to death.

[30]   18 U.S.C. § 3593(b).
[31]   18 U.S.C. § 3593(c).
[32]   18 U.S.C. § 3593(d).
[33]   18 U.S.C. § 3593(e).
[34]   18 U.S.C. § 3593(f).
[35]   18 U.S.C. § 3591(b).
[36]   18 U.S.C. § 3596(b).
[37]   18 U.S.C. § 3596(c).
[38]   18 U.S.C. § 3598.
[39]   18 U.S.C. § 3595.
[40]   18 U.S.C. § 3596(a).
[41]   18 U.S.C. § 3597.

In: Crime and Law Enforcement Issues ISBN 978-1-61122-877-9
Editor: James E. Hirsch © 2011 Nova Science Publishers, Inc.

Chapter 3

JUVENILE JUSTICE: RIGHTS DURING THE ADJUDICATORY PROCESS

Alison M. Smith

ABSTRACT

As more attention is being focused on juvenile offenders, some question whether the justice system is dealing with this population appropriately. Since the late 1960s, the juvenile justice system has undergone significant modifications resulting from U.S. Supreme Court decisions, changes in federal and state law, and the growing belief that juveniles were increasingly involved in more serious and violent crimes. Consequently, at both the federal and states levels, the juvenile justice system has shifted from a mostly rehabilitative system to a more punitive one, with serious ramifications for juvenile offenders. Despite this shift, juveniles are generally not afforded the panoply of rights afforded to adult criminal defendants. The U.S. Constitution requires that juveniles receive many of the features of an adult criminal trial, including notice of charges, right to counsel, privilege against self-incrimination, right to confrontation and cross-examination, proof beyond a reasonable doubt, and double jeopardy. However, in *McKeiver v. Pennsylvania*, the Court held that juveniles do not have a fundamental right to a jury trial during adjudicatory proceedings.

The Sixth Amendment explicitly guarantees the right to an impartial jury trial in criminal prosecutions. In *Duncan v. Louisiana*, the U.S. Supreme Court held that this right is fundamental and guaranteed by the Due Process Clause of the Fourteenth Amendment. However, the Court has since limited its holding in *Duncan* to adult defendants by stating that the right to a jury trial is not constitutionally required for juveniles in juvenile court proceedings. Some argue that because the Court has determined that jury trials are not constitutionally required for juvenile adjudications, courts should not treat or consider juvenile adjudications in subsequent criminal proceedings. In addition, some argue that the use of non-jury juvenile adjudications in subsequent criminal proceedings violates due process guarantees, because juvenile justice and adult criminal proceedings are fundamentally different.

Has the juvenile justice system changed in such a manner that the Supreme Court should revisit the question of jury trials in juvenile adjudications? Are the procedural safeguards in the juvenile justice system sufficient to ensure their reliable use for sentence enhancement purposes in adult criminal proceedings? To help address these questions, this report provides a brief background on the purpose of the juvenile system and discusses procedural due process protections provided by the Court for juveniles during adjudicatory hearings. It also discusses the Court's emphasis on the jury's role in criminal proceedings and will be updated as events warrant.

As attention continues to focus on juvenile offenders, some question the way in which they are treated in the U.S. criminal justice system. Since the late 1960s, the juvenile justice system has undergone significant modifications as a result of United States Supreme Court decisions, changes in federal and state law and the growing perception that juveniles were increasingly involved in more serious and violent crimes [1]. As a result, federal and state juvenile justice systems have focused less on rehabilitation and more on punishment, which may have significant ramifications for juvenile offenders once they reach adulthood. For example, recidivist statutes such as the Armed Career Criminal Act (ACCA) [2] impose mandatory minimums based on prior convictions, including juvenile adjudications [3]. As such, adult criminal defendants are exposed to longer terms of imprisonment based on prior juvenile misconduct. Despite this shift in focus to one more closely resembling the adult criminal justice system, juvenile offenders are not generally afforded the full panoply of rights provided to adult criminal defendants.

BACKGROUND: THE JUVENILE JUSTICE SYSTEM

The establishment of a juvenile court in Cook County, Illinois, in 1899 marked the first statewide implementation of a separate judicial framework whose sole concern was the problems and misconduct of children. The juvenile court was designed to be more than a court for children. The underlying theory behind a separate juvenile court system was that the state has a duty to assume a custodial and protective role over individuals who cannot act in their own best interest [4]. As such, the separate system for juvenile offenders was predicated on the notion of rehabilitation — not punishment, retribution, or incapacitation. Because the juvenile court focused on protection rather than punishment, the juvenile proceeding was conceptualized as a civil proceeding (not a criminal one), with none of the trappings of an adversarial proceeding [5]

By the mid-20th century, questions arose regarding the fairness and efficacy of the juvenile justice system and its ability to effectively rehabilitate young offenders. Concerns that the differences between the adult and juvenile systems were illusory prompted the need to preserve the legal rights of children adjudicated in the juvenile justice system [6]. As such, state courts began to expand the legal rights of juvenile offenders. The emerging focus on juveniles' rights in the state courts prompted intervention from the U.S. Supreme Court, which had traditionally deferred to the states.

PROCEDURAL DUE PROCESS RIGHTS

Beginning in the mid-1960s, the Court examined the due process rights of minors in four landmark cases: Kent v. United States, [7] In re Gault, [8] In re Winship, [9] and McKeiver v. Pennsylvania [10]. Through these cases, the Court left an indelible mark on the juvenile justice system by restricting the discretion of juvenile court judges and enumerating the constitutional rights retained by juveniles during adjudication. These decisions resulted in a hybrid juvenile justice system that renders some of the procedural rights afforded to adult criminal defendants. Some argue that this hybrid system blurs the historical distinction between the juvenile justice and adult criminal systems.

Kent v. United States

The Court first recognized that the U.S. Constitution guaranteed juveniles due process rights in *Kent v. United States* [11]. In *Kent*, the Court reviewed a District of Columbia case in which the petitioner challenged the validity of the juvenile court's decision to waive jurisdiction over him, on the ground that the procedure used by the court in reaching its decision constituted a denial of due process of law. The U.S. Supreme Court held that the waiver of jurisdiction was a "critically important" stage in the juvenile process and must be attended by minimum requirements of due process and fair treatment required by the Fourteenth Amendment [12]. In reaching its decision, the Court expressed concern that the non-criminal nature of the juvenile proceeding was an invitation to "procedural arbitrariness" [13] including broad judicial fact-finding.

In re Gault

In *In re Gault*, [14] the Court held that the informal procedures of juvenile courts amount to a denial of juveniles' fundamental due process rights [15] Although the Court recognized that juvenile courts were attempting to help juveniles, it reasoned that this worthy purpose failed to justify informal procedure, particularly when a juvenile's liberty was threatened [16]. After a thorough examination of the history of the juvenile court system, the Court reiterated much of the criticism it raised in *Kent*, specifically expressing concern about the juvenile court's informality and the broad discretion of its judges [17] To ensure that juveniles receive the essentials of fair treatment during an adjudicatory hearing, the Court found that juveniles were entitled to certain due process rights afforded to adult criminal defendants under the U.S. Constitution [18]. These rights include the right to reasonable notice of the charges, the right to counsel, the right to confrontation, and the right against self-incrimination [19].

In re Winship

In *In re Winship*, the Court continued to expand the rights of juveniles by holding that the state must show proof beyond a reasonable doubt to adjudicate a minor as delinquent for an act that would be a crime if committed by an adult [20]. The state of New York charged Samuel Winship with delinquency for stealing $112 from a woman's pocketbook in a furniture store [21]. Having already established that juvenile proceedings must conform to due process and fair treatment, the Court considered a single issue: whether due process and fair treatment require a state to demonstrate proof beyond a reasonable doubt to hold a juvenile accountable for committing an adult criminal act [22]

Although a New York juvenile court found Winship to be delinquent under a statute that required the state to show guilt merely by a preponderance of the evidence, the Court reversed, emphasizing that criminal charges have always required a higher burden of persuasion than civil cases [23]. The Court expressly held that the Due Process Clause of the Fourteenth Amendment protects the accused against conviction except upon proof beyond a reasonable doubt of every fact necessary to constitute the crime with which he or she is charged [24]. Finding that juveniles are constitutionally entitled to the reasonable doubt standard, the Court stated, "[t]he same considerations that demand extreme caution in fact-finding to protect the innocent adult apply as well to the innocent child." [25]. The Court rejected the state's argument that the delinquency adjudication is a civil proceeding that did not require due process protections, calling this argument the "civil label of convenience" [26].

McKeiver v. Pennsylvania

By 1970, the Supreme Court had ruled that the due process notion of fundamental fairness entitled juveniles to various procedural protections in juvenile court. However, in *McKeiver v. Pennsylvania*, [27] the Court held that juveniles do not have a fundamental right to a jury trial when being adjudicated in the juvenile justice system [28]. *McKeiver* was a consolidation of three similar appeals involving minors adjudicated delinquent in juvenile court by judges who had rejected their requests for a jury to serve as fact-finder at their hearing [29]. The Court narrowed the issue presented to whether the Due Process Clause of the Fourteenth Amendment ensured the right to trial by jury in the adjudicative phase of a juvenile court delinquency proceeding [30]. After reviewing its previous juvenile court jurisprudence, the Court first considered whether the right to a jury was automatically guaranteed to minors by the Sixth and Fourteenth Amendments [31]. Although it had never expressly characterized juvenile court proceedings as criminal prosecutions within the meaning and reach of the Sixth Amendment, the Court reiterated that the juvenile court system reflected many of the adult criminal court's punitive aspects [32].

However, a plurality of the Court rejected the argument that adjudicatory proceedings were substantively similar to criminal trials, [33] reasoning that a jury trial was only constitutionally required if due process required fact-finding by a jury [34].

In support of its conclusion that a jury is unnecessary for fair fact-finding, the plurality noted that equity cases, workmen's compensation cases, probate matters, deportation cases, and military trials, among others, had been traditionally decided by judges without juries [35]. In reaching its decision, the Court expressed doubt as to whether imposing such a right would improve the fact-finding ability of juvenile courts. In addition, the Court reasoned that imposing such a right would jeopardize the unique nature of the juvenile system and blur the distinctions between juvenile court and adult criminal court [36]. To do so would make the juvenile system obsolcte. The plurality's holding signaled the Court's return to the more paternalistic approach it had rejected in its previous opinions and marked the end of the era of expansion of procedural rights in juvenile adjudications [37].

RIGHT TO JURY TRIAL REVISITED

Arguably, the absence of a jury trial requirement in adjudicatory proceedings presents a host of questions that may warrant a reexamination of the issue. First, some are likely to argue that the increasingly punitive nature of cases adjudicated in the juvenile justice system calls into question the validity of the Court's reasoning underlying its holding in *McKeiver* that juveniles are not entitled to the right to a jury trial [38]. When the Court decided *McKeiver*, it did so to maintain the civil and rehabilitative nature of the juvenile justice system [39]. At the time of the decision, juvenile adjudication hearings were closed to the public, the system was informal, and the records of the juvenile adjudications were confidential and not relied on in criminal prosecutions [40]. Currently, some juvenile adjudication hearings are open to the public, the system is more formal and adversarial, and juvenile adjudications are frequently used in criminal prosecutions for sentence enhancement [41]. From their perspective, the civil and rehabilitative nature of the juvenile justice system has shifted to a more punitive one which more closely resembles the adult criminal justice system.

Central to the *McKeiver's* holding was the Court's conclusion that juries were not essential to accurate fact-finding. However, this premise may be called into question in light of the Court's reemphasis on the importance of a jury. In a series of cases, the U.S. Supreme Court has recognized and emphasized the important role that juries play in criminal proceedings. In *Duncan v. Louisiana,* [42] the U.S. Supreme Court held that the right to jury trial is fundamental and guaranteed by due process.

In *Williams v. Florida*, [43] the Court reaffirmed that the "purpose of the jury trial ... is to prevent oppression by the Government." [44]. The U.S. Supreme Court recognized the superiority of group decision-making over individual judgments in *Ballew v. Georgia*, [45] which defined the constitutional minimum number of jurors that a state must empanel in a criminal prosecution. In *Ballew*, the Court, relying on empirical data, found that a jury composed of less than six members was less likely to foster effective group deliberation and more likely to lead to inaccurate fact-finding and incorrect application of the community's common sense to the facts. In addition, the court concluded that a smaller panel could increase the risk of convicting an innocent person. More recently, the Court has stressed the constitutional necessity of juries, rather than judges, making factual determinations upon which sentences are based [46]. The Court's reasoning in *Ballew* and subsequent cases regarding fact-finding by juries during sentencing may call into question the Court's conclusion in *McKeiver* that a jury would not improve the fact-finding ability and fairness of juvenile courts [47].

An argument can also be made that the absence of a jury trial in the adjudicatory process could lead to inequities in other criminal proceedings. For example, recidivist statutes such as the Armed Career Criminal Act [48] impose mandatory minimums based on prior convictions, which by definition include juvenile adjudications [49]. As such, adult criminal defendants are subjected to longer terms of imprisonment based on prior juvenile misconduct. Some state and lower federal courts have found that equating juvenile adjudications with a conviction as a predicate offense for the purposes of state recidivism statutes subverts the civil nature of the juvenile adjudication to an extent that makes it fundamentally unfair and, thus, violative of due process [50]. One way to remedy the perceived inequities in using non-jury juvenile adjudication as sentence enhancements, critics of the current system maintain, might be to grant juveniles a right to a jury trial during adjudicatory hearings.

REFERENCES

[1]   The focus of this report is on juvenile offenders adjudicated delinquent within the juvenile justice system and not juvenile offenders tried as adults.

[2]   18 U.S.C. § 924(e) requires the imposition of a minimum 15-year term of imprisonment for unlawful possession of a firearm in violation of 18

U.S.C. § 922(g) by an individual with three prior serious drug or violent
felony convictions.

[3]   18 U.S.C. § 924(e)(2)(C)(defining the term "conviction" to include prior
       juvenile adjudications involving a violent felony).

[4]   *See, Kent v. United States*, 383 U.S. 541, 555 (1966) (stating that theory
       of the state's juvenile court act is "rooted in social welfare philosophy
       rather than in corpus juris.").

[5]   For a historical account of the early efforts toward juvenile reform, see
       Mennel, "Origins of the Juvenile Court: Changing Perspectives on the
       Legal Rights of Juvenile Delinquent," 18 CRIME AND DELINQ. 68
       (1972); See generally, *Ex parte Sharp*, 96 P. 563 (1908).

[6]   *See, e.g., Shioutakon v. District of Columbia*, 236 F.2d 666, 669 (D.C.
       Cir 1956)(recognizing juveniles' right to legal counsel during
       adjudications in the District of Columbia); *In re Contreras*, 241 P.2d
       631,633 (Cal. Dist. Ct. App. 1952)(acknowledging that the claim that a
       delinquency adjudication is not a criminal conviction is "legal fiction"
       and that a delinquency adjudication has future implications on a minor's
       character just as a criminal conviction does); *but see, e.g. In re Holmes*,
       109 A.2d 523, 525 (Pa. 1954)(reaffirming that the civil nature of
       juvenile proceedings justified a denial of constitutional rights guaranteed
       to adults who were charged with a crime).

[7]   383 U.S. 541 (1966).

[8]   387 U.S. 1 (1967).

[9]   397 U.S. 358 (1970).

[10]   403 U.S. 528 (1971).

[11]   383 U.S. 541 (1966).

[12]   *Id.* at 560. Specifically, the Court found that the "essentials of due
       process and fair treatment" require (1) a hearing on the issue of waiver
       with legal representation, (2) juvenile court judges to give juveniles'
       counsel access to records that the judges relied on in making the waiver
       decision, and (3) juvenile court judges to provide a brief statement of the
       facts they considered when making the waiver decision. *Id.* at 561-63.

[13]   *Id.* at 555.

[14]   387 U.S. 1 (1967). The police took Gerald Gault, age 15, into custody
       for allegedly making a lewd and obscene phone call to a neighbor.
       Neither of his parents received notice that the police had taken Gault into
       custody. Gault's mother learned that her son was in custody only when
       she returned home from work and sent her other son to look for him.
       Gault's brother learned from friends that Gault was in custody. When

Gault's mother picked him up at the detention home, an officer told her that there would be a hearing the following day. At the hearing, the accuser was not present, the judge did not swear in anyone, and the court did not make a record of the proceeding. At a subsequent hearing, the judge found Gault to be a juvenile delinquent and committed him to an "industrial school" until the age of 21. Because state law did not allow Gault to appeal the decision, he filed a habeas corpus petition.

[15] *Id.* at 30-31.

[16] *Id.* at 26-27.

[17] *Id.* at 17-18 (calling the juvenile court's constitutional and theoretical bases "debatable" and stating that, in practice, the results are unsatisfactory). Further, the Court asserted that principle and procedure cannot be substituted by a judge's vast discretion to determine what is in the child's best interest.

[18] *Id.* at 20 (stating that due process is a fundamental element of the justice system that limits the state's power over the individual). The Court declined to address other pre-trial procedures relating to juveniles. *Id.* at 12-13.

[19] *Id.* at 31-42.

[20] 397 U.S. 358, 368 (1970).

[21] *Id* at 360 (noting that the charge against Winship would have been larceny if he had been an adult).

[22] *Id.* at 359 n. 1 (declining to consider the due process requirement of any stage other than the adjudicatory phase and declining to consider other constitutional issues).

[23] *Id.* at 361-63 (stating that the reasonable doubt standard has always been assumed to be the requisite standard of proof in criminal cases and that there has been ubiquitous adoption of this standard by the states).

[24] *Id.* at 364 (expressing that the reasonable doubt standard is "indispensable" as a safeguard against convictions resting on factual error and to maintain the community's respect and confidence in the criminal law system).

[25] *Id.* at 365.

[26] *Id.* at 365-66 (rejecting the civil nature argument as untenable after *Gault* and discarding the argument that incorporating due process rights in a juvenile proceeding would necessarily equate a delinquency adjudication with a criminal conviction, destroy the confidentiality of the proceeding, formalize the proceeding, and delay the adjudicatory process).

[27] 403 U.S. 528 (1971).

[28] *Id.* at 545.

[29] *Id.* at 534-38.

[30] *Id.* at 541 (stating that the court would limit its analysis to whether the fundamental fairness standard of due process required juveniles the right to elect a jury in delinquency proceedings).

[31] *Id.* at 540 (stating that the Sixth Amendment guarantees the right to an impartial jury in all criminal prosecutions under federal law, and the Fourteenth Amendment compels states to grant a jury trial in state courts if one is held in federal court).

[32] *Id.* at 541.

[33] Id. at 541-42 (arguing that an adjudication mirrored a criminal trial because the petition charged a violation of the penal code in language similar to an indictment, juveniles were detained in facilities similar to adult prisons prior to their hearings, defense counsel and the prosecution conducted plea bargains, similar motions were heard and decided, the same rules of evidence applied, the public could observe both types of proceedings, and the stigma attached to a delinquency adjudication amounted to a criminal conviction).

[34] *Id.* at 545 (refraining from holding that all rights constitutionally ensured to adult criminal defendants extend to minors, and noting that the *Gault* and *Winship* Courts incorporated the right to notice, counsel, confrontation, cross-examination, and reasonable doubt standard of proof because those rights were considered essential to adequate fact-finding and therefore required by due process).

[35] *Id.* at 543 (acknowledging the benefits of a jury but finding that a defendant may be treated as fairly by a judge alone as he or she would be by a jury).

[36] *Id.* at 547. The Court reasoned that the non-criminal juvenile justice system in place provided certain rehabilitative benefits to juveniles. The Court concluded that granting juveniles the right to a jury trial would threaten these rehabilitative benefits to juveniles by creating delay, imposing formality, forcing juvenile courts to be more adversarial, and possibly even resulting in public trials.

[37] Because *McKeiver* held that juveniles are not constitutionally guaranteed the right to a jury, some states have granted this right by statute. Approximately one-third of the states provide juveniles with either a conditional or unconditional right to fact-finding by a jury. See Alaska Stat. § 47.10.070; Mass Gen. Laws Ann. ch. 19, § 55A; Mich. Comp.

Laws Ann. § 712A.17(2); Mont. Code Ann. § 41-5-1502; N.M. Stat. Ann. § 32A-2-16; Okla. Stat. Ann. tit. 10, § 7003-3.8; Tex. Fam. Code Ann. § 54.03(c); W. Va. Code Ann. § 49-5-6; Wis. Stat. Ann. § 48.31(2); Wyo. Stat. Ann. § 14-6-223(c)(codifying an unconditional right to fact-finding by jury in juvenile adjudications in the respective states); see also Colo. Rev. Stat. Ann. § 19-2-107; Idaho Code § 20-509; 705 Ill. Comp. Stat. Ann. 405/5-101; Kan. Stat. Ann. § 38-1656; R.I. Gen. Laws § 14-1-47; S.D. Codified Laws § 26-7A-34; S.D. Codified Laws § 15-6-38(a); Va. Code Ann. § 16.1-272 (providing a conditional right to a jury in juvenile adjudications in the respective states).

[38] Barry C. Feld, "The Constitutional Tension Between Apprendi and McKeiver: Sentence Enhancements Based on Delinquency Convictions and the Quality of Justice in Juvenile Courts," 38 *Wake Forest L. Rev.* 1111, 1156-57 (2003).

[39] 403 U.S. at 547.

[40] *Id.* at 1147.

[41] For example, the Armed Career Criminal Act (ACCA) requires imposition of a minimum 15-year term of imprisonment for unlawful possession of a firearm in violation of 18 U.S.C. § 922(g) by an individual with three prior serious drug or violent felony convictions. Congress defined the term "conviction" to include "a finding that a person has committed an act of juvenile delinquency involving a violent felony." 18 U.S.C. § 924(e)(2)(C).

[42] 391 U.S. 145 (1968).

[43] 399 U.S. 78 (1970)(holding that the constitutional guarantee of a jury trial does not require that jury membership be fixed at 12).

[44] 399 U.S. at 100 (stating that "providing an accused with the right to be tried by a jury of his peers gave him an inestimable safeguard against the corrupt or overzealous prosecutor and against the compliant, biased or eccentric judge").

[45] 435 U.S. 223, 232-39 (1978) (stating that "when individual and group decisionmaking were compared [in social scientific studies], it was seen that groups performed better because prejudices of individuals were frequently counterbalanced, and objectivity resulted. Groups ... exhibited ... self-criticism.... Because juries frequently face complex problems laden with value choices, the[se] benefits are important.... In particular, the counterbalancing of various biases is critical to the accurate application of the common sense of the community to the facts of any given case").

[46] See *Jones v. United States*, 526 U.S. 227 (1999)(holding that under the Sixth Amendment's jury trial guarantee, any fact [other than a prior conviction] that increases the maximum penalty for a crime must be charged in an indictment, submitted to a jury, and proven beyond a reasonable doubt); *Apprendi v. New Jersey*, 520 U.S. 466 (2000); *Ring v. Arizona*, 536 U.S. 584 (2002)(holding that an aggravating circumstance that makes a defendant eligible for a death sentence is the functional equivalent of an element of an offense for purposes of the Sixth Amendment right to jury trial and therefore must be found by a jury); *Blakely v. Washington*, 542 U.S. 296 (2004)(finding that the "statutory maximum" for *Apprendi* purposes is the maximum sentence a judge may impose solely on the basis of facts reflected in the jury verdict or admitted by the defendant); *United States v. Booker*, 543 U.S. 220 (2005)(finding that the mandatory nature of the Federal Sentencing Guidelines violates the Sixth Amendment right to jury trial).

[47] 403 U.S. at 543 (finding that a defendant may be treated as fairly by a judge alone as he or she would be by a jury).

[48] 18 U.S.C. § 924(e) requires the imposition of a minimum 15-year term of imprisonment for unlawful possession of a firearm in violation of 18 U.S.C. § 922(g) by an individual with three prior serious drug or violent felony convictions.

[49] 18 U.S.C. § 924(e)(2)(C)(defining the term "conviction" to include prior juvenile adjudications involving a violent felony).

[50] *Id.*; *State v. Chatman*, 2005 WL 901138 (Tenn. Crim. App. 2005) (Apr. 19, 2005); *Pinkston v. State*, 836 Ne 2d 453 (2005); *United States v. Jones*, 332 F.3d 688 (3d Cir. 2003), *cert. denied*, 540 U.S. 1150 (2004); *United States v. Smalley*, 294 F.3d 1030 (8th Cir. 2002), *cert. denied*, 537 U.S. 1114 (2003); *State v. Hitt*, 42 P.3d 732 (Kan. 2002), *cert. denied*, 537 U.S. 1104 (2003). For a discussion of the constitutionality using non-jury juvenile adjudications in subsequent criminal proceedings for sentence enhancement, refer to CRS Report RS22610, *Armed Career Criminal Act (ACCA): Using Prior Juvenile Adjudications for Sentence Enhancements*, by Alison M. Smith.

In: Crime and Law Enforcement Issues   ISBN 978-1-61122-877-9
Editor: James E. Hirsch   © 2011 Nova Science Publishers, Inc.

Chapter 4

STATUTES OF LIMITATION IN FEDERAL CRIMINAL CASES: AN OVERVIEW

Charles Doyle

ABSTRACT

A statute of limitations dictates the time period within which a legal proceeding must begin. The purpose of a statute of limitations in a criminal case is to ensure the prompt prosecution of criminal charges and thereby spare the accused of the burden of having to defend against stale charges after memories may have faded or evidence is lost.

There is no statute of limitations for federal crimes punishable by death, nor for certain federal crimes of terrorism, nor, since passage of the Adam Walsh Child Protection and Safety Act (P.L. 109-248, H.R. 4472, 2006), for certain federal sex offenses. Prosecution for most other federal crimes must begin within five years of the commitment of the offense. There are exceptions. Some types of crimes are subject to a longer period of limitation; some circumstances suspend or extend the otherwise applicable period of limitation.

Arson, art theft, certain crimes against financial institutions and various immigration offenses all carry statutes of limitation longer than the five year standard. Regardless of the applicable statute of limitations, the period may be extended or the running of the period suspended or tolled under a number of circumstances such as when the accused is a fugitive or when the case involves charges of child abuse, bankruptcy, wartime fraud against the government, or DNA evidence.

Ordinarily, the statute of limitations begins to run as soon as the crime has been completed. Although the federal crime of conspiracy is complete when one of the plotters commits an affirmative act in its name, the period for conspiracies begins with the last affirmative act committed in furtherance of the scheme. Other so-called continuing offenses include various possession crimes and some that impose continuing obligations to register or report.

Limitation-related constitutional challenges arise most often under the Constitution's ex post facto and due process clauses. The federal courts have long held that a statute of limitations may be enlarged retroactively as long as the previously applicable period of limitation has not expired. The Supreme Court recently confirmed that view; the ex post facto proscription precludes legislative revival of an expired period of limitation. Due process condemns pre-indictment delays even when permitted by the statute of limitations if the prosecution wrongfully caused the delay and the accused's defense suffered actual, substantial harm as a consequence.

INTRODUCTION

The Constitution's speedy trial clause, U.S. Const. Amend. VI, protects the criminally accused against unreasonable delays between his indictment and trial. Before indictment, the statutes of limitation, and in extreme circumstances the due process clauses, U.S. Const. Amends. V and XIV, protect the accused from unreasonable delays. The anti-terrorism measures of the USA PATRIOT Act, 115 Stat. 809 (2001), made substantial alterations in the statutes of limitation that govern a number of federal crimes. This is an overview of federal law relating to the statutes of limitation in criminal cases, including those changes produced by the Act.

The phrase "statute of limitations" refers to the time period within which formal criminal charges must be brought after a crime has been committed [1]. "The purpose of a statute of limitations is to limit exposure to criminal prosecution to a certain fixed period of time following the occurrence of those acts the legislature has decided to punish by criminal sanctions. Such a limitation is designed to protect individuals from having to defend themselves against charges when the basic facts may have become obscured by the passage of time and to minimize the danger of official punishment because of acts in the far-distant past. Such a time limit may also have the salutary effect of encouraging law enforcement officials promptly to investigate suspected criminal activity"[2]. Therefore, in most instances, prosecutions are barred if the defendant points out that there was no indictment or other formal charge within the time period dictated by the statute of limitations [3].

Statutes of limitation are creatures of statute. The common law recognized no period of limitation. An indictment could be brought at any time. Limitations are recognized today only to the extent that a statute or due process dictate their recognition [4]. Congress and most state legislatures have enacted statutes of limitation, but declare that prosecution for some crimes may be brought at any time [5].

Federal statutes of limitation are as old as federal crimes. When the Founders assembled in the First Congress, they passed not only the first federal criminal laws but made prosecution under those laws subject to specific statutes of limitation [6]. Similar provisions continue to this day. Federal capital offenses may be prosecuted at any time, [7] but unless some more specific arrangement has been made a general five year statute of limitations covers all other federal crimes [8]. Some of the exceptions to the general rule, like those of the USA PATRIOT Act, identify longer periods for particular crimes [9]. Others suspend or extend the applicable period under certain circumstances such as the flight of the accused, [10] or during time of war [11].

PROSECUTION AT ANY TIME

Aside from capital offenses, [12] crimes which Congress associated with terrorism may be prosecuted at any time if they result in a death or serious injury or create a foreseeable risk of death or serious injury [13] Although the crimes were selected because they are often implicated in acts of terrorism, a terrorist defendant is not a prerequisite to an unlimited period for prosecution [14]. A third category of crimes that may be prosecuted at any time consists of various designated federal child abduction and sex offenses [15].

LIMITS BY CRIME

Although the majority of federal crimes are governed by the general five year statute of limitations, Congress has chosen longer periods for specific types of crimes – 20 years for the theft of art work; [16] 10 years for arson, [17] for certain crimes against financial institutions, [18] and for immigration offenses; [19] and eight years for the nonviolent violations of the terrorism-associated statutes which may be prosecuted at any time if committed under violent circumstances [20]. Investigative difficulties [21] or the seriousness of the crime [22] seem to have provided the rationale for enlargement of the time limit for prosecuting these offenses beyond the five year standard.

SUSPENSION AND EXTENSION

The five year rule may yield to circumstances other than the type of crime to be prosecuted. For example, an otherwise applicable limitation period may be suspended or extended in cases involving child abuse, [23] the concealment of the assets of an estate in bankruptcy, [24] wartime fraud against the government, [25] dismissal of original charges, [26] fugitives, [27] foreign evidence, [28] or DNA evidence [29].

The child protection section, 18 U.S.C. 3283, permits an indictment or information charging kidnapping , or sexual abuse, or physical abuse, of a child under the age of 18 to be filed within the longer of 10 years or the life of the victim [30]. The recent enactment of 18 U.S.C. 3299, discussed earlier, which eliminates the statute of limitations in cases of child abduction and sex offenses against children, obviously limits the sweep of Section 3283.

Prior to the enactment of Section 3299 and the passage of the 2006 Violence Against Women Act, [31] the application of the DNA sections turned on the presence or absence of a crime under Chapter 109A of Title 18 [32]. In the case of a crime under Chapter 109A, Section 3282(b) stated that the statute of limitations could be tolled by the filing of an indictment identifying the accused by his DNA profile, if the accused were otherwise unknown [33]. In the case of felonies other than those of Chapter 109A, the governing section, Section 3297, seemed open to either of two interpretations:

> In a case in which DNA testing implicates an identified person in the commission of a felony, no statute of limitations that would otherwise preclude prosecution of the offense shall preclude such prosecution until a period of time following the implication of the person by DNA testing has elapsed that is equal to the otherwise applicable limitation period. 18 U.S.C. 3297 (language struck by the Violence Against Women Act amendment noted).

It might mean that the otherwise applicable statute of limitations is tolled until DNA testing can be completed. On the other hand, it may mean that the applicable statute of limitations is tolled in the presence of suspect-implicating DNA evidence until the individual implicated is sufficiently identified for indictment other than merely by his DNA profile. Section 3297's enactment in conjunction with legislation designed to eliminate DNA testing backlogs seems to support the first reading; the hearing testimony of Justice Department officials who proposed the language, the second [34]. Dicta in the only case, reported or unreported, to have considered Section 3297 supports the Justice Department's view [35]. Whichever is the case, the Violence Against Women Act struck the exception for Chapter 109A cases from Section 3297 so that it now clearly applies to cases arising under that chapter as well.

Enactment of Section 3299, which eliminates the statute of limitations for prosecutions under Chapter 109A, makes it unnecessary to consider the impact of Section 3282(b) which tolls the statute of limitations in Chapter 109A cases when one applies. Section 3299 overshadows Section 3297 to a lesser extent. Section 3297's DNA tolling of the applicable statute of limitations comes into play in rape and other sex offenses, although it may be implicated in other cases involving DNA evidence. Section 3299 reduced its impact substantially when it eliminated the statute of limitations in most federal sex cases, i.e., those prosecuted under 18 U.S.C. chs. 109A, 110, 117 and 18 U.S.C. 1591. Questions of Section 3297's coverage may still arise in cases brought under other federal statutes.

The statute of limitations on offenses which involve concealing bankruptcy assets does not begin to run until a final decision discharging or refusing to discharge the debtor: "The concealment of assets of a debtor in a case under Title 11 shall be deemed to be a continuing offense until the debtor shall have been finally discharged or a discharge denied, and the period of limitations shall not begin to run until such final discharge or denial of discharge," 18 U.S.C. 3284. When a discharge determination is impossible because of the dismissal of bankruptcy proceedings or want of a timely discharge petition or for any other reason, the statute of limitations runs from the date of the event when discharge becomes impossible [36].

Statutes of limitation for defrauding the United States during wartime do not begin to run until three years after the war is over [37]. The provision "appears to have only been used in cases that involved conduct during or shortly after World War II" and none since [38]. Moreover, even in instances of a declared war, the section applies only to crimes which "involve the defrauding of the United States in [some] pecuniary manner or in a manner concerning property"[39].

The clock stops for statute of limitation purposes when an indictment or information is returned [40]. If the indictment or information is subsequently dismissed, federal law gives the government an additional six months (30 days if the indictment or information is dismissed on appeal and there is a grand jury with jurisdiction in place) [41]. The statute of limitations remains tolled if the original indictment is replaced by a superseding indictment, but only if the superseding indictment does not substantively alter the original charge [42].

Section 3292 was enacted to compensate for the delays the Justice Department experienced when it sought to secure bank records and other evidence located overseas [43]. It provides that:

(a) (1) Upon application of the United States, filed before return of an indictment, indicating that evidence of an offense is in a foreign country, the district court before which a grand jury is impaneled to investigate the offense shall suspend the running of the statute of limitations for the offense if the court finds by a preponderance of the evidence that an official request has been made for such evidence and that it reasonably appears, or reasonably appeared at the time the request was made, that such evidence is, or was, in such foreign country.

(2) The court shall rule upon such application not later than thirty days after the filing of the application.

(b) Except as provided in subsection (c) of this section, a period of suspension under this section shall begin on the date on which the official request is made and end on the date on which the foreign court or authority takes final action on the request.

(c) The total of all periods of suspension under this section with respect to an offense – (1) shall not exceed three years; and (2) shall not extend a period within which a criminal case must be initiated for more than six months if all foreign authorities take final action before such period would expire without regard to this section.

(d) As used in this section, the term "official request" means a letter rogatory, a request under a treaty or convention, or any other request for evidence made by a court of the United States or an authority of the United States having criminal law enforcement responsibility, to a court or other authority of a foreign country.

Construction of Section 3292 has thus far been something less than uniform [44]. The courts are divided over whether the target of the grand jury or the subject of the foreign evidence sought may contest the government's application when it is filed or whether the application may be filed ex parte with an opportunity for the accused to contest suspension following indictment [45]. In either event, the government clearly bears the burden of establishing to the court its right to a suspension by a preponderance of the evidence [46] Yet it is less certain whether the phrase indicating that the application must be filed with "the district court before which a grand jury is impaneled to investigate the offense," means that the application must relate to a specific grand jury investigation or may be filed in anticipation of such an investigation [47]. On the related issue of when an application may be filed, one court has ruled that the government may seek the suspension either to allow it to obtain foreign evidence or to compensate it for time expended to acquire the evidence prior to the application [48]. Yet another has held that the extension cannot be had when the evidence sought by the government is in its possession at the time of the application [49]. Finally, the question of when "final action" occurs and the statute of limitations again begins to run has proven perplexing. Some courts suggest that final action occurs with a dispositive response, i.e., when the United States is satisfied its request has been answered; [50] yet at least one other believes that final action occurs when the foreign government believes it has provided a final response [51].

A provision exempting fugitives accompanied passage of the first federal statute of limitations [52]. The language has changed little since ("no statute of limitations shall extend to any person fleeing from justice," 18 U.S.C. 3290), but its meaning remains a topic of debate [53] Most circuits, taking their lead from *Streep v. United States*, 160 U.S. 128 (1895), have held that the government must establish that the accused acted with an intent to avoid prosecution [54]. Yet two have held that mere absence from the jurisdiction is sufficient [55]. Even in the more demanding circuits, however, flight is thought to include the accused's concealing himself within the jurisdiction, [56] or remaining outside the jurisdiction when he becomes aware of the possibility of prosecution, [57] or fleeing before an investigation begins [58] or to avoid prosecution on another matter, [59] or to avoid civil or administrative justice rather than criminal justice [60].

CONSPIRACIES AND CONTINUING OFFENSES

Statutes of limitation "normally begin to run when the crime is complete" [61] which occurs when the last element of the crime has been satisfied [62]. The rule for conspiracy is a bit different [63]. The general conspiracy statute consists of two elements: (1) an agreement to commit a federal crime or to defraud the United States and (2) an overt act committed in furtherance of the agreement [64]. Conspirators left unimpaired will frequently continue on through several overt acts to the ultimate commission of the underlying substantive offenses which are the objectives of their plots. Thus, the statute of limitations for such conspiracies runs not from the first overt act committed in furtherance of the conspiracy but from the last [65]. The statute of limitations under conspiracy statutes which have no overt act requirement runs from the accomplishment of the objectives of the conspiracy or from its abandonment [66].

Concealment of the criminal plot after its completion is considered a natural component of all conspiracies. Consequently, overt acts of concealment after the objectives of the conspiracy have been accomplished may not be used to delay the running of the statute of limitations [67]. Overt acts of concealment which are among the original objectives of the conspiracy as charged in the indictment, however, may serve as the point at which the statute of limitations begins to run [68]. Distinguishing between the two is sometimes difficult.

There are other crimes, which like conspiracy, continue on long after all the elements necessary for their prosecution are first present. The applicable statute of limitations for these continuing crimes is delayed if either "the explicit language of the substantive criminal statute compels such a conclusion, or the nature of the crime involved is such that Congress must assuredly have intended that it be treated as a continuing one"[69] Continuing federal offenses for purposes of the statutes of limitation include:

- escape from federal custody, *United States v. Bailey*, 444 U.S. 394, 636 (1980); [70]
- flight to avoid prosecution, *United States v. Merino*, 44 F.3d 749, 753-54 (9th Cir. 1994); [71]
- failure to report for sentencing, *United States v. Gray*, 876 F.2d 1411, 1419 (9th Cir. 1989); [72]
- possession of the skin and skull of an endangered species, *United States v. Winnie*, 97 F.3d 975, 975-76 (7th Cir. 1996); [73]

- possession of counterfeit currency, *United States v. Kayfez*, 957 F.2d 677, 678 (9th Cir. 1992); [74]
- kidnapping , *United States v. Denny-Shaffer*, 2 F.3d 999, 1018-19 (10th Cir. 1993); [75]
- failure to register under the Foreign Agents Registration Act, *United States v. McGoff*, 831 F.2d 1071, 1071 (D.C.Cir. 1987); [76]
- failure to register under the Selective Service Act, *United States v. Kerley*, 838 F.2d 932, 935 (7th Cir. 1988); [77]
- being found in the United States having reentered this country after deportation, *United States v. Gomez*, 38 F.3d 1031, 1035 (8th Cir1994); [78] and
- embezzlement under some circumstances, *United States v. Smith*, 373 F.3d 561, 568 (4th Cir. 2004) [79]

CONSTITUTIONAL CONSIDERATIONS

Constitutional challenges to the application of various statutes of limitation perhaps most often claim support from the ex post facto or due process clauses. The Constitution prohibits both Congress and the states from enacting ex post facto laws [80]. More precisely it prohibits:

> 1st. Every law that makes an action done before the passing of the law, and which was innocent when done, criminal; and punishes such action. 2d. Every law that aggravates a crime, or makes it greater than it was, when committed. 3d. Every law that changes the punishment, and inflicts a greater punishment, than the law annexed to the crime, when committed. 4th. Every law that alters the legal rules of evidence, and receives less, or different, testimony, than the law required at the time of the commission of the offense, in order to convict the offender [81].

The lower federal appellate courts had long felt that a statute that extends a period of limitation before its expiration does not offend the ex post facto clauses, but that the clauses ban laws that attempt to revive and extend an expired statute of limitations [82]. Until the United States Supreme Court confirmed that view in *Stogner v. California*, 539 U.S. 607 (2003), however, there were well regarded contrary opinions. The California Supreme Court, for example, at one point concluded that the ex post facto clauses in fact pose no impediment to the revival of an expired statute of limitations [83]. The Justice Department cited the California case, *Frazer*, in its summary of proposed anti-terrorism legislation, [84] suggesting that its retroactive section was intended both to extend the statutes of limitation to cases where the period of limitation had not run and to revive the prospect of prosecution where the period had expired. The USA PATRIOT Act's retroactivity clause used the same language found in the Justice Department's original proposal, [85] arguably reflecting the same intent.

The California court, however, had read too much into then contemporary United States Supreme Court interpretations of the ex post facto clause. *Frazer* involved a statutory amendment which allowed prosecution of certain child sex offense cases within one year after the offense had been reported to authorities even if the otherwise applicable statute of limitations had run. The *Frazer* court pointed out that the Supreme Court had apparently pruned its *Calder* statement so as to define ex post facto laws as "any statute which punishes as a crime an act previously committed, which was innocent when done; which makes more burdensome the punishment for a crime, after its commission, or which deprives one charged with crime of any defenses available according to law at the time when the act was committed," 21 Cal.4th at 755, 982 at 191, 88 Cal.Rptr.2d at 324, *quoting, Beazell v. Ohio*, 269 U.S. 167, 169 (1925). Moreover, as the California court understood it, the Supreme Court had not only indicated that evidentiary changes were beyond the realm of the clauses' protection but that the defenses protected by the clauses were limited to those based on the elements or punishment of the crime when it was committed, 21 Cal.4th at 755-57, 982 at191-92, 88 Cal.Rptr.2d at 324-26, *citing, Collins v. Youngblood*, 497 U.S. 37, 43 n.3, 50 (1990).

The Supreme Court subsequently warned that *Collins* should not be read as a repudiation of *Calder's* four prohibited classes, but instead that "*Collins* held that it was a mistake to stray *beyond Calder's* four categories," *Carmell v. Texas*, 529 U.S. 513, 539 (2000)(emphasis in the original). The Court seemed to further signal its reluctance to reach beyond the limits of *Calder* when it declined to extend the ex post facto proscription to cover a retroactive application of a judicial (rather than a legislative) change in the law, *Rogers v. Tennessee*, 532 U.S. 451, 462 (2001) [86].

These developments did not necessarily undermine the California decision in *Frazer*, however, since its revival of a statute of limitations that had run did not appear to fit easily within any of the *Calder* categories. But the *Frazer* analysis was in error nonetheless.

The U.S. Supreme Court characterized the California legislative revival of an expired period of limitation not only "manifestly unjust and oppressive," but among those laws that run afoul of *Calder's* second standard ("Every law that aggravates a crime, or makes it greater than it was, when committed"), *Stogner v. California*, 539 U.S. 607, 611-12 (2003). As properly understood and alternatively characterized in *Calder*, this second category embraces statutes that like the California statute "inflicted punishments, where the party was not by law, liable to any punishment," at the time, 539 U.S. at 612, *quoting, Calder*, 3 Dall. (3 U.S.) at 389.

Retroactivity aside, the due process clauses may be implicated if a crime is not subject to any statute of limitations or if the period of limitation has not run. Although statutes of limitation generally govern the extent of permissible pre-indictment delay, extraordinary circumstances may trigger due process implications. The Supreme Court in *Marion* observed that even "the Government concedes that the Due Process Clause of the Fifth Amendment would require dismissal of [an] indictment if it were shown at trial that the pre-indictment delay . . . caused substantial prejudice to [a defendant's] rights to a fair trial and that the delay was an intentional device to gain tactical advantage over the accused" [87]. The Court declined to dismiss the indictment there, however, because the defendants failed to show they had suffered any actual prejudice from the delay or to show "that the Government intentionally delayed to gain some tactical advantage over [them] or to harass them" [88].

The Court later made clear that due process contemplates more than a claimant's showing of adverse impact caused by pre-indictment delay: "Thus *Marion* makes clear that proof of prejudice is generally a necessary but not sufficient element of a due process claim, and that the due process inquiry must consider the reasons for the delay as well as the prejudice to the accused" [89].

Perhaps because so few defendants have been able to show sufficient prejudice to necessitate further close inquiry, [90] the lower federal appellate courts seem at odds over exactly what else due process demands before it will require dismissal. Most have held that the defendant bears the burden of establishing both prejudice and government deficiency; [91] others that once the defendant establishes prejudice the burden shifts to the government to negate the second prong; [92] and still others that once the defendant shows prejudice the court must balance the harm against the justifications for delay [93].

APPENDICES
PERIODS OF LIMITATION FOR SPECIFIC FEDERAL CRIMES

No limitation

1. Capital Offenses
7 U.S.C. 2146(b) (killing federal employee engaged in duties with respect to transportation and sale of certain animals)

8 U.S.C. 1324 (1) (bringing in or harboring aliens where death results)

15 U.S.C. 1825(a)(2)(C) (killing those enforcing the Horse Protection Act)

18 U.S.C. 32, 33, 34 (destruction of aircraft, commercial motor vehicles or their facilities where death results)

18 U.S.C. 36 (drive-by shooting resulting in 1st degree murder)

18 U.S.C. 37 (violence at international airports where death results)

18 U.S.C. 43, 3559(f) (animal enterprise terrorism constituting murder of a child))

18 U.S.C. 115 (kidnapping with death resulting of the member of the family of a federal official or employee to obstruct or retaliate)

18 U.S.C. 115 (1st degree murder of the member of the family of a federal official or employee to obstruct or retaliate)

18 U.S.C. 175 (development or possession of biological weapons)

18 U.S.C. 175c, 3559(f) (variola virus offense constituting murder of a child)

18 U.S.C. 229, 229A (use of chemical weapons where death results)

18 U.S.C. 241 (conspiracy against civil rights where death results)

18 U.S.C. 242 (deprivation civil rights under color of law where death results)

18 U.S.C. 245 (discriminatory obstruction of enjoyment federal protected activities where death results)

18 U.S.C. 247 (obstruction of the exercise of religious beliefs where death results)

18 U.S.C. 351 (1st degree murder of a Member of Congress)

18 U.S.C. 351 (conspiracy to kill or kidnap a Member of Congress if death results)

18 U.S.C. 351 (kidnapping a Member of Congress if death results)

18 U.S.C. 794 (espionage)

18 U.S.C. 831, 3559(f) (nuclear material offense constituting murder of a child)

18 U.S.C. 844(d) (use of fire or explosives unlawfully where death results)

18 U.S.C. 844(f)(burning or bombing federal property where death results)

18 U.S.C. 844(i)(burning or bombing property affecting interstate commerce where death results)

18 U.S.C. 924(j)(1) (murder while in possession of a firearm during the commission of a crime of violence or drug trafficking)

18 U.S.C. 930(c) (1st degree murder while in possession of a firearm in a federal building)

18 U.S.C. 1091 (genocide where death results)

18 U.S.C. 1111 (1st degree murder within the special maritime or territorial jurisdiction of the U.S.)

18 U.S.C. 1121(b) (killing a state law enforcement officer by a federal prisoner or while transferring a prisoner interstate)

18 U.S.C. 1114 (1st degree murder of a federal officer or employee)

18 U.S.C. 1116 (1st degree murder of a foreign dignitary)

18 U.S.C. 1118 (murder by a federal prisoner)

18 U.S.C. 1119 (1st degree murder of an American by an American overseas)

18 U.S.C. 1120 (1st degree murder by an escaped federal prisoner)

18 U.S.C. 1121 (1st degree murder of one assisting in a federal criminal investigation)

18 U.S.C. 1201 (kidnapping where death results)

18 U.S.C. 1203 (hostage taking where death results)

18 U.S.C. 1365, 3559(f) (tampering with consumer products constituting murder of a child)

18 U.S.C. 1503 (1st degree murder committed to obstruction of federal judicial proceedings)

18 U.S.C. 1512 (tampering with a federal witness or informant involving murder)

18 U.S.C. 1513 (retaliating against a federal witness or informant involving murder)

18 U.S.C. 1591, 2245 (murder committed during the course of sex trafficking by force, fraud or of a child)

18 U.S.C. 1651, 1652, 3559(f) (piracy involving murder of a child)

18 U.S.C. 1716 (mailing injurious articles with intent to injure or damage property where death results)

18 U.S.C. 1751 (kidnapping the President where death results)

18 U.S.C. 1751 (conspiracy to kill or kidnap the President where death results)

18 U.S.C. 1751 (1st degree murder of the President)

18 U.S.C. 1952, 3559(f) (travel in aid of racketeering involve the murder of child)

18 U.S.C. 1958 (use of interstate facilities in furtherance of a murder-for-hire where death results)

18 U.S.C. 1959 (murder in aid of racketeering activity)

18 U.S.C. 1992 (terrorist attacks on trains and mass transit)

18 U.S.C. 2113(e) (robbing a federally insured bank if death results)

18 U.S.C. 2118, 3559(f) (robbery or burglary involving controlled substances constituting murder of a child)

18 U.S.C. 2119 (carjacking where death results)

18 U.S.C. 2199, 3559(f) (murder of a child by a stowaway)

18 U.S.C. 2241, 2245 (aggravated sexual assault of a child under 12 years of age in the special maritime or territorial jurisdiction of the U.S. where death results)

18 U.S.C. 2242, 2245 (coercing or enticing interstate travel for sexual purposes where death results)

18 U.S.C. 2243, 2245 (transporting minors for sexual purposes resulting in the death of a child under 14 years of age)

18 U.S.C. 2244, 2245 (abusive sexual contact where death results)

18 U.S.C. 2251 (sexual exploitation of children where death results)

18 U.S.C. 2251A, 2245 (selling or buying children where death results)

18 U.S.C. 2260, 2245 (production of material depicting sexually explicit activities of a child where death results)

18 U.S.C. 2261, 2261A, 2262, 3559(f) (murder of a child involved in interstate domestic violence, stalking, or interstate violation of a protective order)

18 U.S.C. 2280 (violence against maritime navigation where death results)

18 U.S.C. 2281 (violence against maritime fixed platform where death results)

18 U.S.C. 2282A (interference with maritime commerce where death results)

18 U.S.C. 2283 (transportation of explosive, nuclear, chemical, biological or radioactive material resulting in death)

18 U.S.C. 2291 (destruction of a vessel or maritime facility)

18 U.S.C. 2332 (terrorist murder of an American outside the U.S.)

18 U.S.C. 2332a (use of weapons of mass destruction where death results)

18 U.S.C. 2332b (acts of terrorism transcending national boundaries where death results)

18 U.S.C. 2332f (bombing public places)

18 U.S.C. 2332g, 3559(f) (anti-aircraft missile offense constituting murder of a child)

18 U.S.C. 2332h, 3559(f) (radiological dispersal device offense constituting murder of a child)

18 U.S.C. 2340A (torture where death results)

18 U.S.C. 2381 (treason)

18 U.S.C. 2441 (war crimes where death results)

18 U.S.C. 2421, 2245 (transportation of illicit sexual purposes where death results)

18 U.S.C. 2422, 2245 (coercion or inducement to travel for illicit sexual purposes where death results)

18 U.S.C. 2423, 2245 (transportation of minors for illicit sexual purposes where death results)

18 U.S.C. 2425, 2245 (interstate transportation of information concerning a minor where death results)

21 U.S.C. 461 (killing a poultry inspector)

21 U.S.C. 675 (killing a meat inspector)

21 U.S.C. 848(c), 3591(b) (major drug kingpin violations)

21 U.S.C. 848(e)(1) (killing in furtherance of a serious drug trafficking violation or killing a law enforcement official in furtherance of a controlled substance violation)

21 U.S.C. 1041(c) (murder of an egg inspector)

42 U.S.C. 2000e-13 (murder of EEOC personnel)

42 U.S.C. 2283 (murder of federal nuclear inspectors)

49 U.S.C. 46502 (air piracy where death results)

49 U.S.C. 46506 (murder in the special aircraft jurisdiction of the United States)

2. Terrorism-Related Offenses Resulting in or Involving the Risk of Death or Serious Injury

18 U.S.C. 32 (destruction of aircraft or aircraft facilities)

18 U.S.C. 37 (violence at international airports)

18 U.S.C. 81 (arson within special maritime and territorial jurisdiction)

18 U.S.C. 175 or 175b (biological weapons offenses)

18 U.S.C. 175c (variola virus)

18 U.S.C. 229 (chemical weapons offenses)

18 U.S.C. 351(a),(b),(c), or (d) (congressional, cabinet, and Supreme Court assassination and kidnapping)

18 U.S.C. 831 (nuclear materials offenses)

18 U.S.C. 832 (participation in a foreign atomic weapons program)

18 U.S.C. 842(m) or (n) (plastic explosives offenses)

18 U.S.C. 844(f)(2) or (3)(arson and bombing of federal property risking or causing death)

18 U.S.C. 844(i) (burning or bombing of property used in, or used in activities affecting, commerce)

18 U.S.C. 930(c) (killing or attempted killing during an attack on a federal facility with a dangerous weapon)

18 U.S.C. 956(a)(1) (conspiracy to murder, kidnap, or maim persons abroad)

18 U.S.C. 1030(a)(1)(protection of computer systems containing classified information)

18 U.S.C. 1030(a)(5)(A)(i)(resulting in damage defined in 1030(a)(5)(B)(ii) through (v) (protection of computers)

18 U.S.C. 1114 (protection of officers and employees of the United States)

18 U.S.C. 1116 (murder or manslaughter of foreign officials, official guests, or internationally protected persons)

18 U.S.C. 1203 (hostage taking)

18 U.S.C. 1361 (destruction of federal property)

18 U.S.C. 1362 (destruction of communication lines, stations, or systems)

18 U.S.C. 1363 (injury to buildings or property within special maritime and territorial jurisdiction of the United States)

18 U.S.C. 1366(a) (destruction of energy facilities)

18 U.S.C. 1751(a),(b),(c), or (d) (Presidential and Presidential staff assassination and kidnapping)

18 U.S.C. 1992 (terrorist attacks on trains and mass transit)

18 U.S.C. 2155 (destruction of national defense materials, premises, or utilities)

18 U.S.C. 2156 (production of defective national defense material)

18 U.S.C. 2280 (violence against maritime navigation)

18 U.S.C. 2281 (violence against maritime fixed platforms)

18 U.S.C. 2332 (certain homicides and other violence against United States nationals occurring outside of the United States)

18 U.S.C. 2332a (use of weapons of mass destruction)

18 U.S.C. 2332b (acts of terrorism transcending national boundaries)

18 U.S.C. 2332f (bombing public places)

18 U.S.C. 2332g (anti-aircraft missiles)

18 U.S.C. 2332h (radiological dispersal devices)

18 U.S.C. 2339 (harboring terrorists)

18 U.S.C. 2339A (providing material support to terrorists)

18 U.S.C. 2339B (providing material support to terrorist organizations)

18 U.S.C. 2339C (financing terrorism)

18 U.S.C. 2339D (receipt of military training from a foreign terrorist organization)

18 U.S.C. 2340A (torture committed under color of law)

21 U.S.C. 960A (narcoterrorism)

42 U.S.C. 2122 (atomic weapons)

42 U.S.C. 2284 (sabotage of nuclear facilities or fuel)

49 U.S.C. 46502 (aircraft piracy)

49 U.S.C. 46504 (second sentence)(assault on a flight crew with a dangerous weapon)

49 U.S.C. 46505(b)(3) or (c)(explosive or incendiary devices, or endangerment of human life by means of weapons, or aircraft)

49 U.S.C. 46506 (if homicide or attempted homicide involved, application of certain criminal laws to acts on aircraft)

49 U.S.C. 60123(b) (destruction of interstate gas or hazardous liquid pipeline facility)

3. Child Abduction and Sex Offenses

18 U.S.C. 1201 (kidnapping a child)

18 U.S.C. 1591 (sex trafficking by force, fraud or of a child)

18 U.S.C. ch.109A

18 U.S.C. 2241 (aggravate sexual abuse)

18 U.S.C. 2242 (sexual abuse)

18 U.S.C. 2243 (sexual abuse of a ward or child)

18 U.S.C. 2244 (abusive sexual contact)

18 U.S.C. 2245 (sexual abuse resulting in death)

18 U.S.C. 2250 (failure to register as a sex offender)

18 U.S.C. ch. 110

18 U.S.C. 2251 (sexual exploitation of children)

18 U.S.C. 2251A (selling or buying children)

18 U.S.C. 2252 (transporting, distributing or selling child sexually exploitive material)

18 U.S.C., 2252A (transporting or distributing child pornography)

18 U.S.C. 2252B (misleading names on the Internet)

18 U.S.C. 2260 (making child sexually exploitative material overseas for export to the U.S.)

18 U.S.C. ch. 117

18 U.S.C. 2421 (transportation of illicit sexual purposes)

18 U.S.C. 2422 (coerce or entice travel for illicit sexual purposes)

18 U.S.C. 2423 (travel involving illicit sexual activity with a child)

18 U.S.C. 2424 (filing false immigration statement)

18 U.S.C. 2425 (interstate transmission of information about a child relating to

illicit sexual activity)

20 Years

18 U.S.C. 668 (major art theft)

10 Years

8 U.S.C. 1324(a) (harboring illegal aliens)
18 U.S.C. 81 (arson in the special maritime or territorial jurisdiction of the United States)
18 U.S.C. 215 (receipt by financial institution officials of commissions or gifts for procuring loans)
18 U.S.C. 656 (theft, embezzlement, or misapplication by ban officer or employee)
18 U.S.C. 657 (embezzlement by lending, credit and insurance institution officers or employees)
18 U.S.C. 844(f)(burning or bombing federal property)
18 U.S.C. 844(h) (carrying explosives during the commission of a federal offense or using fire or explosives to commit a federal offense)
18 U.S.C. 844 (i) (burning or bombing property used in or used in activities affecting commerce)
18 U.S.C. 1005 (fraud concerning bank entries, reports and transactions)
18 U.S.C. 1006 (fraud concerning federal credit institution entries, reports and transactions)
18 U.S.C. 1007 (fraud concerning Federal Deposit Insurance Corporation transactions)
18 U.S.C. 1014 (fraud concerning loan and credit applications generally; renewals and discounts; crop insurance)
18 U.S.C. 1033 (crimes by or affecting persons engaged in the business of insurance)
18 U.S.C. 1344 (bank fraud)
18 U.S.C. 1341 (mail fraud affecting a financial institution)
18 U.S.C. 1343 (wire fraud affecting a financial institution)
18 U.S.C. 1423 (misuse of evidence of citizenship or naturalization) (or conspiracy to commit)

18 U.S.C. 1424 (personation or misuse of papers in naturalization proceedings) (or conspiracy to commit)

18 U.S.C. 1425 (procurement of citizenship or naturalization unlawfully) (or conspiracy to commit)

18 U.S.C. 1426 (reproduction of naturalization or citizenship papers) (or conspiracy to commit)

18 U.S.C. 1427 (sale of naturalization or citizenship papers) (or conspiracy to commit)

18 U.S.C. 1428 (surrender of canceled naturalization certificate) (or conspiracy to commit)

18 U.S.C. 1541 (passport or visa issuance without authority) (or conspiracy to commit)

18 U.S.C. 1542 (false statement in application and use of passport) (or conspiracy to commit)

18 U.S.C. 1543 (forgery or false use of passport) (or conspiracy to commit)

18 U.S.C. 1544 (misuse of passport) (or conspiracy to commit)

18 U.S.C. 1581 (peonage; obstruction of justice)

18 U.S.C. 1583 (enticement into slavery)

18 U.S.C. 1584 (sale into involuntary servitude)

18 U.S.C. 1589 (forced labor)

18 U.S.C. 1590 (slave trafficking)

18 U.S.C. 1592 (document offenses involving slave trafficking)

18 U.S.C. 1963 (RICO violation involving bank fraud)

50 U.S.C. 783 (disclosure of classified information (with suspension until the end of any federal employment of the accused)

8 Years

1. Generally

18 U.S.C. 32 (destruction of aircraft or aircraft facilities)

18 U.S.C. 37 (violence at international airports)

18 U.S.C. 112 (assaults upon diplomats)

18 U.S.C. 175 or 175b (biological weapons offenses)

18 U.S.C. 228 (chemical weapons offenses)

18 U.S.C. 351 (congressional, cabinet, and Supreme Court assassination, kidnapping , or assault)

18 U.S.C. 831 (nuclear materials offenses)

18 U.S.C. 842(m) or (n) (plastic explosives offenses)

18 U.S.C. 930(c) (killing or attempted killing during an attack on a federal facility with a dangerous weapon)

18 U.S.C. 956(a)(1) (conspiracy to murder, kidnap, or maim persons abroad)

18 U.S.C. 1030(a)(1)(protection of computer systems containing classified information)

18 U.S.C. 1030(a)(5)(A)(i)(resulting in damage defined in 1030(a)(5)(B)(ii) through (v) (protection of computers)

18 U.S.C. 1114 (protection of officers and employees of the United States)

18 U.S.C. 1116 (murder or manslaughter of foreign officials, official guests, or internationally protected persons)

18 U.S.C. 1203 (hostage taking)

18 U.S.C. 1361 (destruction of federal property)

18 U.S.C. 1362 (destruction of communication lines, stations, or systems)

18 U.S.C. 1363 (injury to buildings or property within special maritime and territorial jurisdiction of the United States)

18 U.S.C. 1366(a) (destruction of energy facilities)

18 U.S.C. 1751(a),(b),(c), or (d) (Presidential and Presidential staff assassination, kidnapping, or assault)

18 U.S.C. 1992 (terrorist attacks on trains and mass transit)

18 U.S.C. 2155 (destruction of national defense materials, premises, or utilities), 2280 (violence against maritime navigation)

18 U.S.C. 2281 (violence against maritime fixed platforms)

18 U.S.C. 2332 (certain homicides and other violence against United States nationals occurring outside of the United States)

18 U.S.C. 2332a (use of weapons of mass destruction)

18 U.S.C. 2332b (acts of terrorism transcending national boundaries)

18 U.S.C. 2339A (providing material support to terrorists)

18 U.S.C. 2339B (providing material support to terrorist organizations)

18 U.S.C. 2340A (torture committed under color of law)

42 U.S.C. 2284 (sabotage of nuclear facilities or fuel)

49 U.S.C. 46502 (aircraft piracy)

49 U.S.C. 46504 (second sentence)(assault on a flight crew with a dangerous weapon)

49 U.S.C. 46505 (explosive or incendiary devices, or endangerment of human life by means of weapons, or aircraft)

49 U.S.C. 46506 (certain criminal laws to acts on aircraft)

49 U.S.C. 60123(b) (destruction of interstate gas or hazardous liquid pipeline facility)

2. Federal Crimes of Terrorism That Do Not Result in or Involve the Risk of Death or Serious Injury

18 U.S.C. 32 (destruction of aircraft or aircraft facilities)

18 U.S.C. 37 (violence at international airports)

18 U.S.C. 81 (arson within special maritime and territorial jurisdiction)

18 U.S.C. 175 or 175b (biological weapons offenses)

18 U.S.C. 175c (variola virus)

18 U.S.C. 229 (chemical weapons offenses)

18 U.S.C. 351(a),(b),(c), or (d) (congressional, cabinet, and Supreme Court assassination and kidnapping)

18 U.S.C. 831 (nuclear materials offenses)

18 U.S.C. 832 (participation in a foreign atomic weapons program)

18 U.S.C. 842(m) or (n) (plastic explosives offenses)

18 U.S.C. 844(f)(2) or (3)(arson and bombing of federal property risking or causing death)

18 U.S.C. 844(i) (burning or bombing of property used in, or used in activities affecting, commerce)

18 U.S.C. 930(c) (killing or attempted killing during an attack on a federal facility with a dangerous weapon)

18 U.S.C. 956(a)(1) (conspiracy to murder, kidnap, or maim persons abroad)

18 U.S.C. 1030(a)(1)(protection of computer systems containing classified information)

18 U.S.C. 1030(a)(5)(A)(i)(resulting in damage defined in 1030(a)(5)(B)(ii) through (v) (protection of computers)

18 U.S.C. 1114 (protection of officers and employees of the United States),

18 U.S.C. 1116 (murder or manslaughter of foreign officials, official guests, or internationally protected persons)

18 U.S.C. 1203 (hostage taking)

18 U.S.C. 1361 (destruction of federal property)

18 U.S.C. 1362 (destruction of communication lines, stations, or systems)

18 U.S.C. 1363 (injury to buildings or property within special maritime and territorial jurisdiction of the United States)

18 U.S.C. 1366(a) (destruction of energy facilities)

18 U.S.C. 1751(a),(b),(c), or (d) (Presidential and Presidential staff assassination and kidnapping)

18 U.S.C. 1992 (terrorist attacks on trains and mass transit)

18 U.S.C. 2155 (destruction of national defense materials, premises, or utilities),

18 U.S.C. 2156 (production of defective national defense material)

18 U.S.C. 2280 (violence against maritime navigation)

18 U.S.C. 2281 (violence against maritime fixed platforms)

18 U.S.C. 2332 (certain homicides and other violence against United States nationals occurring outside of the United States)

18 U.S.C. 2332a (use of weapons of mass destruction)

18 U.S.C. 2332b (acts of terrorism transcending national boundaries)

18 U.S.C. 2332f (bombing public places)

18 U.S.C. 2332g (anti-aircraft missiles)

18 U.S.C. 2332h (radiological dispersal devices)

18 U.S.C. 2339 (harboring terrorists)

18 U.S.C. 2339A (providing material support to terrorists)

18 U.S.C. 2339B (providing material support to terrorist organizations)

18 U.S.C. 2339C (financing terrorism)

18 U.S.C. 2339D (receipt of military training from a foreign terrorist organization)

18 U.S.C. 2340A (torture committed under color of law)

21 U.S.C. 960A (narcoterrorism)

42 U.S.C. 2122 (atomic weapons)

42 U.S.C. 2284 (sabotage of nuclear facilities or fuel)

49 U.S.C. 46502 (aircraft piracy)

49 U.S.C. 46504 (second sentence)(assault on a flight crew with a dangerous weapon)

49 U.S.C. 46505(b)(3) or (c)(explosive or incendiary devices, or endangerment of human life by means of weapons, or aircraft)

49 U.S.C. 46506 (if homicide or attempted homicide involved, application of certain criminal laws to acts on aircraft)

49 U.S.C. 60123(b) (destruction of interstate gas or hazardous liquid pipeline facility)

7 Years

18 U.S.C. 1031 (major fraud against the United States)

6 Years

26 U.S.C. 6531 (tax crimes)

5 Years
All crimes not otherwise provided for

1 Year

18 U.S.C. 402 (contempt of court)

STATE FELONY STATUTES OF LIMITATION

State	Felonies (Generally)	Various Exceptions
ALABAMA	3 years (Ala. Code §15-3-1)	Any time: (a) capital offense; (b) felony involving: - arson; forgery; drug trafficking; death or serious injury; use, attempted use, or threat to use violence; or counterfeiting; or (c) sex offense w/ victim>16 (Ala. Code §15-3-5)
ALASKA	5 years (Alaska Stat .§12.10.010)	(a) Any time: murder; class A, B, or unclassified felony sexual assault; felony sexual abuse of minor; various sexual offenses w/ a minor victim; (b) 10 years: 1st degree indecent exposure; manslaughter (Alaska Stat§12.10.010)
ARIZONA	7 years (Ariz. Rev. Stat. Ann. §13-107)	Any time: attempted commission or commission of - homicide; class 2 felony sex offense or sexual exploitation of children; violent sexual assault; misuse of public money; felony falsification of public records (Ariz. Rev. Stat. Ann. §13-107)
ARKANSAS	(a) 6 years: Class Y, A (b) 3 years: Class B, C, D, or unclassified (Ark. Code Ann. §5-1-109)	Any time: murder (Ark. Code Ann. §5-1-109)

Table (Continued)

State	Felonies (Generally)	Various Exceptions
CALIFORNIA	3 years (Cal. Penal Code § 801)	(a) Any time: crime punishable by death or life imprisonment; or embezzlement of public money (b) 6 years: felony punishable by imprisonment for 8 years or more (Cal. Penal Code §§799, 800)
COLORADO	3 years (Colo. Rev. Stat. Ann. §16-5-401)	Any time: committing, attempting, conspiring to commit, or soliciting commit - murder, treason, kidnapping , forgery, or sex offenses against a child (Colo. Rev. Stat. Ann. §16-5-401)
CONNECTICUT	5 years (Conn. Gen. Stat. Ann. §54-193)	Any time: capital or class A felony; arson-murder; or 1st degree escape (Conn. Gen. Stat. Ann. §54-193)
DELAWARE	5 years (Del. Code Ann. tit. 11 §205)	Any time: commit or attempt to commit murder, class A felony, or a sexual offense(Del. Code Ann. tit. 11 §205)
FLORIDA	3 years (Fla. Stat. Ann. §775.15)	(a) Any time: capital or life felony, felony resulting in death, or perjury in a capital case; (b) 10 years: felony from use of destructive device resulting in injury; (c) 4 years: 1st degree felony, (Fla. Stat. Ann. §775.15)
GEORGIA	4 years (Ga. Code Ann. §17-3-1)	(a) Any time: murder; (b) 15 years: rape; (c) 7 years: other crimes punishable by death or life imprisonment; or felonies w/ victims >14 (Ga. Code Ann. §17-3-1)

State	Felonies (Generally)	Various Exceptions
HAWAII	3 years (Haw. Rev. Stat. §701-108)	(a) Any time: commit, attempt, conspire to commit, or solicit murder; (b) 10 years: vehicular manslaughter; (c) 6 years: class A felony (Haw. Rev. Stat. §701-108)
IDAHO	5 years (Idaho Code §19-402)	Any time: murder, voluntary manslaughter, rape, sexual abuse of a child, or terrorism (Idaho Code §19-401)
ILLINOIS	3 years (Ill. Comp. Stat. Ann. ch. 720 §5/3-5)	Any time: homicide, attempted murder, treason, arson, or forgery (Ill. Comp. Stat. Ann. ch.720 §5/3-5)
INDIANA	5 years (Ind. Code Ann. §35-41-4-2)	Any time: murder or a Class A felony (Ind. Code Ann. §35-41-4-2)
IOWA	3 years (Iowa Code Ann. §802.3)	(a) Any time: murder; (b) 10 years: sexual abuse (Iowa Code Ann. §§802.1, 802.2, 802.3)
KANSAS	5 years (Kan. Stat. Ann. §21-3106)	Any time: murder or terrorism; (Kan. Stat. Ann. §21-3106)
KENTUCKY	Any time (Ky. Rev. Stat. Ann. §500.050)	
LOUISIANA	4 years(La. Code Crim. P.art. 572)	(a) Any time: crime punishable by death or life imprisonment; (b) 10 years: various sex crimes against minors; (c) 6 years: felony punishable at hard labor) (La. Code Crim. P. arts. 571, 571.1. 572.)
MAINE	(a) 6 years: Class A, B, or C crime; (b) 3 years: Class C or D crime (Me. Rev. Stat. Ann. tit. 17-A §8)	Any time: murder, 1st or 2d degree homicide, or various sexual offenses against a minor (Me. Rev. Stat. Ann. tit. 17-A §8)

Table (Continued)

State	Felonies (Generally)	Various Exceptions
MARYLAND	Any time subject to occasional individual statutory exceptions, e.g., computer crimes (3 years) (Md..Cts. and Jud. Proc. §5-601)	
MASSACHUSETTS	6 years (Mass. Gen. Laws Ann. ch. 277 §63)	(a) Any time: murder (b) 15 years: commit or conspire to commit rape or assault w/ intent to rape or murder; (c) 10 years: commit or conspire to commit robbery or assault w/ intent to rob(Mass. Gen. Laws Ann. ch. 277 §63)
MICHIGAN	6 years (Mich. Comp. Laws Ann. §767.24)	(a) Any time: murder, terrorism, or 1st degree sexual conduct; (b) 10 years: kidnapping , extortion, conspiracy or assault w/ intent to murder(Mich. Comp. Laws Ann. §767.24)
MINNESOTA	3 years (Minn. Stat. Ann. §628.26)	(a) Any time: crime resulting in death, kidnapping ; (b) 6 years: bribery or medicaid fraud; (c) 5 years: arson, riot, theft offenses involving <$35,000 , or environmental false statement offenses (Minn. Stat. Ann. §628.26)
MISSISSIPPI	2 years (Miss. Code Ann. §99-1-5)	Any time: murder, rape, kidnapping , arson, manslaughter,burglary, aggravated assault, forgery, counterfeiting, robbery, larceny, fraud, embezzlement, or various sexual offenses against minors (Miss. Code Ann. §99-1-5)
MISSOURI	3 years (Mo. Ann. Stat. §556.036)	Any time: murder, rape or a class A felony (Mo. Ann. Stat. §556.036)
MONTANA	5 years (Mont. Code Ann. §45-1-205)	(a) Any time: homicide (b) 10 years: sexual assault(Mont. Code Ann. §45-1-205)
NEBRASKA	3 years (Neb. Rev. Stat. §29-110)	Any time: treason, murder, arson, forgery or various sexual offenses(Neb. Rev. Stat. §29-110)

State	Felonies (Generally)	Various Exceptions
NEVADA	3 years (Nev. Rev. Stat. Ann. §171.085)	(a) Any time: murder; (b) 4 years: theft, arson, robbery, burglary, sexual assault, or forgery (Nev. Rev. Stat. Ann. §§171. 080, 171.085)
NEW HAMPSHIRE	6 years (N.H. Rev. Stat. Ann. §625:8)	Any time: murder (N.H. Rev. Stat. Ann. §625:8)
NEW JERSEY	5 years (N.J. Stat. Ann. §2C:1-6)	(a) Any time: murder, manslaughter, sexual assault (b) 10 years: environment offenses; (c) 7 years: bribery or certain other offenses involving misconduct in office (N.J. Stat. Ann. §2C:1-6)
NEW MEXICO	(a) 6 years: 2d B felony; (b) 5 years: 3d or 4th B felony (N.M. Stat. Ann. §30-1-8)	Any time: capital or 1st degree felony (N.M. Stat. Ann. §30-1-8)
NEW YORK	5 years (N.Y. Crim. P. Law §30.10)	Any time: class A felony or 1st degree rape, sexual criminal act, or sexual conduct against a child (N.Y. Crim. P. Law §30.10)
NORTH CAROLINA	Any time (N.C. Gen. Stat. §15-1)	
NORTH DAKOTA	3 years (N.D. Cent. Code §29-04-02)	Any time: murder (N.D. Cent. Code §29-04-01)
OHIO	6 years (Ohio Rev. Code Ann. §2901.13)	(a) Any time: murder; (b) 20 years: commit, attempt, or aid and abet kidnapping , robbery, riot, manslaughter, sexual assault, burglary, or arson (Ohio Rev. Code Ann. §2901.13)
OKLAHOMA	3 years (Okla. Stat. Ann. tit. 22 §152)	(a) Any time: murder; (b) 12 years: rape, sodomy, or certain other sexual offenses (Okla. Stat. Ann. tit. 22 §§151, 152)

Table (Continued)

State	Felonies (Generally)	Various Exceptions
OREGON	3 years (Ore. Rev. Stat. §131.125)	(a) Any time: commit, attempt, conspire to commit, or solicit murder; (b) 6 years: arson or various sexual offenses against minors (Ore. Rev. Stat. §131.125)
PENNSYLVANIA	2 years (Pa. Stat. Ann. tit. 42 §5552)	(a) Any time: commit, conspire to commit, or solicit murder; or manslaughter; (b) 12 years: major sex offenses; (c) 5 years: commit, conspire to commit or solicit, assault, arson, terroristic threats, arson, robbery, kidnapping , burglary, forgery, theft, perjury, fraud, gambling, drug trafficking, racketeering, or obstruction of justice (Pa. Stat. Ann tit. 42 §§5551, 5552)
RHODE ISLAND	3 years (R.I. Gen. Laws §12-12-17)	(a) Any time: treason, homicide, arson, burglary, counterfeiting, forgery, robbery, rape, assault, drug trafficking, or any other felony punishable by life imprisonment; (b) 10 years: larceny, bribery, racketeering, perjury, or extortion (R.I. Gen. Laws§12-12-17)
SOUTH CAROLINA	Any time	
SOUTH DAKOTA	7 years (S.D. Cod. Laws §23A-42-2)	Any time: Class A, B, or C felonies (S.D. Cod. Laws§23A-42-2)
TENNESSEE	(a) 15 years: Class A felony; (b) 8 years: Class B felony; (c) 4 years: Class C or D felony; (d) 2 years: Class E felony (Tenn. Code Ann. §40-2-101)	Any time: crime punishable by death or life imprisonment (Tenn. Code Ann. §40-2-101)
TEXAS	3 years (Tex. Code Crim. P. art. 12.01)	(a) Any time: murder or manslaughter; (b) 10 years: forgery, embezzlement, various sexual offenses against minors; (c) 7 years: bank fraud or tax fraud; (d) 5 years: theft or arson (Tex. Code Crim. P. art. 12.01)

State	Felonies (Generally)	Various Exceptions
UTAH	4 years (Utah Code Ann. §76-1-302)	Any time: capital felony, murder, or manslaughter (Utah Code Ann. §76-1-301)
VERMONT	3 years (Vt. Stat. Ann. tit.13 §4501)	(a) Any time: rape, murder, arson(causing death), or kidnapping ; (b) 11 years: arson; (c) 6 years: certain sexual offenses, grand larceny, robbery, burglary, embezzlement, forgery, bribery, false claims, fraud, or felony tax offenses (Vt. Stat. Ann. tit.13 §4501)
VIRGINIA	Any time (Va. Code §19.2-8)	
WASHINGTON	3 years (Wash. Rev. Code Ann. §9A.04.080)	(a) Any time: homicide; (b) 10 years: arson, rape, or certain offenses involving misconduct in office; (c) 7 years: certain sexual offenses against minors; (d) 6 years: racketeering; (e) 5 years: medicaid or tax fraud (Wash. Rev. Code Ann. §9A.04.080)
WEST VIRGINIA	Any time (W.Va. Code §61-11-9)	
WISCONSIN	6 years (Wis. Stat. Ann. §939.74)	Any time: homicide (Wis. Stat. Ann. §939.74)
WYOMING	Any time	

REFERENCES

[1]   BLACK'S LAW DICTIONARY 927 (6th ed. 1990).

[2]   *Toussie v. United States*, 397 U.S. 112, 114-15 (1970).

[3]   The statute of limitations is an affirmative defense that can be waived either explicitly or by failure to raise it at or before trial on the untimely charge, *United States v. Baldwin*, 414 F.3d 791, 795 (7th Cir. 2005); *United States v. Titterington*, 374 F.3d 453, 458 (6th Cir. 2004); *United*

States v. Smith, 373 F.3d 561, 563 (4th Cir. 2004); *United States v. Koonin*, 361 F.3d 1250, 1252 (9th Cir. 2004); *United States v. Thurston*, 358 F.3d 51, 62 (1st Cir. 2004); *United States v. Spero*, 331 F.3d 57, 60 (2d Cir. 2003); *United States v. Gilchrist*, 215 F.3d 333, 339 (3d Cir. 2000); *United States v. Mulderig*, 120 F.3d 534, 540 (5th Cir. 1997); *United States v. Cooper*, 956 F.2d 960, 961 (10th Cir. 1992); *United States v. Wild*, 551 F.2d 418, 424-25 (D.C. Cir. 1977).

[4]   At some point events pass into history and due process restricts the extent to which they may be resurrected to build a criminal accusation, with or without an applicable statute of limitations, *United States v. Marion*, 404 U.S. 307, 324 (1971).

[5]   Capsulized descriptions of the various state criminal statutes of limitation governing felony prosecutions are appended.

[6]   "Except for murder and forgery, the statute of limitations for the prosecution of all federal capital offenses is three years; the statute of limitations for all noncapital crimes is two years," 1 Stat. 119 (1790).

[7]   18 U.S.C. 3281.

[8]   "Except as otherwise expressly provided by law, no person shall be prosecuted, tried, or punished for any offense, not capital, unless the indictment is found or information is instituted within five years next after such offense shall have been committed," 18 U.S.C. 3282.

[9]   18 U.S.C. 3286.

[10]   18 U.S.C. 3290,

[11]   18 U.S.C. 3287.

[12]   "An indictment for any offense punishable by death may be found at any time without limitation," 18 U.S.C. 3281. Between the Supreme Court's decision in *Furman v. Georgia*, 408 U.S. 238 (1972), and passage of the Violent Crime Control and Law Enforcement Act of 1994, 108 Stat. 1796, the death penalty authorized by federal capital offense statutes could not be constitutionally imposed. The question arose whether the term "offenses punishable by death" in the statute of limitations referred to offenses made capital by statute or only to offenses for which the death penalty might constitutionally be imposed. The courts concluded that Congress intended the term to refer to offenses which it made capital by statute. *United States v. Emery*, 186 F.3d 921, 924 (8th Cir. 1999); *United States v. Edwards*, 159 F.3d 1117, 1128 (8th Cir. 1998); *United States v. Manning*, 56 F.3d 1188, 1196 (9th Cir. 1995). A list of the federal capital offenses is appended. The list includes those crimes made capital by operation of other provisions of law such as 18 U.S.C.

3559(f)(murder of a child during the course a federal crime of violence) and 18 U.S.C. 2245 (murder committed during the course of designated federal sex offenses).

[13] 18 U.S.C. 3286(b)("Notwithstanding any other law, an indictment may be found or an information instituted at any time without limitation for any offense listed in Section 2332b(g)(5)(B), if the commission of such offense resulted in, or created a foreseeable risk of, death or serious bodily injury to another person"). A list of crimes cross referenced in 18 U.S.C.2332b(g)(5)(B) is appended.

[14] 18 U.S.C. 2332b(g)(5) defines a federal crime of terrorism as "an offense that – (A) is calculated to influence or affect the conduct of a government by intimidation or coercion, or to retaliate against government conduct; and (B) is a violation of" one of list of terrorism-associated offenses. The list of crimes which Section 3286(b) makes prosecutable at any time consists of those crimes listed in 18 U.S.C. 2332b(g)(5)*(B)*. Had Congress wished the waiver of the statutes of limitation to apply only to terrorists accused of these offenses presumably it would have referred to 18 U.S.C. 2332b(g)(5), i.e., both 2332b(g)(5)(A) and (B), rather than simply to 18 U.S.C. 2332b(g)(5)(B) as it did.

[15] 18 U.S.C. 3299 ("Notwithstanding any other law, an indictment may be found or an information instituted at any time without limitation for any offense under Section 1201 [kidnapping] involving a minor victim, and for any felony under Chapter 109A, 110 (except for Section 2257 and 2257A), or 117, or Section 1591 [sex trafficking of an adult by force or fraud or of a child]"). The felonies in Chapters 109A, 110 and 117 include violations of 18 U.S.C. 2241 (aggravate sexual abuse), 2242 (sexual abuse), 2243 (sexual abuse of a ward or child), 2244 (abusive sexual contact), 2245 (sexual abuse resulting in death), 2250 (failure to register as a sex offender), 2251 (sexual exploitation of children), 2251A (selling or buying children), 2252 (transporting, distributing or selling child sexually exploitive material), 2252A (transporting or distributing child pornography), 2252B (misleading names on the Internet), 2260 (making child sexually exploitative material overseas for export to the U.S.), 2421 (transportation of illicit sexual purposes), 2422 (coerce or entice travel for illicit sexual purposes), 2423 (travel involving illicit sexual activity with a child), 2424 (filing false immigration statement), 2425 (interstate transmission of information about a child relating to illicit sexual activity).

[16] "No person shall be prosecuted, tried, or punished for a violation of or conspiracy to violate Section 668 unless the indictment is returned or the information is filed within 20 years after the commission of the offense," 18 U.S.C. 3294.

[17] "No person shall be prosecuted, tried, or punished for any non-capital offense under Section 81 [arson in the special maritime or territorial jurisdiction of the United States] or subsection (f), (h), or (i) of Section 844 [use of fire or explosives to commit a federal offense, and burning or bombing of federal property or property used in or in activities affecting interstate or foreign commerce] unless the indictment is found or the information is instituted not later than 10 years after the date on which the offense was committed," 18U.S.C. 3295.

[18] "No person shall be prosecuted, tried, or punished for a violation of, or a conspiracy to violate – (1) Section 215, 656, 657, 1005, 1006, 1007, 1014, 1033, or 1344; (2) Section 1341 or 1343 [mail and wire fraud], if the offense affects a financial institution; or (3) Section 1963 [(RICO) racketeer influenced and corrupt organizations], to the extent that the racketeering activity involves a violation of Section 1344 [bank fraud] – unless the indictment is returned or the information is filed within 10 years after the commission of the offense," 18 U.S.C. 3293.

[19] "No person shall be prosecuted, tried, or punished for violation of any provision of Sections 1423 to 1428, inclusive, of Chapter 69 [nationality and citizenship offenses] and Sections 1541 to 1544, inclusive, of Chapter 75 [passport and visa offenses] of Title 18 of the United States Code, or for conspiracy to violate any of such Sections, unless the indictment is found or the information is instituted within 10 years after the commission of the offense," 18 U.S.C. 3291

[20] "Notwithstanding Section 3282, no person shall be prosecuted, tried, or punished for any noncapital offense involving a violation of any provision listed in Section 2332b(g)(5)(B) [terrorist offenses], or a violation 112, 351(e), 1361, or 1751(e) of this title, or Section 46504, 46505, or 46506 of Title 49, unless the indictment is found or the information is instituted within eight years after the offense was committed. . . ." 18 U.S.C. 3286(a).

[21] *See e.g.,* H.REP.NO. 82-167, at 2-3 (1951); H.REP.NO. 98-907, at 2 (1984), *reprinted in,* 1984 U.S.C.C.A.N. 3578, 3578-579.

[22] *Administration's Draft Anti-Terrorism Act of 2001: Hearings Before the House Comm. on the Judiciary,* 107th Cong., 1st Sess. at 60 (2001).

[23] 18 U.S.C. 3283.

[24]   18 U.S.C. 3284.

[25]   18 U.S.C. 3287.

[26]   18 U.S.C. 3288, 3289.

[27]   18 U.S.C. 3290.

[28]   18 U.S.C. 3292.

[29]   18 U.S.C. 3282(b), 3297.

[30]   "No statute of limitations that would otherwise preclude prosecution for an offense involving the sexual or physical abuse, or kidnapping , of a child under the age of 18 years shall preclude such prosecution during the life of the child, or for 10 years after the offense, whichever is longer," 18 U.S.C. 3283.

[31]   P.L. 109-162, 119 Stat. 2960 (2006); officially, the Violence Against Woman and Department of Justice Reauthorization Act of 2005.

[32]   18 U.S.C. 2241-2248 (relating to federal sexual abuse offenses).

[33]   "(1) *In general*. – In any indictment for an offense under Chapter 109 for which the identity of the accused is unknown, it shall be sufficient to describe the accused as an individual whose name is unknown, but who has a particular DNA profile. "(2) *Exception*. – (An indictment described under paragraph (1) which is found not later than five years after the offense under Chapter 109A is committed, shall not be subject to – (A) the limitations period described under subsection (a) [of five years]; and (B) the provisions of Chapter 208 [relating to speedy trial] until the individual is arrested or served with a summons in connection with the charges contained in the indictment. "(3) *Defined term*. – For purposes of this subsection, the term 'DNA profile' means a set of DNA identification characteristics," 18 U.S.C. 3282(b).

[34]   *DOJ Oversight: Funding Forensic Sciences – DNA and Beyond: Hearing Before the Subcomm. on Administrative Oversight and the Courts of the Senate Comm. on the Judiciary*, 108th Cong., 1st Sess. (statement of Director Sarah V. Hart)("As noted, we have recommended remedial legislation to provide that, in felony cases in which the defendant is implicated through DNA testing, the statute of limitations does not begin to run until the DNA identification occurs. Even where crime scene DNA evidence is available, unavoidable delay may occur before the offender can be identified through DNA matching, if he is not convicted until years later for some other offense which results in a DNA sample being taken and entry of his DNA profile into CODIS. The proposed tolling provision will help to ensure that prosecution will not be barred by an arbitrary time limit in such cases").

[35] *United States v. Martinez*, 2007 WL 709015 (D.N.M. Feb. 16, 2007)(emphasis added) ("The United States contends that the application of 18 U.S.C. 3297, *which tolls the commencement of any otherwise applicable limitations period until DNA testing implicates an individual*, 'presents an interesting issue from the standpoint of retroactivity'. . . . Because the Court has already determined that 18 U.S.C. 3281 is the proper statute of limitations to apply in this case. . . it need not decide for the purpose of this motion whether 18 U.S.C. 3297 applies in this case").

[36] *United States v. Gilbert*, 136 F.3d 1451, 1454-455 (11th Cir. 1998); *United States v. Dolan*, 120 F.3d 856, 867-68 (8th Cir. 1997), both citing, *United States v. Guglielmini*, 425 F.2d 439 (2d Cir. 1970); and *Rudin v. United States*, 254 F.2d 45 (6th Cir. 1958).

[37] "When the United States is at war the running of any statute of limitations applicable to any offense (1) involving fraud or attempted fraud against the United States or any agency thereof in any manner, whether by conspiracy or not, or (2) committed in connection with the acquisition, care, handling, custody, control or disposition of any real or personal property of the United States, or (3) committed in connection with the negotiation, procurement, award, performance, payment for, interim financing, cancellation, or other termination or settlement, of any contract, subcontract, or purchase order which is connected with or related to the prosecution of the war, or with any disposition of termination inventory by any war contractor or Government agency, shall be suspended until three years after the termination of hostilities as proclaimed by the President or by a concurrent resolution of Congress. Definitions of terms in Section 103 of Title 41 shall apply to similar terms used in this section," 18 U.S.C. 3287.

[38] *United States v. Shelton*, 816 F.Supp. 1132, 1134-135 (W.D.Tex. 1993)(declining to apply the suspension to cases arising out of hostilities in the area of the Persian Gulf).

[39] *Bridges v. United States*, 346 U.S. 209, 220 (1953).

[40] *United States v. Garcia*, 268 F.3d 407, 411 (6th Cir. 2001)("with respect to the charges brought in the indictment, however, the five year limitation period stops running as soon as the indictment is brought"); *United States v. Milstein*, 401 F.3d 53, 67 (2d Cir. 2005); *United States v. Brady*, 67 F.3d 1421, 1426 (9th Cir. 1995); *United States v. O'Bryant*, 998 F.2d 21, 23 (1st Cir. 1993). This is the case even if the indictment is returned under seal and unsealed only after the period of limitation has run, as long as the indictment was sealed for a legitimate prosecutorial

purpose, *United States v. Bracy*, 67 F.3d at 1426; *United States v. Sharpe*, 995 F.2d 49, 51 (5th Cir. 1993); *United States v. Shell*, 961 F.2d 138, 141 (9th Cir. 1992); *United States v. Richard*, 943 F.2d 115, 118-19 (1st Cir. 1991); *United States v. Larkin*, 875 F.2d 168, 170-72 (8th Cir. 1989); *United States v. Srulowitz*, 819 F.2d 37, 40-41 (2d Cir. 1987); *but see, United States v. Wright*, 343 F.3d 849, 857 (6th Cir. 2003)(as long as the indictment was properly sealed *and* the defendant failed to show actual prejudice when the indictment was opened after the expiration of the period of limitation); *United States v. Thompson*, 287 F.3d 1244, 1251-252 (10th Cir. 2002)(declining to permit tolling of a sealed indictment).

[41]   "Whenever an indictment or information charging a felony is dismissed for any reason after the period prescribed by the applicable statute of limitations has expired, a new indictment may be returned in the appropriate jurisdiction within six calendar months of the date of the dismissal of the indictment or information, or, in the event of an appeal, within 60 days of the date the dismissal of the indictment or information becomes final, or, if no regular grand jury is in session in the appropriate jurisdiction when the indictment or information is dismissed, within six calendar months of the date when the next regular grand jury is convened, which new indictment shall not be barred by any statute of limitations. This section does not permit the filing of a new indictment or information where the reason for the dismissal was the failure to file the indictment or information within the period prescribed by the applicable statute of limitations, or some other reason that would bar a new prosecution," 18 U.S.C. 3288. "Whenever an indictment or information charging a felony is dismissed for any reason before the period prescribed by the applicable statute of limitations has expired, and such period will expire within six calendar months of the date of the dismissal of the indictment or information, a new indictment may be returned in the appropriate jurisdiction within six calendar months of the expiration of the applicable statute of limitations, or, in the event of an appeal, within 60 days of the date the dismissal of the indictment or information becomes final or, if no regular grand jury is in session in the appropriate jurisdiction at the expiration of the applicable statute of limitations, within six calendar months of the date when the next regular grand jury is convened, which new indictment shall not be barred by any statute of limitations. This section does not permit the filing of a new indictment or information where the reason for the dismissal was the

failure to file the indictment or information within the period prescribed
by the applicable statute of limitations, or some other reason that would
bar a new prosecution," 18 U.S.C. 3289. Beyond the extension here,
when a timely indictment is dismissed pursuant to a plea agreement
under which the defendant pleads to other charges, the statute of
limitations ordinarily begins again for the dismissed charges unless the
defendant has waived as part of the plea agreement, *United States v.
Midgley*, 142 F.3d 174, 177-79 (3d Cir. 1998); *United States v. Gilchrist*,
215 F.3d 333 (3d Cir. 2000); *United States v. Podde*, 105 F.3d 813, 818-
20 (2d Cir. 1997).

[42] *United States v. Garcia*, 268 F.3d 407, 411 (6th Cir. 2001)("a
      superseding indictment brought outside the five-year limitations period
      while an earlier indictment is still validly pending will nevertheless be
      timely under Section 3282 so long as it does not materially broaden the
      charges of the original indictment. When a superseding indictment is
      filed outside the limitations period but does not broaden the charges set
      forth in the original timely indictment, it is said to relate back to the
      filing of the original indictment"); *see also, United States v. Watford*,
      468 F.3d 891, 908-909 (6th Cir. 2006); *United States v. Qayyum*, 451
      F.3d 1214, 1218 (10th Cir. 2006); *United States v. Daniels*, 387 F.3d 636,
      642 (7th Cir. 2004); *United States v. Ratcliff*, 245 F.3d 1246, 1253 (11th
      Cir. 2001); *United States v. Ben Zvi*, 242 F.3d 89, 98 (2d Cir. 2001);
      United States v. Oliva, 46 F.3d 320, 324 (3d Cir. 1995); *United States v.
      Gomez*, 38 F.3d 1031, 1036 n.8 (8th Cir. 1994); *United States v.
      O'Bryant*, 998 F.2d 21, 23 (1st Cir. 1993); *United States v. Pacheco*, 912
      F.2d 297, 305 (9th Cir. 1990); *United States v. Schmick*, 904 F.2d 936,
      940-41 (5th Cir. 1990); *United States v. Snowden*, 770 F.2d 393, 398 (4th
      Cir. 1985).

[43] H.REP.NO. 98-907, at 2-3 (1984), *reprinted in* 1984 U.S.C.C.A.N.
      3578, 3578-579; *Foreign Evidence Rules Amendment: Hearing Before
      the Subcomm. on Criminal Justice of the House Comm. on the Judiciary*,
      98th Cong., 2d Sess. 15 (1984)(testimony of Dep.Ass't Att'y Gen. Mark
      Richard).

[44] Abramovsky and Edelstein, *Time for Final Action on 18 U.S.C. 3292*, 21
      MICHIGAN JOURNAL OF INTERNATIONAL LAW 941 (2000).

[45] *Compare, In re Grand Jury Investigation*, 3 F.Supp. 2d 82 (D.Mass.
      1998)(denying the government's ex parte application without prejudice),
      with, DeGeroge v. U.S.District Court, 219 F.3d 930, 937 (9th Cir. 2000)
      ("DeGeorge first argues that the government's Section 3292 application

was invalid because it was ex parte and in camera. However, there is no basis in the statute for such an argument"); *see also, United States v. Wilson*, 249 F.3d 366, 371 (5th Cir. 2001)("An application to toll the statute of limitations under §3292 is a preindictment, ex parte proceeding").

[46] 18 U.S.C. 3292(a)(1); *United States v. Wilson*, 249 F.3d at 373; *United States v. Trainor*, 376 F.3d 1325, 1330 (11th Cir. 2004).

[47] *Compare, United States v. O'Neill*, 952 F.Supp. 831, 833 (D.D.C. 1996)("The government can only request that statutes of limitation be tolled for offenses under investigation by the grand jury"), *with, DeGeorge v. U.S.District Court*, 219 F.3d at 939-40 (denial of mandamus)(characterizing the statement in *O'Neill* as dicta and declining to find clear error in a contrary lower court decision), *on appeal*, 380 F.3d 1203, 1214; *but see, United States v. Meador*, 138 F.3d 986, 994 (5th Cir. 1998) ("The purpose of §3292, apparent from its structure and legislative history, is to compensate for delays attendant in obtaining records form other countries. This provision should not be an affirmative benefit to prosecutors, suspending the limitations period, pending completion of an investigation, whenever evidence is located in a foreign land. It is not a statutory grant of authority to extend the limitations period by three years at the prosecutors' option").

[48] *United States v. Miller*, 830 F.2d 1073, 1076 (9th Cir. 1987).

[49] *United States v. Atiyeh*, 402 F.3d 354, 362-67 (3d Cir. 2005).

[50] *United States v. Bischel*, 61 F.3d 1429, 1432-434 (9th Cir. 1995); *United States .v. Torres*, 318 F.3d 1058, 1061-65 (11th Cir. 2003); *United States v. Hagege*, 437 F.3d. 943, 955-56 (9th Cir. 2005).

[51] *Untied States v. Meador*, 138 F.3d at 991-94.

[52] 1 Stat. 119 (1790)("nothing herein contained shall extend to any person or persons fleeing from justice").

[53] *See generally, What Constitutes "Fleeing From Justice" Within the Meaning of 18 U.S.C.A. §3290 Which Provides That No Statute of Limitations Shall Extend to Persons Fleeing From Justice*, 148 ALR FED 573.

[54] *United States v. Florez*, 447 F.3d 145, 150-51 (2d Cir. 2006); *Ross v. U.S. Marshal*, 168 F.3d 1190, 1193-194 (10th Cir. 1999); *United States v. Greever*, 134 F.3d 777, 780 (6th Cir. 1998); *United States v. Foseca-Machado*, 53 F.3d 1242, 1244 (11th Cir. 1995); *United States v. Fowlie*, 24 F.3d 1070, 1072 (9th Cir. 1994); *United States v. Marshall*, 856 F.2d

896, 900 (7th Cir. 1988); *Donnell v. United States*, 229 F.2d 560, 565 (5th Cir. 1956); *Brouse v. United States*, 68 F.2d 294, 295 (1st Cir. 1933).

[55] *In re Assarsson*, 687 F.2d 1157, 1162 (8th Cir. 1982); *McGowen v. United States*, 105 F.2d 791, 792 (D.C. Cir. 1939). *Streep* declared that it "unnecessary, for the purposes of the present case, to undertake to give an exhaustive definition of these words [fleeing from justice]; for it is quite clear that any person who takes himself out of the jurisdiction, with the intention of avoiding being brought to justice for a particular offense, can have no benefit of the limitation, at least when prosecuted for that offense in a court of the United States," 160 U.S. at 133. In context, it might be thought unclear whether the Court meant flight with intent was required or merely sufficient.

[56] *United States v. Florez*, 447 F.3d at 152; *United States v. Greever*, 134 F.3d at 780.

[57] *United States v. Fowlie*, 24 F.3d at 1072-73; *United States v. Rivera-Ventura*, 72 F.3d at 283-84; *United States v. Catino*, 735 F.2d 718, 722-23 (2d Cir. 1984).

[58] *Ross v. U.S.Marshal*, 168 F.3d at 1194-195.

[59] *United States v. Morgan*, 922 F.2d 1495, 1496-497 (10th Cir. 1991); *United States v. Rivera-Ventura*, 72 F.3d at 283; *United States v. Gonzalez*, 675 F.2d 1050, 1052-53 (9th Cir. 1982).

[60] *United States v. Rivera-Ventura*, 72 F.3d at 284.

[61] *Toussie v. United States*, 397 U.S. 112, 115 (1970), quoting, *Pendergast v. United States*, 317 U.S. 412, 418 (1943); *see also, United States v. Reitmeyer*, 356 F.3d 1313, 1317 (10th Cir. 2004); *United States v. Najjor*, 255 F.3d 979, 983 (9th Cir. 2001); *United States v. Acevedo*, 229 F.3d 350, 355 (2d Cir. 2000); *United States v. Dees*, 215 F.3d 378, 380 (3d Cir. 2000); *United States v. Yashar*, 166 F.3d 873, 875 (7th Cir. 1999); *United States v. Lutz*, 154 F.3d 581, 586 (6th Cir. 1998); *United States v. Gilbert*, 136 F.3d 1451, 1453 (11th Cir. 1998); *United States v. Gomez*, 38 F.3d 1031, 1034 (8th Cir. 1994); *United States v. Blizzard*, 27 F.3d 100, 102 (4th Cir. 1994).

[62] *United States v. Reitmeyer*, 356 F.3d 1313, 1317 (10th Cir. 2004); *United States v. Carlson*, 235 F.3d 466, 470 (9th Cir. 2000); *United States v. Crossley*, 224 F.3d 847, 859 (6th Cir. 2000); *United States v. Yashar*, 166 F.3d at 875; *United States v. Vebeliunas*, 76 F.3d 1283, 1293 (2d Cir. 1996).

[63] *See generally, When Is Conspiracy Continuing Offense for Purposes of Statute of Limitations Under 18 USCS §3282*, 106 ALR FED. 616.

[64]   "If two or more persons conspire either to commit any offense against the United States, or to defraud the United States, or any agency thereof in any manner or for any purpose, and one or more of such persons do any act to effect the object of the conspiracy, each shall be fined under this title or imprisoned not more than five years, or both. . . ." 18 U.S.C. 371.

[65]   *Fiswick v. United States*, 329 U.S. 211, 216 (1946); *see also, United States v. Qayyum*, 451 F.3d 1214, 1218 (10th Cir. 2006); *United States v. Arias*, 431 F.3d 1327, 1340 (11th Cir. 2005)("if a conspirator establishes the affirmative defense of withdrawal, the statute of limitations [as to him] will begin to run at the time of withdrawal. Otherwise, the statute will not begin to run until the final act of the conspiracy has occurred"); *United States v. Wren*, 363 F.3d 654, 663 (7th Cir. 2004); *United States v. Hitt*, 349 F.3d 1010, 1015 (D.C.Cir. 2001); *United States v. Monaco*, 194 F.3d 381, 387 n.2 (2d Cir. 1999); *United States v. Perry*, 152 F.3d 900, 904 (8th Cir. 1998); *United States v. Manges*, 110 F.3d 1162, 1169 (5th Cir. 1997); *United States v. Craft*, 105 F.3d 1123, 1127 (6th Cir. 1997). Conspiracies live on as long as the conspirators continue to receive the economic benefits of the scheme, *United States v. Salmonese*, 352 F.3d 608, 614-17 (2d Cir. 2003).

[66]   *United States v. Gagleby*, 420 U.S. 1136, 1145 (10th Cir. 2005); *United States v. Saadey*, 393 F.3d 669, 677 (6th Cir. 2005); *United States v. Therm-All, Inc.*, 373 F.3d 625, 632 (5th Cir. 2004); *United States v. Grimmett*, 236 F.3d 452, 453 (8th Cir. 2001); *United States v. Tocco*, 200 F.3d 401, 425 n.9 (6th Cir. 2000); *United States v. Arnold*, 117 F.3d 1308, 1313 (11th Cir. 1997).

[67]   *Grunewald v. United States*, 353 U.S. 391, 406 (1957); *see also, United States v. Qayyum*, 451 F.3d 1214, 1219 (10th Cir. 2006); *United States v. Grenoble*, 413 F.3d 569, 575-76 (6th Cir. 2005); *United States v. Arnold*, 117 F.3d 1308, 1314 (11th Cir. 1997); *United States v. Maloney*, 71 F.3d 645, 659 (7th Cir. 1995).

[68]   *Grunewald v. United States*, 353 U.S. at 406; *see also, United States v. Qayyum*, 451 F.3d 1214, 1219 (10th Cir. 2006); *United States v. Mann*, 161 F.3d 840, 859 (5th Cir. 1998); *United States v. Arnold*, 117 F.3d at 1314; *United States v. Maloney*, 71 F.3d at 659-60; *United States v. Rabinowitz*, 56 F.3d 932, 934 (8th Cir. 1995).

[69]   *Toussie v. United States*, 397 U.S. at 115; *United States v. Smith*, 373 F.3d 561, 563-64 (4th Cir. 2004); *United States v. Reitmeyer*, 356 F.3d 1313, 1322 (10th Cir. 2004).

[70] "Whoever escapes or attempts to escape from the custody of the Attorney General or his authorized representative, or from any institution or facility in which he is confined by direction of the Attorney General, or from any custody under or by virtue of any process issued under the laws of the United States by any court, judge, or commissioner, or from the custody of an officer or employee of the United States pursuant to lawful arrest, shall, if the custody or confinement is by virtue of an arrest on a charge of felony, or conviction of any offense, be fined under this title or imprisoned not more than five years, or both; or if the custody or confinement is for extradition, or for exclusion or expulsion proceedings under the immigration laws, or by virtue of an arrest or charge of or for a misdemeanor, and prior to conviction, be fined under this title or imprisoned not more than one year, or both," 18 U.S.C. 751(a).

[71] "Whoever moves or travels in interstate or foreign commerce with intent either (1) to avoid prosecution, or custody or confinement after conviction, under the laws of the place from which he flees, for a crime, or an attempt to commit a crime, punishable by death or which is a felony under the laws of the place from which the fugitive flees, or (2) to avoid giving testimony in any criminal proceedings in such place in which the commission of an offense punishable by death or which is a felony under the laws of such place, is charged, or (3) to avoid service of, or contempt proceedings for alleged disobedience of, lawful process requiring attendance and the giving of testimony or the production of documentary evidence before an agency of a State empowered by the law of such State to conduct investigations of alleged criminal activities, shall be fined under this title or imprisoned not more than five years, or both. . . ." 18 U.S.C. 1073.

[72] "Whoever, having been released under this chapter knowingly — (1) fails to appear before a court as required by the conditions of release; or (2) fails to surrender for service of sentence pursuant to a court order; shall be punished as provided in subsection (b) of this section," 18 U.S.C. 3146(a).

[73] "It is unlawful for any person subject to the jurisdiction of the United States to engage in any trade in any specimens contrary to the provisions of the Convention [on International Trade in Endangered Species], or to possess any specimens traded contrary to the provisions of the Convention, including the definitions of terms in article I thereof," 16 U.S.C. 1538(c)(1).

[74] "Whoever, with intent to defraud, passes, utters, publishes, or sells, or attempts to pass, utter, publish, or sell, or with like intent brings into the United States or keeps in possession or conceals any falsely made, forged, counterfeited, or altered obligation or other security of the United States, shall be fined under this title or imprisoned not more than 15 years, or both," 18 U.S.C. 472.

[75] "(a) Whoever unlawfully seizes, confines, inveigles, decoys, kidnaps, abducts, or carries away and holds for ransom or reward or otherwise any person, except in the case of a minor by the parent thereof, when — (1) the person is willfully transported in interstate or foreign commerce, regardless of whether the person was alive when transported across a State boundary if the person was alive when the transportation began; (2) any such act against the person is done within the special maritime and territorial jurisdiction of the United States;(3) any such act against the person is done within the special aircraft jurisdiction of the United States as defined in Section 46501 of Title 49; (4) the person is a foreign official, an internationally protected person, or an official guest as those terms are defined in Section 1116(b) of this title; or (5) the person is among those officers and employees described in Section 1114 of this title and any such act against the person is done while the person is engaged in, or on account of, the performance of official duties; shall be punished by imprisonment for any term of years or for life and, if the death of any person results, shall be punished by death or life imprisonment," 18 U.S.C. 1201(a); *see also, United States v. Garcia*, 854 F.2d 340, 343 (9th Cir. 1988)(the statute of limitations does not begin to run until the victim is released); if the victim is killed, the offense is a capital crime and the prosecution may be brought at any time.

[76] "Failure to file any such registration statement or supplements thereto as is required by either Section 612(a) or Section 612(b) of this title [relating to registration requirements] shall be considered a continuing offense for as long as such failure exists, notwithstanding any statute of limitation or other statute to the contrary ," 22 U.S.C. 618(e).

[77] "No person shall be prosecuted, tried, or punished for evading, neglecting, or refusing to perform the duty of registering imposed by Section 3 of this title [Section 453 of this Appendix] unless the indictment is found within five years next after the last day before such person attains the age of twenty-six, or within five years next after the last day before such person does perform his duty to register, whichever

shall first occur," 50 U.S.C.App. 462(d); *see also, United States v. Jacob*, 781 F.2d 643, 648-49 (8th Cir. 1986).

[78] "Subject to subsection (b) of this section, any alien who — (1) has been denied admission, excluded, deported, or removed or has departed the United States while an order of exclusion, deportation, or removal is outstanding, and thereafter (2) enters, attempts to enter, or is at any time found in, the United States, unless (A) prior to his reembarkation at a place outside the United States or his application for admission from foreign contiguous territory, the Attorney General has expressly consented to such alien's reapplying for admission; or (B) with respect to an alien previously denied admission and removed, unless such alien shall establish that he was not required to obtain such advance consent under this chapter or any prior Act, shall be fined under Title 18, or imprisoned not more than two years, or both," 8 U.S.C. 1326(a); *see also, United States v. Santana-Castellano*, 74 F.3d 593, 597 (5th Cir. 1996)("Likewise, the five year statute of limitations under Sec. 1326 begins to run at the time the alien is found barring circumstances that suggest that the INS should have known of his presence earlier, such as when he reentered the United States through an official border checkpoint in the good faith belief that his entry was legal"); *United States v. DiSantillo*, 615 F.2d 128, 132 (3d Cir. 1980).

[79] "We believe that the specific conduct at issue here is more properly characterized as a continuing offense rather than a series of separate acts. The facts found by the district court were sufficient to prove that he set into place and maintained an automatically recurring scheme whereby funds were electronically deposited in his account and retained for his own use without need for any specific action on his part," *Id.*

[80] "No Bill of Attainder or ex post facto Law shall be passed . . . . No State shall . . . pass any Bill of Attainder, [or] ex post facto Law . . . . U.S. Const. Art. I, §§9, 10.

[81] *Stogner v. California*, 539 U.S. 607, 612 (2003), quoting, *Calder v. Bull*, 3 Dall. (3 U.S.) 386, 390 (1798) (*seriatim* opinion of Chase, J.).

[82] *United States v. De La Mata*, 266 F.3d 1275, 1286 (11th Cir. 2001); *United States v. Grimes*, 142 F.3d 1342, 1351 (11th Cir. 1998); *United States v. Morrow*, 177 F.3d 272, 294 (5th Cir. 1999); *United States v. Chandler*, 66 F.3d 1460, 1467 (8th Cir. 1995); *United States v. Taliaferro*, 979 F.2d 1399, 1402-403 (10th Cir. 1992); *United States v. Knipp*, 963 F.2d 839, 844 (6th Cir. 1992); *United States ex rel. Massarella v. Elrod*, 682 F.2d 688, 689 (7th Cir. 1982); *United States v.*

Richardson, 512 F.2d 105, 196 (3d Cir. 1975); *United States v. Clemens*, 266 F.2d 397, 399 (9th Cir. 1959); *Falter v. United States*, 23 F.2d 420, 425-26 (2d Cir. 1928).

[83]   *People v. Frazer*, 24 Cal.4th 737, 759, 982 P.2d 180, 194, 88 Cal.Rptr.2d 312, 327 (1999).

[84]   *Section 301. No Statute of Limitations For Prosecuting Terrorism Offenses, Consultation Draft of September 20, 2001, Anti-Terrorism Act of 2001, Section-by-Section Analysis,* printed in, *Administration's Draft Anti-Terrorism Act of 2001: Hearing Before the House Comm. on the Judiciary,* 107th Cong., 1st Sess. 60 (2001)("This section expressly provides that it is applicable to offenses committed before the date of enactment of the statute, as well as those committed thereafter. . . . The constitutionality of such retroactive applications of changes in statutes of limitation is well settled. See, e.g., *United States v. Grimes,* 142 F.3d 1342, 1350-51 (11th Cir. 1998); *People v. Frazer,* 982 P.2d 180 (Cal. 1999)"). *Grimes* cited the earlier lower federal case law and declared, "We now join our fellow circuits in holding that application of a statute of limitations extended before the original limitations period has expired does not violate the ex post facto clause," 142 F.3d at 1351. Note that *Grimes* said nothing of cases reviving the possibility of prosecution *after* the original limitations period had expired.

[85]   "The amendments made by this section shall apply to the prosecution of any offense committed before, on, or after the date of the enactment of this section,"§809(b), P.L. 107-56, 115 Stat. 272, 380 (2001); *Section 301(c). No Statute of Limitations For Prosecuting Terrorism Offenses, H.R. , Anti-Terrorism Act of 2001,* printed in, *Administration's Draft Anti-Terrorism Act of 2001: Hearing Before the House Comm. on the Judiciary,* 107th Cong., 1st Sess. 82 (2001). This same text appeared in the version of the bill reported out of the House Judiciary Committee, §301(c), H.R. 2975, reprinted in H.REP.NO. 107-236, at 26 (2001).

[86]   "Justice Scalia makes much of the fact that at the time of the framing of the Constitution, it was widely accepted . . . that (according to Justice Scalia) there is no doubt that the ex post facto clause would have prohibited a legislative decision identical to the Tennessee court's decision here. This latter argument seeks at bottom merely to reopen what has long been settled by the constitutional text and our own decisions: that the ex post facto clause does not apply to judicial decisions," *Rogers v. Tennessee,* 532 U.S. 451, 462 (2001). The case arose when the Tennessee Supreme Court abrogated a previously

common law rule that barred a murder prosecution unless the victim died within a year and a day of the defendant's assault upon the victim.

[87] *United States v. Marion*, 404 U.S. 307, 324 (1971); *see also, United States v. Gouveia*, 467 U.S. 180, 192 (1984)("But applicable statutes of limitations protect against the prosecution's bringing stale criminal charges against any defendant, and, beyond that protection, the Fifth Amendment requires the dismissal of an indictment, even if it is brought within the statute of limitations, if the defendant can prove that the Government's delay in bringing the indictment was a deliberate device to gain an advantage over him and that it caused him actual prejudice in presenting his defense").

[88] *United States v. Marion*, 404 U.S. at 325.

[89] *United States v. Lovasco*, 431 U.S. 783, 790 (1977); *see also, Arizona v. Youngblood*, 488 U.S. 51, 57 (1988) ("Our decisions in related areas have stressed the importance for constitutional purposes of good or bad faith on the part of the Government when the claim is based on the loss of evidence attributable to the Government").

[90] This initial burden has been described as heavy and rarely met, *United States v. Gilbert*, 266 F.3d 1180, 1187 (9th Cir. 2001); *United States v. Cornielle*, 171 F.3d 748, 752 (2d Cir. 1999). The defendant must show more than mere speculative harm; he "must specifically identify witnesses or documents lost during the delay properly attributable to the government, relate the substance of the testimony which would have been offered by the missing witnesses or the information contained in lost documents in sufficient detail to permit a court to assess accurately whether the information was material to his defense, and show that the missing testimony or other evidence is not available from alternative sources," *United States v. Al-Muqsit*, 191 F.3d 928, 938 (8th Cir. 1999); *see also, United States v. Beckman*, 183 F.3d 891, 895 (8th Cir. 1999); *United States v. Trammell*, 133 F.3d 1343, 1351 (10th Cir. 1998); *United States v. Crouch*, 84 F.3d 1497, 1514-516 (5th Cir. 1996).

[91] *United States v. Galdney*, 474 F.3d 1027, 1030 (8th Cir. 2007)("Galdney must establish the delay resulted in actual and substantial prejudice to the presentation of the defense and the government intentionally delayed Galdney's indictment either to gain a tactical advantage or to harass him. The court will inquire into the reasons for delay only where actual prejudice has been established"); *United States v. Atchley*, 474 F.3d 840, 852 (6th Cir. 2007); *United States v. Abdush-Shakur*, 465 F.3d 458, 465 (10th Cir. 2006); *United States v. Gomez-Rasario*, 418 F.3d 90, 108 (1st

Cir. 2005); *United States v. Jimenez*, 256 F.3d 330, 345 (5th Cir. 2001); *United States v. Beckett*, 208 F.3d 140, 150 (3d Cir. 2000); *Aleman v. Honorable Judges*, 138 F.3d 302, 309 (7th Cir. 1998); *United States v. Miner*, 127 F.2d 610, 615 (7th Cir. 1997).

[92] *United States v. Henderson*, 337 F.3d 914, 920 (7th Cir. 2003); *United States v. McMutuary*, 217 F.3d 477, 481 (7th Cir. 2000); *United States v. Spears*, 159 F.3d 1081, 1084 (7th Cir. 1999); *United States v. Benshop*, 138 F.3d 1229, 1232 (8th Cir. 1998).

[93] *United States v. Barken*, 412 F.3d 1131, 1134 (9th Cir. 2005); *United States v. Al-Muqsit*, 191 F.3d 928, 938 (8th Cir. 1999); *United States v. McDougal*, 133 F.3d 1110, 1113 (8th Cir. 1998); *United States v. Ross*, 123 F.3d 1181, 1184 (9th Cir. 1997); *Jones v. Angelone*, 94 F.3d 900, 904 (4th Cir. 1996); *see also, United States v. DeGeorge*, 380 F.3d 1203, 1210-211 (9th Cir. 2004)("DeGeorge must satisfy a two-part test to establish that pre-indictment delay has violated his due process rights: 1) he must prove that he suffered actual, non-speculative prejudice from the delay; and 2) he must show that the delay when balanced against the government's reasons for it, offends those fundamental conceptions of justice which lie at the base of our civil and political institutions").

In: Crime and Law Enforcement Issues   ISBN 978-1-61122-877-9
Editor: James E. Hirsch   © 2011 Nova Science Publishers, Inc.

Chapter 5

THE ILLICIT DRUG MARKET IN TAIWAN

James O. Finckenauer and Ko-Lin Chin

INTRODUCTION

Definition: "Drug crime organization" in this analysis refers to criminal organizations that are engaged in trafficking, transporting, producing and distributing large quantities of drugs in Taiwan. Individual drug dealers and drug users are excluded from this analysis.

Main Sources for Drugs in Taiwan

Heroin

Opium poppy is not cultivated in Taiwan. Heroin in Taiwan is mainly from the Golden Triangle, the border area between Thailand and Burma, and is trafficked into Taiwan from Thailand, mainland China and Hong Kong, or directly from mainland China. Over the past six years, it has been found that North Korea grows opium poppy and produces heroin with the support of the government. Through contacts with drug barons in other countries, North Korean officials sell drugs to East Asia, European countries, and North America. North Korean heroin has gradually become the main staple in Taiwan's market.

Amphetamine

Taiwanese drug dealers have the ability to produce a large amount of good quality amphetamine with their superior techniques. Besides supplying Taiwan's local market, they also export their drugs to Japan. Ephedrine, the precursor chemical for amphetamine production, is almost always trafficked from mainland China. Six years ago, in reaction to Taiwanese law enforcement crackdowns, drug dealers moved their amphetamine laboratories to the southeast coastal provinces in mainland China, especially to Fujian Province. They produced amphetamines there, and then trafficked them back to Taiwan. However, in the past two years, mainland China has begun to crackdown on drug crimes as well. Taiwanese drug dealers were deterred by the severe punishments for drug crimes in mainland China. Therefore, they have gradually moved their amphetamine laboratories back to Taiwan.

Marijuana

Marijuana is not produced in Taiwan. From cases solved in the past, all marijuana in Taiwan has been trafficked by mail parcels from America. But recently it has been found that drug dealers are growing marijuana in some remote districts in Taiwan on a large scale basis, or growing it within some buildings on a small scale basis.

Ecstasy

In the early years, ecstasy, FM2 and other controlled drugs were trafficked into Taiwan from Holland, the United States, and Malaysia. Because these drugs are relatively easy to produce and raw materials are abundant, local gang members are working with college or graduate students to produce ecstasy. In one incident, equipment and raw material from a school lab were utilized to produce ecstasy.

RELATIONSHIPS BETWEEN GANGS AND DRUG DEALERS IN TAIWAN

In the traditional drug markets of heroin and amphetamine, it has not been found that Taiwan's local gangs are involved in them in a systematic way. Most gang members are pure drug users, and only a few of them are involved in the drug business.In the new drug market of ecstasy and ketamine, city gangs such as the Bamboo United, the Four Seas, and the Pine Union are the main forces in the market. Recently, profits from this drug trade have become an important financial resource for some gangs.

HONG KONG GANGS IN THE TAIWAN DRUG MARKET

Due to its free market and well-developed economic system, Hong Kong was a trading hub for South Asia during the time when there was tension across the Taiwan Strait. Just like ordinary businessmen, triad members were able to travel to China, Taiwan and other countries in Southeast Asia. Relying on their tight organization and sufficient money supply, they connected drug producing places and costumers and quickly established a huge international heroin trafficking and trade network. This network even reached Europe and America. Between 1960 and 1998, Taiwan's heroin sources were mostly controlled by gang members from Hong Kong. Triad societies such as the San Yee On, Wo on Lok and 14K all sent their members to Taiwan. These members were highly professional. They divided their jobs expertly. They were in charge of trafficking drugs into Taiwan, setting up storage houses and negotiating with local drug dealers. They were not permitted to contact each other. They followed the orders from their bosses in Hong Kong individually. These actions resemble international espionage. After 1998, Taiwanese businessmen who went to mainland China and Thailand to conduct business were able to contact foreign drug producers. These businessmen established a direct channel of heroin trading and trafficking from producers to Taiwan. Since then, the supply channel of Hong Kong gangs has been gradually replaced.

THE STRUCTURE OF ORGANIZATIONS

Internal Division of Labor and Order (Different Roles, Orders and Aims)

The organizational structure of drug crime groups in Taiwan is formed naturally by the needs of drug producing, trafficking and trading. The division of labor is divided into six parts as follows:

1. Coordinator: He or she is the key man in every group who is in charge of contacting money suppliers (money men), collecting money, looking for drug resources, arranging drug supply channels and storage houses and negotiating drug sales. He is the general coordinator of the entire process.
2. Drug producer: He is in charge of producing, taking care of and safeguarding amphetamine and ecstasy factories, and harvesting marijuana.
3. Trafficker: He is knowingly and voluntarily involved in drug trafficking. He carries drugs either on himself, or takes vehicles or airplanes to specific places or to specific persons.
4. Receiver: He is in charge of receiving drugs from international or domestic express mail services, aviation cargos, hidden parts of containers or consigned baggage, or from third persons, who may or may not be aware they are trafficking drugs to specific destinations.
5. Warehouseman: He is in charge of storing and safeguarding the highly valuable drugs.
6. Dealer: Drug suppliers sell drugs to buyers. It is possible for these buyers and suppliers to contact each other directly, or to use drug brokers (middlemen). The money may be paid before, during or after a deal, and in cash or via an overseas remittance.

It should be noted that there is no one group in Taiwan can perform all six of these roles and complete the whole process on their own. One group may take one to three roles, for example, one group may take roles 1, 2 and 3, and then may cooperate with other group(s), who look for buyers, introduce drug brokers, sell drugs, and collect drug money. In other words, the drug crime groups in Taiwan have scattered roles.

The Ability to Recruit New Members

Drug groups in Taiwan are structured much like the local jiaotou groups; few of them are formal or enterprise-like in their structural patterns. The head or principal in a group leads "little brothers,"follows orders from a "big brother;" and is in charge of some trivial as well as dangerous jobs such as safeguarding, trafficking and selling drugs. "Big brother" must offer them housing, transportation, and good salaries, or share a bonus with them. Most members join a group for economic reasons. Also, some Taiwanese businessmen in mainland China or Thailand, because of business failures or financial difficulties, became vulnerable to the local drug criminal organizations. Consequently, they went back to Taiwan to traffick in or selldrugs.

Qualifications and Regulations

Drug groups in Taiwan recruit members based on whether a person has the connections and the ability to contribute in the drug trade. Having a fishing boat or a crew license, owning a company with a legal permit for exporting and a customs declaration, maintaining good relationswith local drug dealers, or engaging in the business of chemical materials or medical equipments -- all these characteristics may decide whether a person has the potential to join. There is no strict discipline or set of rules. Among all the actions or interactions of members, the most important thing is to keep the drug trade moving smoothly. Making money is their priority. Meanwhile, as ordinary businessmen, they also emphasize prompt delivery, quality of drugs, and on-time payment.

The Mechanism of Market-Division and Dispute-Solving

In Taiwan, different drugs have different dealers, so there is a market division by type of drug. The heroin market is controlled by Hong Kong gang members in Taiwan, and by Taiwanese businessmen in mainland China and Southeast Asia. The amphetamine market is controlled by Taiwan jiaotou group leaders and those who are in possession of the techniques to produce amphetamine. The ecstasy market is controlled by young gang members who are of mainland China descent. Interactions among different kinds of drug groups are rare, but drug groups dealing in the same drug compete with each other. As in any other legitimate business transaction, a buyer may first inquire about prices from a few sellers, and then eventually buy the drug from a dealer who has relatively low prices and good quality. Disputes arise from late delivery, late payment, or so-called "black eating black" (one side delivered the drugs, but the other party did not want to pay the money; or one side paid the money, but the other party did not want to deliver the drugs). When such disputes occur, usually both sides are willing to negotiate. If they cannot resolve the dispute through negotiation, they may solve it by violence. There is no effective mechanism of dispute resolution, or an arbitrator in a group or between different groups.

VIOLENCE

The Inclination to Use Violence

In a relatively large, professionaldrug trafficking or manufacturing group, most members do not use drugs. Their behavior patterns are similar to ordinary businessmen. They rarely use violence against other drug group members or law enforcement authorities. But in the case of solving trade deputes, gaining revenge for "black eating black," or actually carrying out "black eating black", they will use violence. As for local, middle-sized and small-sized drug dealers, they usually are drug users, who are more likely to use violence against their partners, competitors, or law enforcers.

Hiring Roughnecks or Killers

Recently, drug criminal organizations in Taiwan often hire killers from mainland China to murder competitors for snatching drug money. These are all professional killers who are cheap, cruel and efficient. After they fulfill their contract, they abscond back to mainland China so that they can escape punishment from law enforcement authorities in Taiwan. "Little brothers" who are on the lower levels of a group will perform the role of "bouncers" during normal times.

Use of Weapons

No matter what the size of their groups, drug dealers are commonly equipped with weapons. Moreover, because of abundant funds, they have the capacity to buy semi-automaticand submachine guns. They don't use revolvers or locally made handguns. The leaders of groups do not take care of or bring guns themselves. They appoint their trusted followers to store weapons together in certain places, and to distribute them to other members when it is necessary. This way, these leaders will not be arrested for gun possession.

MONEY RESOURCES

Initial Money Resources

The startup monies of drug criminal organizations in Taiwan come from investors with whom the gang members have personal connections. The planners and coordinators usually contact 3 to 6 investors (called money men), and the coordinator will buy or produce the drugs. The profits will be distributed among them in certain proportions, or by just distributing drugs to the money men who want to sell the drugs by themselves. Attracted by the lucrative returns from the drug trade, these money men are very willing to invest. Moreover, after making a large amount of money from the drug trade, drug dealers on the frontline may become money men in order to reduce the risk of being arrested.

Diversification of Economic Activities

After they make big money, the money men and members of a drug group mainly spend their money on cars, gambling, food, and women. Some prudent persons among them may buy real estate, invest in the stock market or set up companies for disguising the drug trafficking and trading. Most of the above activities are carried out individually. It has not been found that drug crime groups systematically invest or engage in legal or illegal underground economic activities in Taiwan as a group.

The Degrees of Control of Illegal Markets

In Taiwan, because of severe punishment for drug offenses and aggressive law enforcement measures against drug crimes, people who are involved in the informal economy are reluctant to be associated with drug dealers. However, the main costumers for ecstasy are youngsters gathering in underground dance halls, so the illegal dance hall owners usually cooperate with the dealers, even themselves selling ecstasy. Underground foreign currency exchange dealers on both sides of the Taiwan Strait are the very people the local money men or drug buyers rely on to send money over to mainland China. The money laundering business is the one industry that is closely affiliated with the drug business.

Degree of Involvment in Legal Economic Activities

In Taiwan, leaders of the drug groups usually disguise themselves as legitimate businessmen. Some of them were recruited into the drug business after their legitimate businesses collapsed. Most of them often travel to China or Southeast Asia. Occasionally, local politicians such as town representatives or councilors are involved in the drug trade. It has not been found that drug crime groups in Taiwan invest or engage in legal economic activities in a systematic way.

POLITICAL CAPITAL

Corruption and Penetration into Law Enforcement

Taiwan's law enforcement authorities are, as a whole, very tough on drug crimes. If a law enforcement member becomes involved in drug crimes, he will face severe punishment. Even though there iscorruption in the law enforcement community, this not related to drug crime groups. Occasionally, some judges let off drug dealers after receiving bribes, but this is not systematic or group corruption.

Controlling Political Parties through Participating in Local or National Administrative Mechanisms

Some local politicians, like town representatives or county councilors, are drug users or are involved in the drug trade, but the number is small. Members of national level representative bodies are highly unlikely to be involved in drug offenses. In the view of Taiwanese society and the media, if a politician became involved in drug use or drug sales, it would be a big scandal. His or her political career would end. So no political parties or politicians want to be involved in drugs. They do not even dare to suggest that punishment for drug offenders should be more lenient. It has not been found that drug crime groups have participated in local or national representative bodies.

Electing Group Members to Legislative Bodies

Drug trafficking groups are neither integrated nor business-like. Most of these groups are small, local groups with members who are mainly concerned with making money and avoiding being prosecuted. To date, there is no evidence to suggest that members of these drug groups are ambitious enough to penetrate into national politics.

The Nexus with Terrorist Groups

There are no terrorist groups in Taiwan.

LAW ENFORCEMENT REACTIONS TO DRUG CRIME

The Reconstruction of Law Enforcement Organizations

After the mid-1980s, Taiwan's economy developed rapidly, and people in Taiwan began to pursue excitement and comfort. As a result, drug use also began to spread. In 1993, police solved a heroin trafficking case involving the greatest quantity of drug in Taiwan's history. Meanwhile, youngsters could buy amphetamines at a very cheap price. The drug problem was getting out of control. At that time, Lian Chan, Director of Administrative Yuan, declared a "War on Drugs." The entire law enforcement community was mobilized to fight against drugs. By 1997, most amphetamine factories in Taiwan had been shut down by the authorities. The remaining drug group members moved their factories to mainland China. The quantity of seized heroin increased and the circulation of drugs decreased. The situation appeared to be under control. But in January of 1998, five privately owned mobile phone companies started to operate their businesses. At that time, law enforcement authorities did not have the equipment to monitor cell phone calls. Nearly all criminals in Taiwan changed to the use of mobile phones almost immediately. Law enforcement could not monitor and investigate their phone conversations, and the quantity of drugs seized for that year (1998) was reduced to a low level. The drug market in Taiwan thus entered a second 4-year golden period (1998-2001). In the meantime,violence and property crimes rose drastically. In March 2000, "Rules for Implementation of Telecommunication Safeguarding and Monitoring" entered into force, requiring that telecommunication practitioners must cooperate actively to establish a telecommunications monitoring system. It forced telecommunication practitioners to cooperate with law enforcement authorities to establish a phone monitoring system, and this system began to work that year. The quantity of drugs being seized increased greatly in 2001 and 2002.

Since 2002, mainland China began to strike hard on drug crimes by sentencing a large number of drug producers and traffickers to death. As a result, Taiwanese drug groups moved their amphetamine factories back to Taiwan. Since then, about twenty amphetamine factories have been dismantled by law enforcement authorities. Meanwhile, ecstasy use has been spreading among youngsters. Taiwan's law enforcement authorities have heightened their attention to this problem.

Changes in Law Enforcement Measures

Taiwan's law enforcement officials usually investigate drug related-cases by means of relying on anonymous reports, using informants, monitoring phone calls, and collecting evidence through actions. As to undercover operations, which have always been employed by law enforcement authorities in the United States, because of the lack of any legal basis for waiving criminal responsibility with respect to any undercover operation, this method is rarely used in Taiwan. Even those informants who are involved in drug crimes in order to obtain information for law enforcement are not immune from prosecution. As a result, a "Witness Protection Law" was formulated in Taiwan in 2000. It clearly stipulated many provisions: "dirty witnesses," waiver of the criminal responsibility of a witness, protection of witnesses, and temporary living arrangements. This law is very helpful for investigating drug crime cases. Arrested drug dealers are especially willing to "flip" and become a dirty witness for the government in order to reduce their criminal responsibility. Many major drug cases were solved this way.

A draft of an "Undercover Agents Law" was sent to the legislature for its deliberation in July 2003. The Judicial Committee of the Legislature Yuan finished its initial review in October of 2003.

Recently, the Internet and other new types of telecommunication products such as PHS, 3G, MSN, Yahoo Messenger and Internet phones are spreading rapidly in Taiwan. Based on the depressing lessons from the past four years, an article was stipulated in advance in the "Law for Implementation of Safeguarding and Monitoring Telecommunication." It says that those who plan to engage in the business of third generation mobile phones (3G), before applying for a permit to constructthe phone system, must cooperate with law enforcement. This entails discussing the construction plan, and seeking the legal documents necessary for granting permission to construct a monitoring system and obtaining the necessary equipment. As a result, law enforcement agencies may be able to prepare for future criminal investigations. On the other hand, it is really difficult to monitor the Internet. Recently, it has been found that some drug dealers use Internet phones to contact each other. This will be a big challenge to law-enforcements authorities.

All heroin in Taiwan is from mainland China and Thailand. Amphetamine produced in Taiwan is exported to Japan. Criminal organizations in Taiwan also provide technological knowhow about the manufacture of amphetamines to America and the Philippines. After gaining access to heroin resources in Southeast Asia, Taiwanese drug organizations have partly replaced the Hong Kong gangs' role in Taiwan. These groups traffick heroin to Australia, Japan and America. Their criminal activities have extended to the international community. Therefore, there is an urgent need for international law enforcement cooperation. In recent years, Taiwan's law enforcement authorities have maintained frequent connections with their counterparts in surrounding countries and solved many cross-border drug cases.

Legal Changes in Drug Crime

The major law against drug crimes in Taiwan is the "Regulations on the Prevention of Drug Harms" act. Its predecessor was the "Regulations of Drug Offenses during the Period of Mobilization" that was enacted on June 3, 1955. The latter was renamed "Regulations of Eliminating Drug Harms" on July 27, 1992, and renamed again to "Regulations on the Prevention of Drug Harms" on Oct 30, 1997. Its revised version has 36 articles. In April 1999, March 2000, June 2001 and January 2002, the Executive Yuan released several modifications to increase or decrease some parts of the classification of drugs and the quality of drugs. On July 9, 2003, Article 32-1 and 31-2 were added and named "Delivery of Drug under Control". On January 9, 2004, another modification was added and ecstasy and cocaine drugs were categorized as the fourth class drugs.

EXTERNAL ENVIRONMENT

The Degree of Acceptance of Drug Crimes

In today's Taiwan, people hold strongly negative attitudes toward drug dealers and users. The degree of acceptance is almost zero. Most Taiwanese citizens support the government's policy of harsh punishments and thorough investigations.

Current Social Movements for Strengthening the Recognition of Drug Crimes

Anti-drug movements in Taiwan are organized by citizen groups mainly focused on "say no to drugs," and providing drug treatment assistance. However, their methods make it hard to attract the attention of youths and drug users. Thus, their effects are very limited.

The Media's Functions in Shaping the Public's Recognition of the Harms of Drug Crime

Taiwan's media have not paid much attention to drug-related crimes. The common news reports on drug crimes are concentrated on disclosing information from law enforcement. After one or two days of a "hot" news wave, everything cools down. It is very rare to see any further and deeper reports tracking criminal activities in terms of drug trafficking and drug users.

In: Crime and Law Enforcement Issues   ISBN 978-1-61122-877-9
Editor: James E. Hirsch   © 2011 Nova Science Publishers, Inc.

Chapter 6

POSITIVE LIFE CHANGES FOLLOWING SEXUAL ASSAULT: A REPLICATION AND EXTENSION

Patricia Frazier, Amy Conlon, Michael Steger,
Ty Tashiro, and Theresa Glaser*
University of Minnesota, Minneapolis, MN

ABSTRACT

Posttraumatic life change was investigated in a sample of nonrecent sexual assault survivors. An average of 16 years postassault, most survivors identified positive changes that had resulted from the assault, particularly in the domains of self (e.g., increased assertiveness), spirituality (e.g., spiritual well-being), and empathy (e.g., concern for others' suffering). Negative changes in beliefs about the fairness and safety of the world also were common, however. Controlling for recent life stressors and personality, positive changes were associated with fewer symptoms of depression, anxiety and Post Traumatic Stress Disorder (PTSD) and greater life satisfaction. Self-reported positive changes generally were related to personality, social support, coping, and control appraisals in hypothesized directions. Coping and control appraisals

* Patricia Frazier, Ph.D. Department of Psychology, University of Minnesota, N218 Elliott Hall, Minneapolis, MN 55455; Phone: 612/625-6863; Fax: 612/626-2079; Email: pfraz@umn.edu

(particularly control over the recovery process) mediated the relations among personality and social support and positive life change.

INTRODUCTION

Surveys of community samples (e.g., Breslau et al., 1998) indicate that most individuals experience some kind of major traumatic event in their lives. It thus is not surprising that the psychological effects of trauma have been the focus of much research attention. Most research has focused on negative consequences, such as Posttraumatic Stress Disorder (PTSD). However, a growing body of research demonstrates that many survivors report positive life changes following various traumatic events. This phenomenon is referred to by several names including posttraumatic growth, stress-related growth, and perceived benefits or benefit-finding (Tedeschi & Calhoun, 2004). Common areas of growth reported by survivors of various traumas reflect changes in three general life domains: changes in one's sense of self (e.g., increased strength and maturity), changes in relationships (e.g., increased closeness to others), and changes in spirituality or life philosophy (e.g., increased sense of purpose in life) (Tedeschi & Calhoun, 1995). Additionally, trauma survivors often report an increased sense of empathy with others' suffering (e.g., McMillen & Fisher, 1998). While not denying the distress associated with traumatic events, posttraumatic growth research reflects the potential for traumatic events to serve as the impetus for positive transformation.

Although sexual assault is a relatively common traumatic event that has a high conditional risk for PTSD (e.g., Kessler, Sonnega, Bromet, Hughes, & Nelson, 1995), few studies have examined posttraumatic growth following sexual assault. In two previous reports we have investigated the prevalence, timing, and correlates of posttraumatic growth among recent sexual assault survivors (Frazier, Conlon, & Glaser, 2001; Frazier, Tashiro, Berman, Steger, & Long, 2004). One goal of our previous research and the research reported here is to broaden the scope of events examined in the posttrauma growth literature, which has focused heavily on individuals struggling with health concerns. Additionally, unlike many studies on posttraumatic growth that have focused exclusively on positive changes, we have assessed both positive and negative life changes (e.g., negative changes in self worth), which provides a more comprehensive picture of the aftermath of the traumatic experience (McMillen & Fisher, 1998). We first briefly review the results of this initial longitudinal study, and the goals and hypotheses of the present study.

OUR PREVIOUS LONGITUDINAL STUDY
OF SEXUAL ASSAULT SURVIVORS

Because of the limited data on sexual assault survivors, in our first paper (Frazier et al., 2001), we focused primarily on documenting the prevalence of various self-reported positive and negative life change in recent survivors. With regard to prevalence, the majority of the survivors in this initial study reported positive life changes, even as soon as 2 weeks postassault. The most common positive life change at all time points (2 weeks, and 2, 6, and 12 months postassault) was increased empathy for others' suffering. Positive changes in the domains of self (e.g., ability to be assertive, ability to recognize strengths) and spirituality (e.g., greater life appreciation, closer to God) also were common. Nonetheless, negative life changes also were reported frequently. For example, across all four time periods, the majority of participants reported negative changes in beliefs about the fairness and safety of the world and the goodness of other people.

A second goal of the first paper was to assess the time course of perceived positive and negative life changes. One assumption in the literature is that the number of positive life changes reported will increase over time, as the term posttraumatic "growth" implies (see O'Leary, Alday, & Ickovics, 1998, for a review). Using hierarchical linear modeling (HLM), we found that on average positive changes increased and negative life changes decreased over time. However, there was also significant individual variability in the time course of self-reported positive and negative life changes. In other words, not all individuals followed the typical pattern: Some survivors reported fewer positive changes and more negative life changes from 2 weeks to 12 months postassault.

Our third goal in this first paper was to assess the relations among positive and negative life change and standard measures of posttraumatic distress (i.e., depression and PTSD). Individuals who reported more positive life changes reported lower levels of depression at both 2 weeks and 1 year postassault, and fewer PTSD symptoms at 2 weeks postassault. Those who reported more negative life changes reported more symptoms of depression and PTSD at both time periods. Changes in self and spirituality were more strongly related to the distress measures than were changes in empathy, relationships, or beliefs about the world. In addition, the relations among negative changes and distress were stronger than those between positive changes and distress (see also Joseph, Williams, & Yule, 1993; Lehman et al., 1993). Finally, because there were individual differences in patterns of positive and negative change over time, we compared individuals with different patterns in terms of 12 month distress levels. These analyses revealed that those who reported higher than average levels of positive change at both 2 weeks and 12 months were less distressed than those with lower than average levels at both time periods. In addition, those who reported higher levels at 2 weeks but not 12 months (i.e., those who "lost" their positive changes) were as distressed as those who never reported positive change (i.e., those who reported lower than average levels at both time periods). Thus, finding benefits early and maintaining them over time appeared important to the recovery process. Conversely, those who reported higher levels of negative change at both time periods were more distressed than those who never reported negative change. There also was a trend for those who reported fewer negatives over time (lost negatives) to be less distressed than those who reported higher levels of negatives changes at both time periods.

In our second paper based on this first longitudinal study (Frazier, Tashiro, et al., 2004), we examined factors that were related to self-reported life changes, focusing on positive life changes.[1] As described above, our first paper highlighted the importance of both early reports of positive change and patterns of self-reported positive changes over time for later distress levels. Thus, the purpose of this second paper was to assess factors associated with reporting positive life change soon after the assault and with individual differences in patterns of self-reported positive changes over time.

Several researchers have developed models of factors that may either facilitate or hinder positive life change following traumatic events (see O'Leary et al., 1998, for a review). These include personal resources, environmental resources, and the individual's coping strategies and appraisal of the event. In this second study (Frazier, Tashiro, et al., 2004), we assessed the relations among variables in each of these categories and both early reports of positive change and changes in self-reported positive life changes over time. The specific correlates measured in each category were: personal characteristics (prior sexual victimization, ethnicity), environmental resources

---

[1] As described in the Method section our life change items assess both negative and positive life change. In the first paper (Frazier et al., 2001), we created scales representing the total number of positive and negative life changes reported. In the second paper (Frazier, Tashiro, et al., 2004), we scored the items on a continuous scale so that higher scores represent more positive life changes and lower scores represent more negative life change. To be consistent with this more recent work, in this paper we use the scoring system used by Frazier, Tashiro, et al. (2004). The correlation between the two scoring systems (number of positive changes reported and total scores on the scale) is .91.

(social support), coping (approach, avoidant, and religious), and control appraisals (behavioral self-blame [past control], control over the recovery process [present control], and taking precautions to prevent future assaults [future control]). The environmental, coping, and control appraisal measures were gathered at all four time points. The significant correlates of early (2 week) positive change were higher early levels of social support, approach coping, religious coping, and control over the recovery process. With regard to predictors of patterns of change over time, the trajectories of social support, approach coping, religious coping, control over the recovery process, and taking precautions were all positively associated with positive-change trajectories, suggesting that, within individuals, increases in these variables were associated with increases in self-reported positive life changes over time. Avoidant coping and behavioral self-blame trajectories were negatively associated with positive-change trajectories, suggesting that decreases in avoidant coping and behavioral self-blame were associated with increases in self-reported positive life changes over time.

Consistent with Schaefer and Moos' (1998) model, we also assessed whether the significant relations between any of the personal (i.e., ethnicity, prior victimization) and environmental (i.e., social support) resource variables and positive change were mediated by coping and control appraisals. None of the personal resource variables were significantly related to positive life change, although social support was significant. The potential mediators (i.e., variables related to both social support and positive life change) were approach and avoidant coping, taking precautions, and control over the recovery process. Regression analyses revealed that control over the recovery process was the strongest mediator of the relation between social support and positive change trajectories. In other words, the primary reason that increases in social support were associated with increases in positive life change was because increases in social support were associated with increased control over the recovery process.

Although this first longitudinal study provided useful data regarding posttrauma life change among sexual assault survivors, it was limited in terms of the make-up of the sample and the range of variables examined. First, all participants had reported to an emergency room following the assault and hence were not necessarily representative of most sexual assault victims. Moreover, the study focused exclusively on recent assault victims, which precluded investigation of long-term changes resulting from sexual assault. Second, the outcome variables were limited to measures of distress, which is an important limitation given that posttrauma growth tends to be more strongly related to positive well-being than to distress (e.g., McMillen, Smith, & Fisher, 1997). Finally, some potentially important correlates of growth were not assessed, such as personality traits.

These limitations were addressed in the current study in which we examined self-reported posttrauma life change in a sample of nonrecent sexual assault survivors recruited through a random phone survey of community women. Specifically, the current study was designed to replicate Frazier et al.'s (2001) findings regarding the prevalence and types of positive and negative life change among sexual assault survivors and the association between posttrauma life change and distress. These earlier findings also were extended by examining the relations among positive life change and a broader range of outcomes, including life satisfaction and perceived health, and by accounting for the effects of recent life stressors and personality in these relationships. We also sought to replicate Frazier, Tashiro, et al.'s (2004) findings regarding the correlates of positive life change, and extended this work by examining additional correlates. The research questions are explained more fully in the following sections along with the study hypotheses.

PREVALENCE AND TYPES OF POSTTRAUMA LIFE CHANGE

Consistent with our previous research on sexual assault (Frazier et al., 2001) and other traumatic events (see Linley & Joseph, 2004, for a review), we predicted that the majority of participants in the current study would identify positive life changes resulting from the assault. Changes in empathy, self, and spirituality were expected to be the most frequently endorsed areas of positive change, whereas changes in beliefs about the fairness and safety of the world were expected to be the least common type of positive change and the most common type of negative change reported.

POSITIVE LIFE CHANGE, DISTRESS AND WELL-BEING

Also consistent with Frazier et al. (2001), we expected more positive change to be associated with less distress (see also Linley & Joseph, 2004). Based on previous research (e.g., McMillen et al., 1997), we also expected positive change to be more strongly related to measures of well-being (i.e., life satisfaction) than to measures of distress (i.e., depression, anxiety, PTSD). We also assessed perceived health because sexual assault often is associated with significant health concerns (Frazier, 2002). Self-reported growth is associated with better health outcomes (e.g., Affleck, Tennen, Croog, & Levine, 1987), including better immune functioning (e.g., McGregor et al., 2004), and we expected a positive relation between self-reported positive change and perceived health in our study as well.

In examining the relations between positive life change and adjustment (i.e., distress, life satisfaction, perceived health), we controlled for the effects of both recent life stressors and personality. Given that most participants in the current study had been sexually assaulted several years previously, it seemed important to account for the contribution of recent life events to current adjustment. Similarly, because variability in adjustment may be accounted for partly by basic personality traits (Watson & Hubbard, 1996), we examined the associations between positive life change and adjustment controlling for both neuroticism and extraversion. These are considered the "Big Two" personality traits and have received the most attention in the stress and coping literature (Watson & Hubbard, 1996). Although we hypothesized that accounting for these variables would decrease the strength of the correlations between positive change and adjustment, we anticipated that self-reported positive life change would still account for unique variance in distress, life satisfaction, and perceived health.

CORRELATES OF POSITIVE CHANGE

The final research question concerned identifying significant correlates of self-reported positive change. As mentioned, conceptual frameworks tend to view the process of posttrauma growth as emerging from several conceptually distinct classes of variables, including personal characteristics, environmental resources, and appraisal and coping responses (e.g., O'Leary et al., 1998). Schaefer and Moos (1998) further hypothesized that the relations among personal and environmental resources and growth are mediated by appraisals and coping. A brief review of the literature linking these variables to posttrauma growth follows.

Personal Characteristics

In our earlier study of correlates (Frazier, Tashiro, et al., 2004), neither of the personal characteristics we assessed (i.e., ethnicity and prior victimization) were associated with positive life change. Thus, in this study we assessed basic personality traits, which may be more important determinants of responses to stressful life events. In their recent review, Tedeschi and Calhoun (2004) concluded that two basic personality qualities (extraversion and openness to experience) are associated with the tendency to grow following trauma. Although neuroticism was not associated with perceived growth in their research (Tedeschi & Calhoun, 1996), it was negatively related to growth in another study (Evers et al., 2001). In addition, positive reinterpretation coping, which is related to posttraumatic growth (e.g., Mohr, Dick, Russo, Likosky, & Goodkin, 1999), has been linked to lower levels of neuroticism in several studies (see Watson & Hubbard, 1996, for a review). We thus predicted that participants higher in extraversion and openness, and lower in neuroticism, would report more positive life changes.

Environmental Resources

Models of posttrauma growth typically include environmental resources, such as social support, as factors that account for variability in the extent to which individuals report positive change. As mentioned, Schaefer and Moos (1998) hypothesized that social support may be associated with outcomes because it is associated with more adaptive coping and event appraisals (see also Tedeschi & Calhoun, 2004). More specifically, supportive others can help individuals process their thoughts and feelings about a trauma, which is necessary for finding benefits in it. Although social support measures have varied, positive relationships between support and growth have been found in several studies (see e.g., Armeli, Gunthert, & Cohen, 2001; Evers et al., 2001; Park, Cohen, & Murch, 1996; Revenson, Wollman, & Felton, 1983) as well as our own prior research (Frazier, Tashiro, et al., 2004). Thus, we expected social support to be related to more self-reported positive changes.

Coping and Event Appraisals

Coping resources and event appraisals play a central role in many theories of positive change (O'Leary et al., 1998). With regard to coping, in general, individuals who engage in more active approach-oriented coping (which involves processing thoughts and feelings about the trauma) are hypothesized to be more likely to report positive changes following a trauma, whereas those who engage in more avoidant coping (which involves avoiding thoughts and feelings about the trauma)should report fewer positive changes (Schaefer & Moos, 1998). Several studies support these hypothesized relations between positive change and various approach-oriented coping strategies (Aldwin, Sutton, & Lachman, 1996; Collins, Taylor, & Skokan, 1990; Cordova, Cunningham, Carlson, & Andrykowski, 2001; Evers et al., 2001; Mohr et al., 1999; Park et al., 1996). In the Park et al. study, approach coping strategies explained more variance in positive life change than any of the other categories of variables (e.g., personal resources, social support). However, results for avoidant coping have been more mixed. Specifically, avoidant strategies have been negatively related (Aldwin et al., 1996), positively related (Collins et al., 1990), and not related (Park et al., 1996; Mohr et al., 1999) to reporting positive change.

A recent review and critique of the broader coping literature recommended that researchers assess "core families" of coping rather than the higher-order dimensions (e.g., problem vs. emotion focused, approach vs. avoidance) typically used to measure coping (Skinner, Edge, Altman, & Sherwood, 2003). They identified five "clearly core" families (i.e., cognitive restructuring, problem solving, support seeking, distraction, avoidance) and four additional "strong candidates" (e.g., social withdrawal, emotional regulation/expressing emotions, rumination, helplessness). Thus, in this study we assessed the same forms of coping as Frazier, Tashiro, et al. (2004), which are all either "clearly core" (i.e., cognitive restructuring, [problem] avoidance) or "strong candidates" (i.e., expressing emotions, social withdrawal) but examined them separately rather than as combined measures of approach and avoidant coping. We expected cognitive restructuring and expressing emotions to be associated with more positive life change and problem avoidance and social withdrawal to be associated with fewer self-reported positive life changes.

Although Schaefer and Moos (1998) focused on approach and avoidant coping, another coping-related variable that appears to be related to positive life change is religiosity. A religious worldview may help survivors to make sense of and find meaning in a traumatic event. Various aspects of religiosity are positively related to positive life change following traumatic events (Aldwin et al., 1996; Calhoun, Cann, Tedeschi, & McMillan, 2000; Park et al., 1996; Tedeschi & Calhoun, 1996), including sexual assault (Frazier, Tashiro, et al., 2004; Kennedy, Davis, & Taylor, 1998). We expected greater use of religious coping to be positively related to self-reported positive life change in this study as well.

Several aspects of event appraisals have been studied in relation to posttraumatic growth (see Linley & Joseph, 2004, for a review). The event appraisal we studied was the perceived controllability of the event, in part because of the centrality of perceived control in theories of trauma recovery and PTSD (see e.g., Foa, Zinbarg, & Rothbaum, 1992). There are various aspects of a trauma over which survivors may feel that they have control, including the occurrence of the trauma (past control), the current impact of the trauma (present control), and whether they will experience future traumas (future control). In their review of the literature on perceived control and trauma, Frazier, Berman, and Steward (2002) found that these three aspects of control had differing relations with measures of posttrauma distress, with present control being the most adaptive. They hypothesized that survivors who feel that they have more control over the recovery process (which is one aspect of present control) may be particularly likely to report positive life changes posttrauma. Indeed, this was the only form of control related to positive life change in a study of bereaved individuals (Frazier, Steward, & Mortensen, 2004). Control over current symptoms (another form of present control) also was associated with reporting more positive life change in a study of arthritis patients (Tennen, Affleck, Urrows, Higgins, & Mendola, 1992). With regard to the other types of control, Tedeschi (1999) hypothesized that self-blame (which can be thought of as control over the past event; see Frazier et al., 2002) would hinder positive change, but that a sense of future control would be associated with reporting more positive changes. In our previous longitudinal study (Frazier, Tashiro, et al., 2004) past control (i.e., behavioral self-blame) was negatively associated with self-reported growth whereas present control (i.e., control over the recovery process) and future control (i.e., engaging in behaviors to try to prevent future assaults) were associated with more self-reported growth, and we expected the same relations here.

In sum, we predicted that the following variables would be associated with reporting more positive life changes after a sexual assault: higher extraversion and openness, lower neuroticism, greater social support, more use of cognitive restructuring and expression emotions and less use of problem avoidance and social withdrawal as coping strategies, greater use of religious coping strategies, less behavioral self-blame, and greater perceived control over the recovery process and future assaults. In addition, when any of the personal (personality traits) or environmental (social support) resources were associated with self-reported positive changes, we assessed whether those relations were mediated by coping strategies or control appraisals. The following conditions must be met to establish mediation: (1) the predictor variable (e.g., personality) must be associated with the outcome variable (positive change); (2) the predictor variable must be associated with the mediator (e.g., coping); (3) the mediator must be associated with the outcome variable, after controlling for the relation between the predictor and outcome; and (4) the addition of the mediator variable must significantly decrease the association between the predictor and outcome variable (Kenny, Kashy, & Bolger, 1998). The data are consistent with complete mediation when the relation between the predictor and the outcome is not significantly different from zero when the mediator is added to the model. Partial mediation occurs when there is a significant reduction in the relation between the predictor and the outcome when the mediator is added but that relation is still significantly different from zero.

METHOD

Participants and Procedure

Participants initially were contacted through a random phone survey regarding stressful life events completed by 894 women (response rate = 72%) residing in Hennepin County (which includes Minneapolis, MN and its immediate suburbs). Of these 894 women, 198 (22%) reported having been sexually assaulted (defined as nonconsensual sexual intercourse involving threats or physical force) and 190 (96%) agreed to participate in a follow-up study that involved completing a mailed questionnaire regarding the assault for which they were paid $25. We received 135 completed follow-up questionnaires (response rate = 71%). Comparisons between participants (n = 135) and nonparticipants (n = 63) revealed no significant differences in race, education, income, relationship status, or age. Data from this sample also have been used in two prior reports (Frazier, Mortensen, & Steward, in press; Frazier, Steward, & Mortensen, 2004).

Respondents ranged in age from 18 to 78 (mean = 39 years). Most (79%) were Caucasian, 16% were African Americans, and the remaining 5% represented other racial groups. The assaults had occurred an average of 16 years previously (range = 1 month to 62 years). The modal education level was "completed some college" (36%), and the modal income was $20,000-$30,000 (26%). Fifty-seven percent of the sample was employed full-time and 59% were married or in a long-term relationship.

Measures

Posttraumatic Life Change

To identify specific aspects of life that had changed as a result of the assault, participants completed a 17-item life change measure. Respondents rated each item on a five-point scale (1 = much worse now, 2 = a little worse now, 3 = no change, 4 = a little better now, 5 = much better now). Items were grouped to reflect the four domains of positive change most often identified in previous research: changes in self, relationships, life philosophy/spirituality, and empathy. Additionally, three items assessed changes in beliefs about the world (e.g., safety), which were expected to change primarily in a negative direction. For analyses of correlates of positive change, we used the 14-item scale used by Frazier, Tashiro, et al. (2004) in which scores on the 14 items dealing with change in self, spirituality, relationships and empathy are totaled so that higher scores indicate more positive change. The alpha coefficient for that scale in this sample was 91.

Psychological Distress

Distress was assessed via measures of depression, anxiety, and PTSD, commonly reported sequelae of sexual assault (Frazier, 2002). Subscales of the Brief Symptom Inventory (BSI; Derogatis, 1993) were used to assess depression (6 items; α = .88) and anxiety (6 items; α = .85). Participants indicated the degree to which they were distressed by each symptom (e.g., feeling blue) over the past month. Responses were made on a 5-point scale (0 = not at all to 4 = extremely). Past research has demonstrated the reliability and validity of the BSI as a measure of psychological distress (Derogatis, 1993). A 17-item checklist developed for this study was used to assess the symptoms of PTSD listed in the DSM-III-R (APA, 1987). Participants were asked to check the symptoms they had experienced in the past month (e.g., "I often have bad dreams about the rape"). The internal consistency reliability coefficient (Kuder-Richardson 20) for the 17-item checklist was .86.

Life Satisfaction

Life satisfaction was assessed with a 9-item measure developed for this study that asked respondents to rate their degree of satisfaction in various life domains within the past month (e.g., "work," "relationships with family members," "life in general"). Responses were made on a 5-point scale (1 = very dissatisfied to 5 = very satisfied; $\alpha = .72$).

Perceived Health

Perceived health was assessed via the General Health scale of the Medical Outcomes Study Health Survey – Short Form 36 (SF-36; Ware & Sherbourne, 1992). The General Health scale consists of 5 items that assess perceived health (e.g., My health is excellent; I am as healthy as anybody I know) on 5 point scales. The SF-36 in general, and the General Health scale in particular, has excellent psychometric properties (see e.g., Stewart, Hays, & Ware, 1988). The alpha coefficient in this sample was .85.

Personality

Neuroticism, openness, and extraversion were assessed using subscales from Saucier's (1994) Mini-Markers, a self-report measure based on the Big Five model of personality. Respondents rated (1 = extremely inaccurate to 9 = extremely accurate) the extent to which adjectives related to extraversion (e.g., energetic), openness (e.g., imaginative) and neuroticism (e.g., moody) described them at the present time. The 8-item subscales were used to assess extraversion and neuroticism and 3 of the 8 items were used to assess openness. The alpha coefficients were .83 (Extraversion), .78 (Openness) and .85 (Neuroticism).

Social Support

Social support was assessed with two items. Respondents rated the helpfulness and caring demonstrated by individuals who provided support following the assault (0 = not at all to 10 = very) and the amount of support they had received since the assault (0 = no support to 10 = a lot of support). The social support index was the average of these two ratings ($\alpha = .79$).

Coping

The Coping Strategies Inventory (CSI; Tobin, Holroyd, & Reynolds, 1984) was used to assess the coping behaviors used in dealing with the assault in the past month. Tobin et al. provided evidence of the predictive, criterion-related, and structural validity, and of the internal consistency and stability, of the CSI. The CSI contains eight 9-item subscales that measure various forms of problem and emotion focused approach and avoidance coping. Four subscales from the CSI were chosen that capture coping behaviors considered "core" or "strong candidates" by Skinner et al. (2003). These include cognitive restructuring (CR) (e.g., "I tried to get a new angle on the situation"), expressing emotions (EE) (e.g., "I found ways to blow off steam"), problem avoidance (PA) (e.g., "I went along as if nothing were happening"), and social withdrawal (SW) (e.g., "I avoided being with people"). Two items that are confounded with distress (Stanton, Danoff-Burg, Cameron, & Ellis, 1994) were removed from the expressing emotions scale. All items were rated on a 1 (Not at all) to 5 (Very much) scale to reflect the extent to which each strategy was used to cope with the assault in the past month. The alpha coefficients for the four scales were as follows: CR (.90), EE (.87), PA (.78), and SW (.85).

Ten items assessed religious coping thoughts and behaviors. These items were adapted from other measures of religious coping, including the Religious Coping Activities Scale (Pargament et al., 1990), religious problem-solving styles questionnaire (Pargament et al., 1988), and the religious coping subscale from the COPE (Carver, Scheier, & Weintraub, 1989). Sample items include "I sought God's help in dealing with the situation," and "I took control over what I could and let God help me with the rest." All items were rated from 1 (not at all) to 5 (very much) in terms of how much they were used in handling the stress of the assault. Coefficient alpha for the religious coping scale was .93.

Control Appraisals

Three scales from the Rape Attribution Questionnaire (RAQ; Frazier, 2002) were used to assess the extent to which survivors attributed the assault to their past behaviors (5 items), felt control over the recovery process (4 items), and reported engaging in behaviors to try to prevent future assaults (5 items) in the past month. Respondents rated the behavioral self-blame items on a 1 (never) to 5 (very often) scale using the following stem: "How often have you thought: I was assaulted because...[I used poor judgment]." Items for the other two scales were rated from 1 (Strongly Disagree) to 5 (Strongly Agree). Sample items include "I know what I must do to help myself recover from my assault" (control over the recovery process) and "Since the assault I try not to put myself in potentially dangerous situations" (taking precautions). All items were judged by a panel of experts to be good indicators of the constructs (see Frazier, 2003, for more information, including all scale items). The alpha coefficients for the three scales were .88 (behavioral self-blame), .78 (control over recovery), and .66 (taking precautions).

Past year Life Stressors

Participants in the random phone survey were asked whether they had experienced a list of 7 stressors in the past year (e.g., relationship loss, non-life threatening illness). The stressors were taken from the Potential Stressful Events Interview (PSEI; Kilpatrick, Resnick, & Freedy, 1991). These data were used to create a variable representing the total number of previous year stressors experienced (range = 0 to 6, $M = 2.60$, $SD = 1.53$).

RESULTS

Prevalence and Domains of Life Change

Participants reported an average of approximately seven positive changes and four negative changes resulting from the assault (see Table 1). Increased empathy for others in similar situations was the most commonly reported positive change. A considerable percentage of respondents also reported positive changes in self such as increased assertiveness and a greater ability to recognize their strengths. Similarly, positive changes in spirituality were frequently reported (e.g., appreciation of life and spiritual well-being). Slightly less than one-third of respondents reported that their relationships with friends and family had changed positively as a result of the assault. Positive changes in beliefs about the fairness and safety of the world were reported by relatively few participants, whereas a substantial proportion reported negative changes in these beliefs. Negative changes in mental health also were common. The average score on the 14-item positive life change scale used in the following analyses was 3.52 (SD = .85), which again reflects that survivors perceive more positive than negative life change.

Table 1. Percentages of Respondents Reporting Positive and Negative Change in each Domain

	% positive change[a]	% negative change[b]
Self		
Ability to be assertive	60	20
Ability to recognize strengths	61	11
Sense of self-worth	41	28
Sense of personal control	46	33
Ability to take care of self	54	16
Beliefs in own judgments	37	37
Mental health	33	44
Mean	*47*	*27*
Relationships		
Relationships with family	31	21
Relationships with friends	29	20
Mean	*30*	*20.5*
Spirituality		
Appreciation of life	56	13
Sense of closeness to God	43	11
Sense of purpose in life	42	18
Spiritual well-being	47	19
Mean	*47*	*15*
Beliefs		
Goodness of people	16	32
Safety of the world	11	48
Fairness of the world	8	44
Mean	*12*	*41*
Empathy		
Concern for others in similar situations	78	3
Number of changes		
Mean	6.94	4.15
Standard Deviation	5.10	4.27

[a] Percentage answering 4 or 5 for each item [b] Percentage answering 1 or 2 for each item
$N = 123$ due to missing data.

Correlations Among Positive Life Change and Distress, Life Satisfaction, and Perceived Health

Correlations among the positive life change scale and measures of distress, life satisfaction, and perceived health are shown in Table 2. Interpretation of the strength of these correlations followed Cohen's (1992) effect size conventions (.10 = small, .30 = medium, .50 = large effect). Survivors who reported more positive life changes reported fewer symptoms of depression, anxiety, and PTSD with correlations in the medium to large range (r's = -.37 to -.51). There also was a large correlation between positive life change and life satisfaction (r = .49). The correlation with better perceived health was significant but small (r = .18). All correlations were reduced after controlling for previous year stressors and personality although they remained significant (except perceived health).

Table 2. Bivariate Correlations and Partial Correlations Among Positive Life Change and Adjustment Measures

| | Positive Life Changes[a] | |
		Controlling for Current Stressors and Personality[b]
Depression	-.51[‡]	-.32[‡]
Anxiety	-.38[‡]	-.18[*]
PTSD symptoms	-.37[‡]	-.22[*]
Perceived Health	.18[*]	.05
Life Satisfaction	.49[‡]	.32[‡]

n's = 116 to 130 due to missing data.
[*]$p < .05$ [‡]$p < .001$
[a] 14-item positive life change scale [b] Neuroticism and Extraversion

Correlates of Positive Life Change

Mean scores on the various personal, environmental, coping, and appraisal variables are in Table 3 and their correlations with self-reported positive life change are in Table 4. The correlational analyses revealed that reporting more positive changes was associated as hypothesized with less neuroticism, more extraversion, more social support, more cognitive restructuring and expressing emotions and less problem avoidance and social withdrawal, greater religious coping, and more perceived control over the recovery process. These correlations generally were in small to medium range (r's = .19 to .44). The strongest correlates were neuroticism (which was negatively associated with self-reported positive life change) and perceived control over the recovery process. Contrary to predictions, three variables - openness, behavioral self-blame, and taking precautions – were not associated with self-reported positive change.

Mediation Analyses

We next assessed whether the coping and appraisal variables mediated the relations among any of the personality or social support variables and positive life change. As shown in Table 3, all three personal and environmental resource variables – extraversion, neuroticism, and social support - met the first criterion for mediation (a significant relation with positive life change). The second criterion is that these predictors are significantly related to the proposed mediators (coping and control appraisals). Analyses assessing this second criterion are in Table 5. Behavioral self-blame and taking precautions were not included because their bivariate correlations with positive life change were not significant. Based on these analyses, social withdrawal and control over the recovery process were tested as potential mediators of the relation between both extraversion and neuroticism and positive change. These two variables, along with expressing emotions, problem avoidance, and religious coping, were tested as mediators of the relation between social support and positive change. To meet the third criterion for mediation, the mediator variable must be significantly related to the outcome with the predictor variable in the equation. Three of the above variables did not meet this criterion. Specifically, expressing emotions, problem avoidance, and social withdrawal were not related to positive life change when social support was included in the model.

Table 3. Mean Scores on Personal, Environmental, Coping, and Appraisal Variables

	Mean	SD
Extraversion	5.80	1.44
Neuroticism	4.56	1.64
Openness	6.72	1.87
Cognitive Restructuring	2.45	1.08
Expressing Emotions	2.19	.98
Problem Avoidance	2.51	.87
Social Withdrawal	2.73	1.02
Religious Coping	2.39	1.14
Social support	5.69	3.00
Behavioral self-blame	2.45	1.20
Taking precautions	4.13	.69
Control over recovery process	3.85	.83

N's = 112 – 133 due to missing data

Table 4. Correlates of Self-Reported Positive Life Change

	Positive Life Change[a]
Extraversion	.27[†]
Neuroticism	-.43[‡]
Openness	.04
Social support	.31[‡]
Cognitive restructuring	.19[*]
Expressing emotions	.22[*]
Problem avoidance	-.23[*]
Social withdrawal	-.31[‡]
Religious coping	.35[‡]
Behavioral self-blame	-.09
Control over recovery process	.44[‡]
Taking precautions	.06

n's = 109 to 128 due to missing data. [*]$p < .05$ [†]$p < .01$ [‡]$p < .001$ [a]14-item positive life change scale

Table 5. Correlations Among Predictors and Mediators

	Predictors		
	Extraversion	Neuroticism	Social Support
Mediators			
Cognitive Restructuring	.07	-.15	.03
Expressing Emotions	.14	-.06	.28[†]
Problem Avoidance	-.10	.17	-.38[‡]
Social Withdrawal	-.28[†]	.31[‡]	-.39[‡]
Religious coping	.11	-.16	.28[†]
Control over recovery process	.18[*]	-.36[‡]	.27[†]

n's = 100 to 128 due to missing data. [*]$p < .05$ [†]$p < .01$ [‡]$p < .001$

Table 6. Mediation Analyses

	B	SE B	β	Goodman's test
1a. Predictor: Extraversion	.17	.06	.29[†]	
1b. Predictor: Extraversion	.13	.06	.22[*]	
Mediator: Social withdrawal	-.21	.08	.25[†]	1.92[*]
2a. Predictor: Extraversion	.16	.05	.27[†]	
2b. Predictor: Extraversion	.11	.05	.20[*]	
Mediator: Control over recovery	.41	.08	.40[‡]	1.89+
3a. Predictor: Neuroticism	-.26	.05	-.47[‡]	
3b. Predictor: Neuroticism	-.23	.05	-.41[‡]	
Mediator: Social withdrawal	-.16	.07	-.19[*]	-1.77+
4a. Predictor: Neuroticism	-.22	.04	-.41[‡]	
4b. Predictor: Neuroticism	-.15	.04	-.29[‡]	
Mediator: Control over recovery	.34	.09	.33[‡]	2.34[*]
5a. Predictor: Social support	.09	.03	.34[‡]	
5b. Predictor: Social support	.07	.03	.27[†]	
Mediator: Religious coping	.19	.06	.27[†]	2.06[*]
6a. Predictor: Social support	.08	.03	.31[‡]	
6b. Predictor: Social support	.06	.02	.21[*]	
Mediator: control over recovery	.35	.09	.36[‡]	2.34[*]

N's = [*] to [*]. $^* p < .05$; $^† p < .01$; $^‡ p < .001$.

The analyses testing the final criterion for mediation for the six remaining sets of variables are presented in Table 6. For each test, two regressions were performed, one in which positive life change was regressed on the predictor alone and one in which positive life change was regressed on the predictor and the mediator. The significance of the drop in the relation between the predictor and positive life change when the mediator was added to the model was assessed using Goodman's test (see Frazier, Tix, & Barron, 2004, for more information). For all six tests, the relation between the predictor and positive life change was smaller when the mediator was in the model but in all cases the predictor was still significant, which suggests partial mediation. The drop in the relation between the predictor and positive life change was significant in four cases and marginally significant in two cases. Focusing on the significant mediators, social withdrawal partially mediated the relation between extraversion and positive life change and perceived control over the recovery process partially mediated the relations among both neuroticism and social support and positive life change. Finally, religious coping also partially mediated the relation between social support and positive life change.

DISCUSSION

One goal of the present study was to compare the prevalence and types of posttraumatic life changes reported by a sample of nonrecent sexual assault survivors to that reported by a sample of recent assault survivors who had reported to the emergency room following the assault (Frazier et al., 2001). Despite the differences between the two samples, the prevalence of positive change is remarkably similar across the two studies. The mean number of positive changes reported in the current sample an average of 16 years postassault (6.94) is comparable to that reported at 1 year postassault by Frazier et al.'s sample (6.34) although the average number of negative changes reported is slightly lower in this sample (4.15 vs. 6.12). When scored as a 14-item life change scale, the mean in this sample (3.52) also is similar to the mean at 12 months in our initial study (3.24; Frazier, Tashiro, et al., 2004). That survivors report areas of growth many years postassault is consistent with the view that positive changes resulting from traumatic experiences are not simply mechanisms for coping with the immediate effects of the trauma (Tedeschi & Calhoun, 1995). However, as mentioned later, researchers need to take greater pains to establish the validity of these self-reports.

The frequency of the various types of changes reported in the current sample also is quite similar to that reported by Frazier et al. (2001). Across both studies, increased empathy is the most common positive change. After increased empathy, the three most common positive changes years after the assault are in the areas of self (increases in assertiveness and ability to recognize personal strengths) and spirituality (greater appreciation of life), which also is consistent with Frazier et al.'s findings. Positive changes in relationships were slightly less common among the nonrecent assault survivors than among the recent assault survivors. This suggests that the impact of a trauma on relationships may fade over time whereas the impact on the self and spirituality may be more enduring. Alternatively, unlike the participants in Frazier et al.'s study who sought help immediately following the assault, women in the current sample may not have told anyone about the assault and thus their relationships may not have been as affected.

The most common negative changes reported by survivors in the current study are with regard to beliefs about the safety and fairness of the world. Again, despite differences between the two samples, these also were the most commonly reported negative changes in the previous study (Frazier et al., 2001). However, negative changes in beliefs are less common an average of 16 years postassault than in the year following the assault. Nonetheless, that a substantial proportion of nonrecent survivors continue to report negative changes in their views regarding the benevolence of the world is consistent with other findings that basic assumptions about the world can remain shattered for years posttrauma (Janoff-Bulman, 1989).

The relations among positive life changes and traditional distress measures also are quite similar to those reported by recent assault survivors (Frazier et al., 2001). Specifically, sexual assault survivors who report more positive life changes also report less depression, anxiety, and symptoms of PTSD. The magnitudes of the relations also are similar (with the exception of the relation between positive life change and PTSD symptoms at 12 months postassault in the previous study). These relations remain significant even when the effects of personality and current life stress are controlled. The current study thus provides stronger evidence linking positive change to distress by demonstrating that these relations are not accounted for by recent life stressors or personality. They also suggest that measures of positive life change provide incremental validity in explaining posttrauma distress.

The current study also extended Frazier et al.'s (2001) findings by examining self-reported positive life change in relation to life satisfaction and perceived health. As predicted, positive life change was associated with higher levels of life satisfaction, and this relationship remained significant when previous year stressors and personality were taken into account. Thus, rather than simply experiencing lower levels of posttrauma distress, individuals who report posttrauma growth may actually experience enhanced life functioning (see also McMillen & Fisher, 1998). Survivors who report more positive life changes also report better health, although this relation is not significant once the relations among personality and current life stress and positive change are accounted for.

The final purpose of study was to replicate and extend Frazier, Tashiro, et al.'s (2004) findings regarding the correlates of self-reported positive life change, which can help inform developing models of the posttrauma recovery process. We first discuss the relations among the coping and appraisal variables and positive life change, followed by a discussion of the personal and environmental resource variables and whether their associations with positive life change are mediated by the coping and appraisal variables.

First, as predicted, both cognitive restructuring and expressing emotions are associated with more self-reported positive change whereas social withdrawal and problem avoidance are associated with fewer self-reported positive life changes. This is consistent with the findings from our previous study in which the combined approach and avoidant coping scales were positively and negatively associated with positive change, respectively (Frazier, Tashiro, et al., 2004). It is interesting to note that in this study social withdrawal has the strongest (negative) correlation with positive life change and that it is the most frequently reported coping strategy, even though the assaults had occurred many years previously on average. The specific social withdrawal items most frequently endorsed involved keeping one's thoughts and feelings to one's self and not letting others know what was going on. This suggests that even many years after the assault survivors may still be coping with the assault but feel reluctant to talk with others about it. Other studies also report high rates of avoidant coping in rape survivors (Santello & Leitenberg, 1993; Valentiner, Foa, Riggs, & Gershuny, 1996) and more avoidant coping with regard to sexual assault (Santello & Leitenberg, 1993) and sexual abuse (Coffey, Leitenberg, Henning, Turner, & Bennett, 1996) than with regard to other events. Finally, greater use of religious coping also is associated with more positive life change, consistent with our prior research (Frazier, Tashiro, et al., 2004) and other studies (e.g., Park et al., 1996). In fact, it is more strongly related to positive life change than cognitive restructuring or expressing emotions, and is as common as these other more widely discussed strategies.

With regard to event appraisals, we assessed three aspects of the controllability of the event: behavioral self-blame (past control), control over the recovery process (present control), and taking precautions to prevent future assaults (future control). The only form of control associated with positive life change is perceived control over the recovery process. Similarly, this form of control was most strongly associated with positive life change in our previous research (Frazier, Tashiro, et al., 2004), perhaps because the present is in fact more controllable than the past or the future. Perceived control over the recovery process also was the only form of control associated with stress-related growth in a sample of bereaved women (Frazier, Steward, & Mortensen, 2004) and was the strongest correlate of distress in other analyses using data from the two sexual assault studies described here (Frazier, 2003;

Frazier, Steward, & Mortensen, 2004). Other aspects of present control, such as control over physical symptoms of disease, also are associated with positive life changes (Tennen et al., 1992). The differences in the relations between past, present, and future control and self-reported growth underscore the importance, highlighted by several authors (e.g., Frazier et al., 2002; Skinner, 1996), of carefully defining the targets of control efforts.

With regard to personal resource variables, in our first longitudinal study the variables we assessed (ethnicity and prior victimization) were not associated with positive life change. Therefore, in this study we examined three personality variables that we thought might be more related to positive life change. Specifically, individuals higher in extraversion and lower in neuroticism reported more positive life change. Both Tedeschi and Calhoun (1996) and Evers et al. (2001) also reported positive relations between extraversion and positive change. Only Evers et al. found a significant relation between neuroticism and positive change, which was the strongest relation in our study. We did not replicate Tedeschi and Calhoun's finding that greater openness is associated with positive life change. Additional analyses suggest that the primary mediators of the relations among extraversion and neuroticism and positive life change are social withdrawal and control over the recovery process. Specifically, extraversion is associated with positive life change because extraverts are less likely to withdraw from others and more likely to perceive that they have control over their recovery process. The opposite is true of individuals higher in neuroticism: they are more likely to withdraw from others and less likely to perceive that they have control over their recovery process.

Finally, as in our previous study, the environmental resource variable we assessed was social support. Consistent with our own past research (Frazier, Tashiro, et al., 2004) and other studies (e.g., Armeli et al., 2001; Park et al., 1996) individuals who have more social support following the assault also report more positive changes. The mediation analyses suggest that individuals with more social support report more positive change because they use more religious coping and perceive more control over the recovery process. In our previous study, the significant mediators of the relation between social support and positive life change were approach and avoidant coping, taking precautions, and control over the recovery process. Thus, the only consistent finding across the two studies is that control over the recovery process mediates the relation between social support and positive life change.

The conclusions that can be drawn from our data must take into account several study limitations. First, although our goal was to examine posttrauma growth in a sample of nonrecent assault survivors, the large amount of time that had elapsed since most participants were assaulted leaves open the possibility that responses were affected by retrospective bias. Second, given that we did not have data on pre-trauma functioning, we could not assess actual life changes but instead relied on self-reports of posttrauma life change. Because most data on posttraumatic growth consists of self-reports, concerns increasingly are being raised regarding the validity of these self-reports and whether they reflect actual life changes (see e.g., Wortman, 2004). Third, including only women in our sample precluded examination of gender differences in posttrauma growth, which have been reported in other studies (e.g., McMillen & Fischer, 1998). Fourth, given the cross-sectional nature of our data, the direction of the relations among the variables cannot be determined and other models may fit the data (Frazier, Tix, & Barron, 2004). For example, it may be that religious coping is associated with positive change because it is associated with greater social support rather than the other way around. Finally, our sample was too small to conduct structural equation modeling (SEM) analyses, which is the preferred method for testing mediation (Frazier, Tix, & Barron, 2004). Sample sizes of at least 200 are recommended to have sufficient power to detect mediation effects. Because our sample was smaller than that, we may have underestimated the extent to which the coping and appraisal measures were mediators in our study.

   Despite these limitations, our data contribute to the growing body of research on posttraumatic growth by replicating the finding that growth is common even among survivors of traumas involving intentional harm, like sexual assault. Our data also show that self-reported positive changes are associated with traditional distress measures, even after controlling for the effects of recent stressors and personality, which suggests that measures of such changes have incremental validity in explaining individual variability in posttraumatic distress. Self-reported positive life changes also are associated with greater life satisfaction, after controlling for these other variables. Finally, our data on correlates of positive life changes help to fill out the network of relations between these changes and other important constructs in the stress and coping field. For example, our data indicate the importance of assessing specific aspects of perceived control, particularly control over the recovery process, and religious coping, which is a form of coping often overlooked in psychological research.

REFERENCES

Affleck, G., Tennen, H., Croog, S., & Levine, S. (1987). Causal attribution, perceived benefits, and morbidity after a heart attack: An 8-year study. *Journal of Consulting and Clinical Psychology, 55*, 29-35.

Aldwin, C. M., Sutton, K. J., & Lachman, M. (1996). The development of coping resources in adulthood. *Journal of Personality, 64*, 837-871.

Armeli, S., Gunthert, K. C., & Cohen, L. H. (2001). Stressor appraisals, coping, and post-event outcomes: The dimensionality and antecedents of stress-related growth. *Journal of Social and Clinical Psychology, 20*, 366-395.

Breslau, N., Kessler, R., Chilcoat, H., Schultz, L., Davis, G., & Andreski, P. (1998). Trauma and posttraumatic stress disorder in the community: The 1996 Detroit area survey of trauma. *Archives of General Psychiatry, 55*, 626-632.

Calhoun, L. G., Cann, A., Tedeschi, R. G., & McMillan, J. (2000). *Journal of Traumatic Stress, 13*, 521-527.

Carver, C., Scheier, M., & Weintraub, J. (1989). Assessing coping strategies: A theoretically based approach. *Journal of Personality and Social Psychology, 56*, 267-283.

Coffey, P., Leitenberg, K., Henning, K., Turner, T., & Bennett, R. (1996) The relation between methods of coping during adulthood with a history of childhood sexual abuse and current psychological adjustment. *Journal of Consulting and Clinical Psychology, 64*, 1090-1093.

Cohen, J. (1992). A power primer. *American Psychologist, 112*, 155-159.

Collins, R. L., Taylor, S. E., & Skokan, L. A. (1990). A better world or a shattered vision? Changes in life perspectives following victimization. *Social Cognition, 8*, 263-285.

Cordova, M., Cunningham, L., Carlson, C., & Andrykowski, M. (2001). Posttraumatic growth following breast cancer: A controlled comparison study. *Health Psychology, 20*, 176-185.

Derogatis, L. (1993). *Manual for the Brief Symptom Inventory*. National Computer Systems. Minneapolis, MN.

Evers, A.W.M., Kraaimaat, F.W., van Lankveld, W., Jongen, P.J.H., Jacobs, J.W.G., & Bijlsma, J.W.J. (2001). Beyond unfavorable thinking: The illness cognition questionnaire for chronic diseases. *Journal of Consulting and Clinical Psychology, 69*, 1026-1036.

Foa, E., Zinbarg, R., & Rothbaum, B. (1992). Uncontrollability and predictability in Post-traumatic Stress Disorder: An animal model. *Psychological Bulletin, 112,* 218-238.

Frazier, P. (2003). Perceived control and distress following sexual assault: A longitudinal test of a new model. *Journal of Personality and Social Psychology, 84,* 1257-1269.

Frazier, P. (2002). The scientific status of research on rape trauma syndrome: Rape trauma syndrome, § 13-2.0. In D. Faigman, D. Kaye, M. Saks, & J. Sanders (Eds). *Modern scientific evidence: The law and science of expert testimony, 2nd. Ed.* (pp. 117-143. St. Paul, MN: West.

Frazier, P., Berman, M., & Steward, J. (2002). Perceived control and posttraumatic distress: A temporal model. *Applied and Preventive Psychology, 10,* 207-223.

Frazier, P., Conlon, A., & Glaser, T. (2001). Positive and negative life changes following sexual assault. *Journal of Consulting and Clinical Psychology, 69,* 1048-1055.

Frazier, P., Mortensen, H., & Steward, J. (in press). Coping strategies as mediators of the relations among perceived control and distress in sexual assault survivors. *Journal of Counseling Psychology.*

Frazier, P., Steward, J., & Mortensen, H. (2004). Perceived control and adjustment to trauma: A comparison across events. *Journal of Social and Clinical Psychology, 23,* 303-324.

Frazier, P., Tashiro, T., Berman, M., Steger, M., & Long, J. (2004). Correlates of levels and patterns of posttraumatic growth among sexual assault survivors. *Journal of Consulting and Clinical Psychology, 72,* 19-30.

Frazier, P., Tix, A., & Barron, K. (2004). Testing moderator and mediator effects in counseling psychology research. *Journal of Counseling Psychology, 51,* 115-134.

Janoff-Bulman, R. (1989). Assumptive worlds and the stress of traumatic events: Applications of the schema construct. *Social Cognition, 7,* 113-136.

Joseph, S., Williams, R., & Yule, W. (1993). Changes in outlook following disaster: The preliminary development of a measure to assess positive and negative responses. *Journal of Traumatic Stress, 6,* 271-279.

Kennedy, J. E., Davis, R. C., & Taylor, B. G. (1998). Changes in spirituality and well-being among victims of sexual assault. *Journal for the Scientific Study of Religion, 37,* 322-328.

Kenny, D. A., Kashy, D. A., & Bolger, N. (1998). Data analysis in social psychology. In D. T. Gilbert, S. T. Fiske, & G. Lindzey (Eds.), *The*

Handbook of Social Psychology (4th ed.). New York, NY: Oxford University Press.

Kessler, R., Sonnega, A., Bromet, E., Hughes, M., & Nelson, C. (1995). Posttraumatic stress disorder in the national comorbidity survey. *Archives of General Psychiatry, 52,* 1048-1060.

Kilpatrick D., Resnick H., Freedy J. (1991*). The Potential Stressful Events Interview. Unpublished instrument.* Charleston, SC: National Crime Victims Research and Treatment Center, Department of Psychiatry, Medical University of South Carolina.

Lehman, D., Davis, C., DeLongis, A., Wortman, C., Bluck, S., Mandel, D., & Ellard, J. (1993). Positive and negative life changes following bereavement and their relations to adjustment. *Journal of Social and Clinical Psychology, 12,* 90-112.

Linley, P.A., & Joseph, S. (2004). Positive change following trauma and adversity: A review. *Journal of Traumatic Stress, 17,*11-21.

McGregor, B.A., Antoni, M.H., Boyers, A., Alferi, S.M., Blomberg, B.B., & Carver, C.S. (2004). Cognitive-behavioral stress management increases benefit finding and immune function among women with early-stage breast cancer. *Journal of Psychosomatic Research, 56,* 1-8.

McMillen, J.C., & Fisher, R. (1998). The Perceived Benefit Scales: Measuring perceived positive life changes after negative events. *Social Work Research, 22,* 173-187.

McMillen, J.C., Smith, E., & Fisher, R. (1997). Perceived benefit and mental health after three types of disaster. *Journal of Consulting and Clinical Psychology, 65,* 733-739.

Mohr, D., Dick, L., Russo, D., Likosky, W., & Goodkin, D. (1999). The psychological impact of multiple sclerosis: Exploring the patient's perspective. *Health Psychology,18,* 376-382.

O'Leary, V., Alday, C., & Ickovics, J. (1998). Models of life change and posttraumatic growth. In R. Tedeschi, C. Park, & L. Calhoun (Eds.), *Posttraumatic growth: Positive changes in the aftermath of crisis* (pp. 127-151). Mahwah, NJ: Erlbaum.

Pargament, K., Ensing, D., Falgout, K., Olsen, H., Reilly, B., Van Haitsma, K., & Warren, R. (1990). God help me: (I). Religious coping efforts as predictors of the outcomes to significant negative life events. *American Journal of Community Psychology, 18,* 793-824.

Pargament, K. I., Kennell, J., Hathaway, W., Grevengoed, N., Newman, J., & Jones, W. (1988). Religion and the problem-solving process: Three styles of coping. *Journal for the Scientific Study of Religion, 27,* 90-104.

Park, C. L., Cohen, L. H., & Murch, R. L. (1996). Assessment and prediction of stress-related growth. *Journal of Personality, 64,* 71-105.

Revenson, T. A., Wollman, C. A., & Felton, B. J. (1983). Social supports as stress buffers for adult cancer patients. *Psychosomatic Medicine, 45,* 321-331.

Santello, M., & Leitenberg, H. (1993). Sexual aggression by an acquaintance: methods of coping and later psychological adjustment. *Violence and Victims, 8,* 91-104.

Saucier, G. (1994). Mini-Markers: A brief version of Goldberg's unipolar big-five markers. *Journal of Personality Assessment, 63,* 506-516.

Schaefer, J. A. & Moos, R. H. (1998). The context for posttraumatic growth: Life crises, individual and social resources, and coping. In R. Tedeschi, C. Park, & L. Calhoun (Eds.), *Posttraumatic growth: Positive changes in the aftermath of crisis* (pp. 99-126). Mahwah, NJ: Erlbaum.

Skinner, E. (1996). A guide to constructs of control. *Journal of Personality and Social Psychology, 71,* 549-570.

Skinner, E., Edge, K., Altman, J., & Sherwood, H. (2003). Searching for the structure of coping: A review and critique of category systems for classifying ways of coping. *Psychological Bulletin, 129,* 216-269.

Stanton, A., Danoff-Burg, S., Cameron, C., & Ellis, A. (1994). Coping through emotional approach: Problems of conceptualization and confounding. *Journal of Personality and Social Psychology, 66,* 350-362.

Stewart, A., Hays, R., & Ware, J. (1988). The MOS short-form general health survey: Reliability and validity in patient populations. *Medical Care, 26,* 724-735.

Tedeschi, R. G. (1999). Violence transformed: Posttraumatic growth in survivors and their societies. *Aggression and Violent Behavior, 4,* 319-341.

Tedeschi, R., & Calhoun, L. (2004). Posttraumatic growth: Conceptual foundations and empirical evidence. *Psychological Inquiry, 15,* 1-18.

Tedeschi, R., & Calhoun, L. (1995). *Trauma and transformation: Growing in the aftermath of suffering.* Thousand Oaks, CA: Sage.

Tedeschi, R., & Calhoun, L. (1996). The posttraumatic growth inventory: Measuring the positive legacy of trauma. *Journal of Traumatic Stress, 9,* 455-471.

Tennen, H., Affleck, G., Urrows, S., Higgins, P., & Mendola, R. (1992). Perceiving control, construing benefits, and daily processes in rheumatoid arthritis. *Canadian Journal of Behavioral Science, 24,* 186-203.

Tobin, D. L., Holroyd, K. A., & Reynolds, R. V. C. (1984). *User's Manual for the Coping Strategies Inventory*. Athens, OH: Ohio University.

Valentiner, D., Foa, E., Riggs, D., & Gershuny, B. (1996). Coping strategies and posttraumatic stress disorder in female victims of sexual and nonsexual assault. *Journal of Abnormal Psychology, 105,* 455-458.

Ware, J., & Sherbourne, C. (1992). The MOS 36-item short-form health survery (SF-36): I. Conceptual framework and item selection. *Medical Care, 30,* 473-483.

Watson, D., & Hubbard, B. (1996). Adaptational style and dispositional structure: Coping in the context of the five-factor model. *Journal of Personality, 64,* 737-774.

Wortman, C. (2004). Posttraumatic growth: Progress and problems. *Psychological Inquiry, 15,* 81-92.

In: Crime and Law Enforcement Issues   ISBN 978-1-61122-877-9
Editor: James E. Hirsch   © 2011 Nova Science Publishers, Inc.

Chapter 7

INCREASING ORGANIZATIONAL LEADERSHIP THROUGH THE POLICE PROMOTIONAL PROCESS

Patrick J. Hughes[*]
Central Pennsylvania College

ABSTRACT

Many police organizations across the United States use traditional written assessments to promote individuals to first line supervisor positions. Written assessments are cost effective. Recent research has shown assessments have shown problems with validity. One specific issue is with attempting to predict a candidate's leadership abilities or behavior. Other research uncovers issues relating to the lack of leadership training for aspiring first line supervisors. First line supervisors have been traditionally viewed as managers rather than leaders. The process has deterred many from applying for promotion within the ranks. This meta-analysis offers insight to the improvement of police promotional process may improve the selection of the right candidate and overall organizational leadership, but also aid in succession planning as well.

[*] E-mail: PatrickHughes@centralpenn.edu

INTRODUCTION

Police organizations and their design appear to be like no other organizations. Usually they are closely compared to that of the military. According to Toth (2008), when describing police organizations he refers to them as "hyper-bureaucratic military organizational attributes-those of formal rank, formal hierarchy, and a chain of unquestioned and unquestioning command" (2008, p. 62). Only until a few years the term "police management" was used to describe what police believed to be leadership. It was perceived that this "police management" displayed what is currently known as leadership. This concept was designated for only those who held a title. Members of these police organizations believe strongly in the maintaining of this design. The top down design of communication, coupled with the centralization of decision-making, is what many in the field believe sets them apart. However, more recent years have shown that managers are not necessarily leaders. Rather, people placed into managerial roles should possess leadership skills, behaviors and knowledge. By employing such a process it could improve an officer's connection with his/her department. It would also aid in succession planning when promoting future leaders within the department.

So how do officers obtain a police leadership position and what is done to measure their leadership behavior and skills? Are the right individuals being placed into these positions, and can these individuals be chosen in the future for positions to lead larger numbers of officers? Police research for the past few decades have dealt with topics, such as leadership styles of those already in positions of authority (Dentsen, 1999; Kuykendall and Unsinger, 1982; and Schwarzwald et al, 2000). Others focused on studying leadership as it pertains to gaining organizational commitment (Eisenberger et al, 1990, Maertz et al, 2007; and Rhoades and Eisenberger; 2002). There has been little research studying the promotional process and how it can impact organizational leadership and commitment. Police corruption is being seen more frequently, especially from those in chiefs' and front line supervisory positions. There appears to be a need to research and create changes to both the design of these agencies, as well the process to promote future leaders. There are studies that support and discuss these very concepts.

This article will explore the current assessment process utilized to promote front line police supervisors. It will further discuss leadership education and its availability and applicability to all officers. The last portion draws a connection between desired leadership styles of officers and how a proper assessment processes coupled with leadership education and training of future first line supervisors could enhance these sought styles.

THE PARAMILITARY DESIGN

When focusing specifically on organizational design, police organizations are very structured. Their chart is well defined as well as the roles that accompany those titles. Communication inside these agencies is very top down. It has been debated that this design is needed because the severe situations these men and women encounter. To further that, the liability that accompanies those situations is also great. These organizations and their design do lack wanted items by the officers. Among these are better communication networks, more participation, better decision-making, and better ethical leadership. It is through these officers requesting change that organizational commitment may increase. Jermier and Berkes (1979) write "participative role clarification improved organizational commitment."(p.17). Inside of a militaristic designed organization the levels of rank in management and their importance are often over simplified. Many times they are seen as mere conduit of communication having no real influence on those they manage. It is further argued by Jermier and Berkes (1979) that "obedience socialization and military command supervision across the hierarchal levels appears to distort the nature of police work." (p. 17). Police organizations face change and a changing environment at a faster than normal pace. If this were the case, then the structure must be flexible enough to handle such situations. It must also have the flowing communication and leadership structure firmly embedded into its design. Looking at most police structures the ranks would transcend from Chief, Deputy Chief, Captain, Lieutenant, Sergeant, Corporal, and patrol officer. These levels are seen more in a larger metropolitan or county level department. This is mainly due to the amount of officers employed by the agency. However, in some states, such as Pennsylvania, department size does not allow for such rank design making the levels of sergeant and patrol officer more open to leadership situations. In the 1979 study by Jermier and Berkes it is said the "quasi military model makes no provision for the situational effects of a leaders behavior." (p. 17). Miller, Watson, and Webb (2009) echo this by suggesting:

Although many agencies appear to rely on military arrangements in terms of structure, rank, and hierarchies, this model may not effectively serve police leaders and their respective organizations. Replacing the military model of leadership development with behavioral competency development may be more effectual in leadership and agency performance. (p. 51)

Many in the police arena believe that police organizations differ greatly from their counterparts in the private arena. In a Miller et al study (2009) they compared the scores of police leaders on the California Personality Inventory (CPI) with those from the business world. They found "results indicate very similar scores."(p. 58). Is there truly a difference in how leadership is applied between the policing and business worlds? Some in the police world will argue at their basic cores the two arenas differ in followers, motivation, wanted leadership styles. When the word "entrepreneur" is spoken, many people associate it with the world of business. In a 2008 study by Robert Smith, he introduces the concept of "Entrepreneurial policing" (p. 210). The basis behind such a term is to show that the leadership concepts in policing do not differ greatly from that of business. He suggests

> Entrepreneurial policing is an open style of management linked to, but transcending, individual leadership styles because it can be practiced by everyone within the police service irrespective of rank. This link between the rubrics of entrepreneurship and leadership is vital because for a practical theory of entrepreneurial policing to develop, policing requires the active participation of future generations of police leaders. (2008, p. 212)

This concept not only intertwines the business world with policing, but it also is an example that leadership should be seen at all levels within the police organization. To further support this Smith connects entrepreneurship and policing by reporting it "is action-orientated cognitive human ability, which guides policing as an everyday practice and paradoxically links managerialism and conformity to risk-taking behaviour." (p. 212). Whereas Smith's style is the most recently introduced, other studies (Huberts, Kaptein and Lasthuizen, 2007, Jermier and Berkes, 1979, Krimmel, and Lindenmuth, 2001, Murphy, 2007, and Toch, 2008) have reported other perceived leadership styles versus the most sought by officers. The styles reported were gathered from the perceptions of officers. Some common themes emerged from these studies. The reported findings in Krimmel and Lindenmuth (2001) found the Machiavellian and bureaucratic styles (p. 484). Jermier and Berkes (1979) attached task to the style utilized. Among the tasks "directive" (p. 4) was perceived, however, "support and "participation were positively related to job satisfaction and organizational commitment" (p.13). Other research such as

Huberts et al, (2007) studied how perceived leadership styles effect officer integrity violations. The three styles identified were "openness", "role model", and "strictness" (p. 596). They also concluded "All three aspects of leadership, role modeling, strictness and openness, have a significant effect on the frequency with which corruption occurs." (p. 596). In a 2007 study completed by Murphy he found the most effective perceived style "admired" by officers to be "transformational leadership" (p. 176). Research conducted in 2008 by Toth focused on officers as the "change agents" (p. 60) in police organizations. He argues, "police departments could be well advised to encourage participatory involvement as a vehicle for organizational reform." (p. 61).

As seen above, many studies have researched and identified styles sought by officers of their supervisors. It appears through employing these styles officers may have stronger organizational commitment. By supervisors engaging in these styles it may strengthen integrity and ethical behavior of the organization. It appears by strengthen leadership among supervisors, especially first line supervisors (i.e. sergeants), would benefit many police organizations and their followers.

If police organizations need more flexibility and incorporate leadership at all ranks, what then should change, and who should be involved in that change? Further questions that need to be researched further would be; is the current promotional process truly selecting candidates with these styles, and if not how can that process be improved to do so?

PROMOTIONS AND ASSESSMENT

In this section the questions mentioned in the last section will be discussed. The promotional process first needs to be defined. These processes can differ from department to department given the resources and numbers of employees. Many larger departments usually utilize a process involving; written examination, performance evaluation, oral examination, psychological exam, medical physical, and drug screening. This process is usually created and disseminated by a consulting department. These consultants are a division in many state chiefs of police associations. For example, Pennsylvania departments can administer this exam process for various fees:

- Costs – As of October 15, 2008
- Self-Scoring Exam $15.00 per Test Exams
- Scored by Standard and Associates $24.50 per Test

- Administrator's Guide $10.00 Per Guide
- Study Guide $4.00 per Guide
- Examiner's Manual $10.00 Per Guide
- Proctors $200.00 (Pennsylvania Chiefs of Police As, 2008, testing page)

Departments can expand and contract on these steps if they so choose. From this information it can be seen that this can be a costly process for smaller agencies. For instance, smaller agencies use either years of service, performance evaluations, even the "good old boy" system to promote. This information now allows for inquiry to the questions previously stated: Is the current promotional process truly selecting candidates with the wanted leadership styles, and if not, how can the process be improved to do so?

One of the most difficult tasks is creating standardized testing. Standard testing has been utilized in various areas, such as collegiate admissions, government civil service, psychological measurement, and most currently high school academic proficiency. These exams were a way to bring fairness and equality to all who take them. The exams seek to measure, through written words a person's skill, and or personality. A job task analysis is completed prior and it offers performance dimensions needed to perform in a certain position. Where it has served its purpose current research has shown they do have flaws. In research conducted by Lowry (1997) and most currently Miller, Watson, and Webb (2009) they support this argument. In the Miller et al study, promotional candidates in Texas attending leadership training in were given the California Psychological Inventory (p. 1). Researchers gave both a pretest and posttest. Researchers here confirm " results indicate that the CPI-260 can be utilized to assess change through training and that, in this case, the training seemed effective at helping the law enforcement executives develop their leadership skills, awareness, and abilities." (Miller, et al, 2009, p.58). In the current processes many candidates never attend, nor are given the opportunity to attend, any of the leadership training prior to testing. Some attributing factors may be; cost, shift coverage, availability of training, or simply not viewed as needed.

Assessment centers have also made their place in standardized testing. These centers, like the consulting services used in Pennsylvania, are seen often in the governmental and public sector. According to Lowry (1997, 1996), "Over 62% of the respondents in a recent survey of police and fire chiefs reported that they use assessment centers, especially for promotion." (p.53). Further findings from the 1978 Uniform Guidelines on Employment Selection

Procedures published by the Equal Employment Opportunity Commission show centers "are inappropriate for "selection procedures which purport to measure traits or constructs such as intelligence, aptitude, personality, common sense, judgment, leadership..." (ctd, Lowry, 1997, p. 54) . The study does suggest an alternative to the written assessment. Lowry (1997) suggests the term "task-specific centers." (p.54). He defines this concept as "exercises (work-samples) and not performance dimensions." (Lowry, 1997, p.54). Given the various differences among organizations each organization could design their own "task-specific" assessment utilizing the officers and the administrators and subject matter experts. This would suggest better participation by officers of all levels. One down side to this concept is Lowry (1997) states "assessors....are not determining how much leadership or judgment, etc. a subject has: they are attempting to measure how well the subject handles a specific job-related situation." (p.57). It is interesting to note; Lowry is not saying leadership may not be present in the behavior while completing the task. One would be possibly be able to observe some situational leadership skills emerge while the task is being performed. It is later stated "it would be appropriate, however, to have an exercise where the subject was designated group leader and there was an issue to address."(Lowry, 1997, p.57). It could be then asked if this assessment measures behavior. The answer is yes. Lowry (1997) has a component termed "behavior observation" (p.59) into the assessment process. When discussing the assessment of future leaders, leadership is something that can be observed, thus a behavior. According to Lowry (2009) "checklists can include a short 8-15 list of items considered important.... a method for recording the subject's actions." (p.59). Revisiting the previously mentioned wanted styles by officers, it is suggested this checklist be designed specifically behaviors sought by officers to be led. This would ensure the right person is being chosen to lead. Smith (2009) said it correctly that "Leadership is a behavioural quality which has to be demonstrated in everyday contexts."(p.221). That is the very concept supports the utilization of the behavior observations in task-specific center assessments.

By further investing time into creating a better testing process to observe leadership behavior, law enforcement agencies would be improving their organizational design. Ultimately, they would be providing those being led with their chosen leader. It would also be a positive step into planning for the future for many agencies. The concept of succession planning is not often considered of in law enforcement organizations.

PLANNING FOR THE FUTURE

The last question to be investigated would be how do police organizations plan and train future leaders of their departments? The training issue has already been discussed briefly. Many departments do not invest time or money into sending officers to leadership trainings. This could be at a federal, state, or local level. On a federal level the FBI maintains The Leadership Development Institute. Some states may also have some type of leadership seminars or classes. For example, Pennsylvania, through the Penn State Justice and Safety Institute, offers leadership development courses. They offer nine courses in all. (Penn State Justice and Safety Institute) Of these courses seven require the officer must be a rank of lieutenant or higher, one course requires the officer is in the promotional process or promoted, and one course has nothing noted about who may attend. This concept in offering leadership training does not appear to be in line with the concept of succession planning. Instead of supplying training to those choosing or aspiring to be leaders, the training occurs after the officer is chosen from a list of eligible candidates. By educating in the manner it appears to be "placing the cart before the horse." As mentioned earlier officers are seeking certain styles from those that lead them. These styles do not appear to be measured through the current written assessment process. Rowe (2006) suggests "the quality of police leadership could be improved by more effective methods to identify officers in the middle rankings posts who had the potential to become chief officers" (p.759). He supports that succession planning can increase overall police leadership and it can be done through training the right people. His research sought to "modernise the police workforce, enhancing training and career progression to improve leadership and management skills at all levels of the service." (Rowe, 2006. p.759). This very point seems to contradict the requirements to attend police leadership trainings.

Another issue in succession planning might be that not enough individuals want to be involved. This could be for various reasons such as, satisfaction with the current assignment, monetary loss, lack of support of motivation, poor test taking ability, disconnect with current administration values. In the 2005 study by Murphy officers perceived their promotional process as "not picking the best police officers" and "the testing and selection method" (p. 256). Whatever the reason may be this does not suggest that there is a lack of those that can lead given the right tools. Sometimes as stated in 2001 study by Whetstone officer have the "perception that promotions are not based on merit and reflect a hidden administrative agenda."(p.153). However, in the same study "black test takers indicate leadership as a prominent concern." (Whetstone, 2001, p.152). While this is a positive sign of those focusing on leadership, this very notion needs to be permeated through all in the organization. Through proper succession planning this can be possible. According to Murphy (2005), Kesner and Sebora (1994) they agreed on "the importance of creating a seamless continuity in leadership development and succession planning." (p. 254). By law enforcement changing the admission and availability of currently offered leadership training, simultaneously with the current promotional processes, police organizations can begin to assure the right leaders are being chosen.

CONCLUSION

The purpose of this paper is to open a dialogue on the concept of increasing police leadership and promoting to improve succession planning. It attempted to show connectivity of the research of many. Research has shown that the current design of police organizations does not support change easily. However, research also suggests change is wanted by officers. They state how future leaders are chosen, as well the style they wish them to exhibit needs to be improved. By making leadership training available to those aspiring to be leaders prior to testing, as well as making testing task behavior exams rather than written, could improve the wanted changes. Further research could be warranted specifically focusing on the leadership trainings offered from states. It also can be built into the organizations overall succession planning of police organizations improving their overall leadership throughout the organization. In this day and age where police corruption is increasing, especially among administration, these changes seemed warranted. Future research could focus solely of succession planning and if in fact it is successful for police agencies who utilize it. As Ian Blair (2003) states about policing in the 21st century " 'our job now is to go out and garner learning from wherever it exists and increase the richness of our leadership culture . . . Police leadership is not essentially different' from all other forms of leadership." (ctd, Ginger, 2003, p. 112).

REFERENCES

Ginger, J. D. (2003). Book Review: Police Leadership in the Twenty-First Century: Philosophy, Doctrine, And Developments (R. Adlam and P. Villiers, Eds.). *International Journal of Police Science and Management*, *6*(2), 112-114. Retrieved May 28, 2009, from Academic Search Premier.

Huberts, L., Kaptein, M., and Lasthuizen, K. (2007). A study of the impact of three leadership styles on integrity violations committed by police officers. *Policing: An International Journal of Police Strategies and Management*, *30*(4), 587-607.

Jermier, J. M., and Berkes, L. J. (1979). Leader Behavior in a Police Command Bureaucracy: A Closer Look at the Quasi-Military Model. *Administrative Science Quarterly*, *24*(1), 1-23. Retrieved June 15, 2009, from http://www.jstor.org/stable/2989873

Lowry, P. E. (1997). Journal of Social Behavior and Personality. *The Assessment Center Process: New Directions*, *12*(5), 53-62. Retrieved May 21, 2009, from Academic Search Premier.

Miller, H. A., Watkins, R. J., and Webb, D. (2009). The use of psychological testing to evaluate law enforcement leadership competencies and development. *Police Practice and Research*, *10*(1), 49-60.

Murphy, S. A. (2007). The role of emotions and transformational leadership on police culture: an autoethnographic account. *International Journal of Police Science and Management*, *10*(2), 165-178. Retrieved May 26, 2009, from Academic Search Premier.

Murphy, S. A. (2006). Executive development and succession planning: qualitative evidence. *International Journal of Police Science and Management*, *8*(4), 253-265. Retrieved May 21, 2009, from Academic Search Premier.

Penn State Justice and Safety Institute. (n.d.). Retrieved July 01, 2009, from http://jasi.outreach.psu.edu/#index.php?lawenf/Programs

Pennsylvania Chiefs of Police As. (2009, June 25). Retrieved June 25, 2009, from http://www.pachiefs.org/testing.aspx

Pennsylvania State Troopers Association v. Pennsylvania's Labor Relations Board (Commonwealth Court of Pennsylvania December, 2002).

Rowe, M. (2006). Following the leader: front-line narratives on police leadership. *Policing*, *29*(4), 757-767. Retrieved May 21, 2009, from Academic Search Premier.

Smith, R. (2009). Entrepreneurship, Police Leadership, and the. *Journal of Investigative Psychology and Offender Profiling*, *5*, 209-225. *Wiley InterScience*. Retrieved May 28, 2009, from www.interscience.wiley.com

Toch, H. (2008). Police officers as change agents in police reform. *Policing and Society*, *18*(1), 60-71.

Whetstone, T. S. (2001). Copping out: Why police officers decline to participate in the sergeant's promotional process. *American Journal of Criminal Justice: AJCJ*, *25*(2), 147-159. Retrieved May 21, 2009, from Criminal Justice Periodicals.

Whetstone, T. S. (2000). Getting Stripes: Educational and Achievement and Study Strategies Used by Sergeant Promotional Candidates. *American Journal of Criminal Justice*, *24*(2), 247-257. Retrieved May 21, 2009, from Academic Search Premier.

White, M. D. (2008). Identifying Good Cops Early: Predicting Performance in the Academy. *Police Quarterly*, *11*(1), 27-49.

In: Crime and Law Enforcement Issues
Editor: James E. Hirsch
ISBN 978-1-61122-877-9
© 2011 Nova Science Publishers, Inc.

Chapter 8

ACCESSORIES TO THE CRIME: "SECONDARY SERVERS" AND ALCOHOL SALES TO OBVIOUSLY INTOXICATED BARROOM PATRONS

*James C. Roberts**

ABSTRACT

The primary goal of this study was to identify characteristics of licensed drinking establishments that predict alcohol sales to obviously intoxicated barroom patrons. Of particular interest was the relationship between "secondary servers" of alcohol and irresponsible alcohol service. Relying on a structured observation guide listing a large number of variables believed to be related to irresponsible alcohol service, trained observers spent a total of 444 hours collecting data in 25 licensed drinking establishments in Hoboken, New Jersey. Observations took place at two separate time periods, 7:30pm – 10:30pm and 11:00pm – 2:00am, on Thursday, Friday, and Saturday nights. Ordinary least squares (OLS) regression analyses revealed "number of secondary servers" as the strongest predictor of alcohol service to obviously intoxicated patrons in Hoboken barrooms. Another significant predictor of alcohol service to

* James C. Roberts, Ph.D. The University of Scranton, Department of Sociology/Criminal Justice Scranton, PA 18510-4605, Direct dial: (570) 941-7435, Fax: (570) 941-6485, E-mail: robertsj7@scranton.edu.

intoxicated patrons in this study was the presence of "aversive environmental stimuli" within licensed premises, such as excessive heat, smoke, and crowding. Several prevention strategies aimed at reducing irresponsible alcohol service in bars and associated problems with alcohol-related harm are proposed.

Keywords: Alcohol, intoxication, licensed premises, bar staff, responsible beverage service

INTRODUCTION

Despite the passage of laws in most countries that prohibit alcohol sales to obviously intoxicated individuals, barroom patrons are regularly served alcohol to the point of intoxication and beyond (McKnight, 1991; Nusbaumer and Reiling, 2003; Toomey, Wagenaar, Kilian, Fitch, Rothstein, and Fletcher, 1999; Toomey, Wagenaar, Erickson, Fletcher, Patrek, and Lenk, 2004). Furthermore, there is growing body of research that links continued alcohol service to obviously intoxicated patrons to alcohol-related harm occurring in and around licensed drinking establishments. Graham, La Rocque, Yetman, Ross, and Guistra (1980) conducted one of the first and most influential observational studies of barroom aggression. Teams of observers (male-female pairs) spent three months and a total of 633 hours conducting unobtrusive observations in 185 licensed premises in Vancouver, Canada. In addition to variables such as poor ventilation and shabby décor, these researchers identified irresponsible alcohol service and patron intoxication as important predictors of aggression in Vancouver barrooms. In describing the prototypical aggressive bar, Graham et al. (1980) state, "...extreme drunkenness is common and usually acceptable. The only reason for refusal of service seems to be that the person is unconscious – and some instances were seen in which a person was awakened to be served another drink" (p. 290).

It is important to note that research on alcohol-related harm occurring in and around licensed premises is grounded in the belief that social contexts have a direct effect on the behaviors of bar patrons. Furthermore, this research takes for granted that individuals bring to drinking episodes a variety of unique characteristics, including unique propensities for problem behavior, including acts of violence and aggressive alcohol consumption (Graham, 1980; Graham, Schmidt, and Gillis, 1996; Graham et al., 1998; Graham, West, and Wells,

2000). Homel, Tomsen, and Thommeny (1992) used insights from Graham et al.'s (1980) study of Vancouver barrooms as a starting point for their research in Sydney, Australia. They too relied on structured observations within barrooms to identify predictors of naturally occurring alcohol-related aggression. Teams of observers spent 300 hours conducting unobtrusive observations in 23 sites within 17 Sydney barrooms. Like Graham et al. (1980), Homel et al. (1992) identified high drunkenness, which is a byproduct of staff members' willingness to serve bar patrons to the point of intoxication and beyond, as one of the chief variables present during violent episodes. These researchers suggest that crowding, boredom, discounted drinks, high cover charges, and the absence of substantial amounts of food in most bars exacerbate problems with irresponsible alcohol service and high levels of intoxication. In their replication of the 1989 Sydney study, Home and Clark (1994) also identified irresponsible alcohol service and intoxication as key situational factors that increase the risk of violence in and around licensed drinking establishments.

Stockwell, Lang, and Rydon (1993) relied on a household survey of adults in Perth, Western Australia to explore drinkers' reports about the setting in which they drank and their experiences with alcohol-related harm, including involvement in violent arguments and fights, accidents, and drunk driving offenses. Findings from this study revealed that most experiences with alcohol-related harm occurred after the respondent had been drinking at licensed premises. Furthermore, these researchers identified bar staff continuing to serve "obviously intoxicated" patrons as the strongest predictor of whether drinkers themselves experienced some kind of harm. While discounted drinks and crowding were also found at places where intoxication was permitted, these variables did not significantly predict increased alcohol consumption or increased risk of harm to drinkers. However, as in Homel et al.'s (1992) study of Sydney barrooms, both drink discounting and crowding demonstrated small but significant associations with continued alcohol service to intoxicated patrons, which, according to these researchers, may be of significance from a preventative point of view. Lang, Stockwell, Rydon, and Lockwood (1995), who analyzed the same survey results used by Stockwell et al. (1993), identified additional predictors of irresponsible alcohol service and high risk consumption, such as the presence of musical entertainment and dancing in bars.

Donnelly and Briscoe (2003) conducted a telephone-based survey of young adults in New South Wales, Australia in order to examine the extent of irresponsible alcohol service to patrons showing signs of intoxication in licensed drinking establishments. Individuals who indicated that they had shown at least one sign of intoxication during their last drinking occasion in a bar, such as loss of coordination or slurred speech, were asked how serving staff responded to their observable intoxication. Possible staff reactions included:

1. they refused to serve me any more alcoholic drinks;
2. they asked me to leave the premises;
3. they called the police;
4. they suggested I buy low- or non-alcoholic drinks;
5. they suggested that I buy some food;
6. they advised me on or organized transport home;
7. they suggested that I stop drinking; and
8. they continued to serve me alcoholic drinks" (Donnelly and Briscoe, 2003, p. 1289).

Findings from this study revealed that few individuals who said that they showed visible signs of intoxication during their last bar visit reported any attempt by serving staff to stop them from consuming alcohol. In fact, of those individuals who reported showing at least one sign of intoxication, less than 3% were refused alcohol and less than 4% were asked to leave the bar. Of those who reported three or more signs of intoxication, less than 4% were refused alcohol and only about 6% were asked to leave. The most common server response to visibly intoxicated patrons was continued alcohol service.

In addition to surveys with and observations of actual bar patrons, researchers have employed the use of "pseudo-intoxicated" bar patrons in an attempt to better understand the nature of irresponsible alcohol service in barrooms. McKnight (1991) was among the first to use covert actors trained in exhibiting signs of intoxication as a means of evaluating responsible beverage service (RBS) training programs. While the RBS program examined in this study led to significant overall changes in knowledge of, attitudes toward, and practices and policies pertaining to responsible alcohol service among bar staff, there was little increase in the refusal of alcohol service to observers feigning intoxication. Rydon, Stockwell, Lang, and Beel (1996) also employed pseudo-intoxicated patrons in a study of licensed premises in Western Australia. Over the course of 120 visits to 23 different establishments, pairs of pseudo-drunk actors placed more than 350 drink orders. Bar staff in this study refused alcohol service during only 10% of the visits and implemented partial interventions, such as offering food or low-alcohol or non-alcoholic drinks, during only 5% of the visits.

In yet another study employing the use of pseudo-intoxicated bar patrons, Lang, Stockwell, Rydon, and Beel (1998) examined the effectiveness of an RBS program implemented in a popular entertainment area in Western Australia. Like McKnight (1991), these researchers found the server training resulted in significant changes in knowledge about responsible beverage service practices and alcohol laws and regulations, but had little impact on actual server responses to obviously intoxicated patrons. Pseudo-drunks in this study were rarely refused alcohol service and their identification was rarely checked on most occasions. Toomey et al. (1999) report similar findings in their evaluation of Project ARM, a server training program implemented in Minnesota, USA. The majority of purchase attempts by pseudo-drunks in this study resulted in alcohol sales. Despite these rather disappointing evaluations of interventions aimed at reducing problem serving in bars, several studies employing the use of pseudo-intoxicated patrons have shown positive changes in responsible alcohol service following the implementation of RBS training (Geller, Russ, and Delphos, 1987; Gliksman, McKenzie, Single, Douglas, Brunet, and Moffatt, 1993; McKnight and Streff, 1994; Russ and Geller, 1987; Toomey, Wagenaar, Gehan, Kilian, Murray, and Perry, 2001; Wallin, Gripenberg, and Andreasson, 2002).

While there is a good deal of research that examines the extent of irresponsible alcohol service in bars, as well as that which links alcohol service to obviously intoxicated patrons to incidents of alcohol-related harm occurring in and around licensed premises, few studies have examined factors that "predict" alcohol sales to intoxicated bar patrons. This relatively new area of research was influenced by studies that have attempted to identify predictors of alcohol sales to underage patrons. For example, several studies suggest that younger servers are more likely to sell alcohol to underage patrons than are older servers (Forster, McGovern, Wagenaar, Wolfson, Perry, and Anstine, 1994; Forster, Murray, Wolfson, and Wagenaar, 1995). Other studies have found alcohol service to underage patrons to be more problematic in busier establishments (Forster et al., 1995) and in those without visible bar managers (Wolfson, Toomey, Forster, Wagenaar, McGovern, and Perry, 1996).

Andreasson, Lindewald, and Rehman (2000) offer one of the first studies to examine factors believed to predict alcohol sales to intoxicated bar patrons. These researchers employed pseudo-intoxicated patrons to illicit server responses to obvious alcohol impairment. The purpose of this study was to see whether intoxicated patrons would be served additional alcohol and whether variables such as age and gender of server, level of bar crowding, and general order within licensed premises affected server responses to alcohol impairment. Findings from this study revealed that pseudo-drunks were served alcohol at 95% of the licensed premises they visited. However, none of the independent variables examined in this study, such as lighting, music, and age and sex of servers, affected this outcome. Like Andreasson et al. (2000), Toomey et al. (2004) attempted to assess the likelihood of alcohol sales to obviously intoxicated patrons and whether server and/or establishment characteristics were related to the likelihood of illegal sales. These researchers also employed pseudo-intoxicated patrons to illicit server responses to obvious alcohol impairment. As in Andreasson et al.'s (2000) study, the likelihood of alcohol sales to obviously intoxicated bar patrons was very high. Findings from this study revealed age of alcohol servers to be an important predictor of alcohol service to intoxicated patrons, as servers who appeared to be less than 31 years of age were 2.7 times more likely to serve alcohol to pseudo-drunks than those who appeared to be age 31 or older.

Reiling and Nusbaumer (2006) relied on survey data collected from 911 alcoholic beverage servers in Indiana, USA to examine willingness to serve bar patrons beyond intoxication. These researchers examined the influence of various personal factors, location factors, management policies and practices, and external social control efforts on willingness to over-serve. Findings from this study revealed servers' personal drinking patterns as important predictors of alcohol service to obviously intoxicated patrons. Specifically, servers who reported drinking frequently, who reported frequently drinking to intoxication, and who reported drinking on-the-job were more likely to serve alcohol to obviously intoxicated bar patrons. Findings from this study also suggest that servers who are heavy drinkers might have distorted definitions of intoxication, which can further affect their ability to serve responsibly. According to Nusbaumer and Reiling (2002), "…previous research indicating the heavier one drinks, the more drinks they require for a definition of intoxication, draws into question their ability, as heavy drinkers, to accurately or appropriately evaluate intoxication" (p. 740). Finally, while some servers may be less capable of responsible alcohol service due to their personal drinking patterns, these researchers suggest that others may simply be choosing to over-serve because of economic incentives. As discussed by Reiling and Nusbaumer (2006), problems associated with the latter group are much more difficult to address and put added pressure on owner and managers to run an orderly bar.

Like Andreasson et al. (2000), Roberts (1998) focused on the characteristics of bars themselves rather than characteristics of serving staff in his attempt to identify predictors of alcohol service to obviously intoxicated bar patrons. This study entailed unobtrusive observations in several bars located in four different beach towns in Southern New Jersey, as well as semi-structured interviews with bar staff and managers working in these establishments. As in Homel et al.'s (1992) study of Sydney barrooms, drink specials and the absence of food in most bars were found to exacerbate problems with irresponsible alcohol service. Like Reiling and Nusbaumer (2006), Roberts (1998) identified serving staff drinking on-the-job as an important predictor of alcohol service to obviously intoxicated patrons. However, the strongest predictor of alcohol service to intoxicated patrons in this study was the presence of "secondary servers" of alcohol.

According to Roberts (1998), secondary servers distribute alcohol in areas within licensed premises away from "traditional bartenders" and bar stations and cater primarily to obviously intoxicated patrons who are either unable or unwilling to wait in long lines in order to purchase alcoholic beverages. "Shot-girls," one of the four types of secondary servers identified in this study, travel throughout barrooms carrying trays of pre-poured, attractively packaged "shots" of alcohol. One popular pre-poured shot in South Jersey barrooms was the "test tube" shot, which consisted of alcohol combined with different mixers and served in a plastic test tube. "Tub-girls" served two to three options of bottled beer from stationary, metal or plastic beer tubs strategically positioned throughout bars. "Cocktail waitresses" traveled throughout bars taking drink orders, placing them with traditional bartenders, and then running drinks back out to bar patrons. Finally, "service bar attendants" worked from behind compact, moveable bar stations that offered two to three choices of bottled beer and two to three choices of alcohol shots. Each of these secondary servers were found to reduce the effort it took for obviously intoxicated bar patrons to continue drinking, as in the case of shot-girls and waitresses, patrons did not have to move from where they were sitting, standing, or in some cases, leaning, to purchase alcoholic beverages.

It is important to note that the names given to secondary servers in Roberts' (1998) study were those used by staff members and management in South Jersey barrooms. In fact, many of the secondary servers interviewed in this study reported responding to employment advertisements posted by bars seeking shot-girls, tub-girls, etc. These were also the job titles they were instructed to apply for when completing work applications at various South Jersey barrooms. It should also be noted that only females were employed as secondary servers in South Jersey barrooms. Owners and managers interviewed in this study were very open about seeking out females, especially young, attractive females, for these positions, as they believed that they would appeal more to the most aggressive drinkers frequenting their establishments, that being young, college-aged males. Traditional bartenders interviewed by Roberts (1998) reported that the presence of secondary servers made it difficult to monitor patrons' alcohol consumption, which is a key component of RBS training programs. Interestingly, secondary servers interviewed in this study reported being exempt from RBS training, as owners and managers were said to view them not as fully functional servers of alcohol, but rather as "support staff" for traditional bartenders.

The primary goal of the present study was to identify characteristics of licensed drinking establishments that predict alcohol sales to obviously intoxicated barroom patrons. Of particular interest was the relationship between secondary servers of alcohol and irresponsible alcohol service. It was predicted that increased numbers of secondary servers working in barrooms and present during individual observation periods would lead to increased alcohol service to obviously intoxicated patrons. The present study also was also an attempt to investigate a number of other possible predictors of alcohol service to intoxicated patrons identified by past researchers.

METHODS

Sample of Bars

The present study focused on licensed drinking establishments that functioned primarily as entertainment venues for young, college-aged patrons in Hoboken, New Jersey. The total population of bars located in Hoboken's southeast quadrant was included in this study, with the exception of two venues that functioned primarily as restaurants. The southeast quadrant of Hoboken contains over half of the city's licensed drinking establishments, as well as a major hub for public transportation that attracts patrons both from within and outside the city. It should be noted that each of the bars included in this study (n = 25) were within reasonable walking distance from this transportation hub and were therefore capable of being visited by the same population of patrons. Bars ranged in capacity from about 100 to over 900 patrons. While the primary entertainment in most venues was prerecorded music, several bars also attracted patrons with televised sporting events, live bands, and disc jockeys. Bars included in this study catered primarily to young (e.g., 20s), white, professionals and college students from Hoboken and the surrounding areas. Male patrons outnumbered female patrons in most Hoboken barrooms.

Procedures

Observations took place at two separate time periods, 7:30pm – 10:30pm and 11:00pm – 2:00am, on Thursday, Friday, and Saturday nights. Each bar, with the exception of one venue that was only open on Fridays and Saturdays, was visited on six separate evenings, allowing for observations on each of the above-mentioned days and time periods. In total, the study entailed 148 individual observation periods lasting a total of 444 hours. Barrooms were assigned to nights and times of observation using a random start, the final result being a structured observation schedule. The present study employed one primary observer who participated in all 148 observation periods. In order to measure the reliability of observer responses in completing the data collection instrument, a second observer was employed who participated in approximately one third of the total number of observation periods. Once the observation schedule had been devised, indicating the days and times each bar was to be observed, the second observer was randomly assigned to 50 observation periods. The primary observer conducted observations alone during the remaining 98 observation periods.

During the months leading up to the study, the two observers studied the contents of a structured observation guide containing a large number of variables related to the physical and social setting of barrooms (e.g., smokiness, temperature, crowding, dancing, etc.), as well as numerous variables related to alcohol service and consumption (e.g., drink specials, drinking in rounds, servers of alcohol drinking on-the-job, etc). They also studied guidelines for identifying and recording the service of alcohol to obviously intoxicated bar patrons. Signs of intoxication included slurred speech, loss of coordination, stumbling, staggering, spilling drinks, crude or quarrelsome behavior, etc. While this list of intoxication signs is not exhaustive, it incorporates those identified by past researchers as being key behavioral indicators of persons who are "obviously intoxicated" (See Donnelly and Briscoe, 2003; Lang et al., 1995). Observers focused exclusively on those patrons who displayed multiple signs of intoxication and appeared severely intoxicated. It is important to note that the primary researcher in this study had seven years of experience as a bartender prior to the start of data collection and had been certified in several alcohol management programs that train serving staff to identify signs of intoxication and monitor patron drinking. In addition to counting the number of times obviously intoxicated patrons were served alcohol, observers also recorded other server responses to intoxicated patrons attempting to purchase alcoholic beverages, which included cutting the patron off and allowing them to stay in the bar, cutting the patron off and asking them to leave the bar, and refusing alcohol service but offering non-alcoholic beverages or food.

In the present study, each alcoholic beverage sold to an obviously intoxicated patron was considered an individual incident of serving intoxicated patrons. Therefore, a single encounter with an intoxicated patron may have resulted in multiple incidents of serving intoxicated patrons. In addition, there were occasions in which sober patrons purchased rounds of drinks for groups of intoxicated patrons. Each drink distributed to an obviously intoxicated patron, whether by a server or patron, was also considered an individual incident of serving intoxicated patrons. Therefore, each incident of serving intoxicated patrons does not necessarily represent a patron-server encounter. Observers in the present study moved from server to server and attempted to spend an equal amount of time observing the serving practices of each. During observation periods with two observers, the protocol was to stay together and observe the same server together. On nights with two observers, the average of their individual counts for the variable "number of incidents of serving intoxicated patrons" was recorded for analysis.

During observation periods, observers circulated throughout the premises, paying particular attention to situational variables contained in the observation guide. They did not consume any alcoholic beverages while conducting observations, but instead purchased beverages that closely resembled mixed drinks (e.g., sodas with lemons or limes, etc.). As in previous observational studies conducted in bars (Graham et al., 1980; Homel et al., 1992; Homel and Clark, 1994), only limited note taking was conducted while inside licensed premises and was done so in places that would not draw any unwanted attention, the most common location being bathroom stalls. Written recordings taken inside barrooms were limited to items in the observation guide that required observers to make counts of particular phenomena, including server responses to obviously intoxicated patrons.

Immediately following each observation period, observers independently rated items in the observation guide. For observation periods in which both observers were present, a third and final observation guide was prepared for analysis after differences in individual coding were resolved. The two observers maintained a high degree of inter-rater reliability throughout the study, with individual responses to items in the observation guide never varying to such a degree as to cause concern. For example, if individual coding of variables did vary, it rarely did so by more than a single response category (e.g., somewhat smoky vs. smoky).

RESULTS

Server Responses to Obviously Intoxicated Patrons

An examination of observed server responses to obviously intoxicated bar patrons revealed that traditional bartenders were the only servers to "cut a patron off," or refrain from serving them alcohol. However, there was only one such incident observed over the course of the entire study. There were no incidents observed in which any server of alcohol offered obviously intoxicated patrons food or non-alcoholic beverages. Even more surprising was the extent of alcohol service to obviously intoxicated bar patrons. Traditional bartenders averaged 58.54 incidents of serving intoxicated patrons per observation period. Secondary servers of alcohol averaged 61.30 incidents of serving intoxicated patrons during those observation periods in which they were present (n = 56). There was a combined average of 81.74 incidents of serving intoxicated patrons per observation for "all servers" of alcohol over the course of the 148 observation periods. It is important to note that many Hoboken barrooms employed more than one type of secondary server of alcohol, including each of those identified by Roberts (1998) in his study of licensed drinking establishments in South Jersey (i.e., shot-girls, tub-girls, cocktail waitresses, and service bar attendants). However, the present study only examined the collective serving practices of this group of servers. As was the case in South Jersey barrooms, only females were hired as secondary servers in licensed drinking establishments throughout Hoboken.

While counts of alcohol service to intoxicated patrons in the present study were quite high, they are partly explained by the phenomenon of "drinking in rounds." Drinking in rounds involves a single patron purchasing three or more alcoholic beverages at one time. Furthermore, as already mentioned, each alcoholic beverage an obviously intoxicated patron was served was considered an individual incident of serving intoxicated patrons. In addition, there were occasions in which sober patrons purchased rounds of drinks for groups of intoxicated patrons. Each drink distributed to an obviously intoxicated patron, whether by a server or patron, was also considered an individual incident of serving intoxicated patrons.

Bivariate Analyses

Table 1. "Number of incidents of serving intoxicated patrons" by variables related to the physical and social environment (N = 148 observation periods)

	N	# incidents of serving intoxicated patrons		F (df)
		Mean	sd	
Appearance of bar				$43.21_{(2)}$**
Attractive	66	29.71	37.70	
Somewhat unattractive	46	56.37	91.73	
Unattractive	36	209.53	157.17	
Smokiness in bar				$45.86_{(2)}$**
Mostly smoke free	91	34.86	65.53	
Somewhat smoky	34	96.24	99.54	
Smoky	23	245.78	164.08	
Temperature in bar				$48.97_{(2)}$**
Cool	70	26.16	34.57	
Somewhat warm	40	57.65	62.10	
Hot	38	209.47	167.61	
Crowding (maximum capacity) in bar				$64.76_{(2)}$**
Low[2]	95	29.88	46.16	
Medium	28	104.46	102.15	
High[3]	25	253.32	163.80	
Movement throughout bar				$47.11_{(2)}$**
Easy to move about	76	23.51	33.18	
Somewhat difficult to move about	35	75.71	85.79	
Difficult to move about	37	207.03	163.24	
Overall comfort of bar				$84.85_{(2)}$**
Comfortable	82	21.29	22.73	

---

[2] Low = approximately 1/3 bar's maximum capacity.
[3] High = at or exceeding bar's maximum capacity.

	N	# incidents of serving intoxicated patrons		F (df)
		Mean	sd	
Somewhat uncomfortable	31	66.42	68.36	
Uncomfortable	35	236.91	153.41	
Clearing of tables and ledges				$42.27_{(2)}$**
Mostly kept clear	85	25.13	31.00	
Somewhat cluttered	29	106.10	151.17	
Cluttered	34	202.47	137.73	
Clearing of bar surfaces				$30.84_{(2)}$**
Mostly kept clear	89	30.81	42.98	
Somewhat cluttered	25	122.24	129.23	
Cluttered	34	185.26	168.07	
Overall cleanliness of bar				$49.85_{(2)}$**
Mostly clean	91	25.57	32.37	
Somewhat unclean	22	112.73	90.17	
Unclean	35	208.29	171.33	
Dancing				$89.81_{(1)}$**
No	100	30.42	40.38	
Yes	48	188.65	157.00	
Time				$35.35_{(1)}$**
T1 = 7:30pm – 10:30pm	74	28.74	67.05	
T2 = 11:00pm – 2:00am	74	134.73	137.89	
Bar type				$37.80_{(1)}$**
Watering hole	117	53.72	77.59	
Other (e.g., band bars, sports bars, dance clubs, etc.)	31	187.48	182.10	

$* p < .05. ** p < .01.$

Table 1 presents the relationship between the dependent variable, number of incidents of serving intoxicated patrons, and several variables related to the physical and social environment within barrooms. As indicated, the average number of times intoxicated patrons were served alcohol was significantly higher during observation periods in which barrooms were unattractive, smoky, hot, crowded, difficult to move around in, uncomfortable, and unclean. There was also more frequent alcohol service to intoxicated patrons during observation periods in which tables, ledges, and bar surfaces were rarely cleared or cleaned and left littered with discarded trash and empty bottles.

As indicated in Table 1, the average number of times intoxicated patrons were served alcohol was higher during observation periods taking place between 11:00 pm and 2:00 am, as well as during those taking place in bars other than "watering holes." Watering holes, which represented most of the establishments included in the present study, offered little in the way of entertainment, musical or otherwise. "Other" Hoboken barrooms, on the other hand, attracted patrons through some specialized, and usually well advertised, entertainment, such as live bands, disc jockeys, or televised sporting events. Dancing, a common feature of other bar types, also demonstrated a statistically significant relationship with number of incidents of serving intoxicated patrons ($p<.01$).

Table 2 presents the relationship between number of incidents of serving intoxicated patrons and several variables related to alcohol service and consumption. As indicated, the average number of times intoxicated patrons were served alcohol was higher during observations periods in which patrons were checked for identification at entry points into barrooms. Some of the more stringent door policies were observed at establishments that local law enforcement identified as being on probation for serving underage patrons. Alcohol service to intoxicated patrons was also significantly higher during observation periods in which there were cover charges, drink specials, and patrons frequently purchasing rounds of alcoholic beverages, as well as during those in which there was no food or snacks made available to bar patrons.

Table 2 also reveals statistically significant relationships between number of incidents of serving intoxicated patrons and the variables "bouncers and doormen drinking alcoholic beverages" ($p < .01$) and "servers of alcohol (any) drinking alcoholic beverages" ($p < .01$). As indicated, the average number of times obviously intoxicated patrons were served alcohol was 200.48 during observation periods in which bouncers were present ($N = 107$) and drinking alcohol, but only 60.74 during those in which they were present and not drinking alcohol. Similarly, the average number of times obviously intoxicated patrons were served alcohol was 155.09 during observation periods in which servers of alcohol (any) were drinking alcohol on-the-job, but only 35.79 during those in which they were not.

Table 2. "Number of incidents of serving intoxicated patrons" by variables related to alcohol service and consumption (N = 148 observation periods)

	N	# incidents of serving intoxicated patrons		F (df)
		Mean	sd	
Cover Charge				$52.00_{(1)}$**
No	120	52.03	75.55	
Yes	28	209.07	181.83	
ID check				$57.74_{(1)}$**
No	108	42.85	62.36	
Yes	40	186.73	168.82	
Drink specials				$17.76_{(1)}$**
No	94	51.78	71.70	
Yes	54	133.89	163.83	
Food				$5.37_{(1)}$*
No	82	102.02	135.01	
Yes	66	56.53	94.42	
Drinking in rounds				$30.66_{(1)}$**
Infrequent	68	27.50	54.73	
Frequent	80	127.84	140.57	
Bouncers and doormen drinking alcoholic beverages (N = 107)				$27.30_{(1)}$**
No	80	60.74	88.23	
Yes	27	200.48	186.14	
Servers of alcohol (any) drinking alcoholic beverages				$44.59_{(1)}$**
No	91	35.79	62.69	
Yes	57	155.09	151.14	

* $p < .05$. ** $p < .01$.

Bivariate correlations revealed significant and positive relationships between number of incidents of serving intoxicated patrons and the variables "number of secondary servers of alcohol" ($p < .01$) and "number of traditional bartenders" ($p < .01$). These analyses also revealed significant and positive relationships between number of secondary servers and number of traditional bartenders ($p < .01$). Relationships between categorical independent variables were examined by running a series of cross-tabulations (chi-square tests). These analyses revealed statistically significant relationships between several variables described as aversive environmental stimuli, including: appearance of bar, smokiness in bar, temperature in bar, crowding (maximum capacity) in bar, movement throughout bar, overall comfort of bar, clearing of tables and ledges, clearing of bar surfaces, and overall cleanliness of bar. In order to address potential problems associated with multicollinearity in the multivariate analyses, a factor analysis was conducted to see if variables could be combined. This analysis resulted in the extraction of a single underlying factor, which explained 67.2% of the variability in the nine variables. This factor, labeled as "aversive environmental stimuli," was substituted into the multivariate analyses.

In preparation of the multivariate analyses, it was also necessary to dummy code the variable "bouncers and doormen drinking alcoholic beverages." To account for observation periods in which bouncers and doormen were not present, this variable was dummy coded into: variable 1 = bouncers and doormen drinking (1 = yes, 0 = no) and variable 2 = bouncers and doormen not present (1 = not present, 0 = present). "Bouncers and doormen not drinking" was used as the reference category in the multivariate analyses.

Multivariate Analyses

Again, the primary hypothesis guiding this study was that increased numbers of secondary servers working in barrooms and present during individual observation periods would lead to increased incidents of serving intoxicated patrons. Testing this hypothesis involved regressing number of incidents of serving intoxicated patrons on number of secondary servers of alcohol while controlling for other variables demonstrating statistically significant relationships with number of incidents of serving intoxicated patrons in the bivariate analyses. Due to the significant and positive correlation between number of secondary servers and number of traditional bartenders, these variables could not be included in the same ordinary least squares (OLS) regression model. Instead, three OLS models were run, the first examining secondary servers independently from number of traditional bartenders, the second examining number of traditional bartenders independently from number of secondary servers of alcohol, and the third examining "total number of servers of alcohol" (i.e., number of secondary servers and number of traditional bartenders combined). By examining the Adjusted R-Square (R^2) for each model, it was possible to see which grouping of variables accounted for the greatest amount of variance in the dependent variable, number of incidents of serving intoxicated patrons.

Table 3 presents the results for the first OLS model examining the relative influence of "number of secondary servers of alcohol" on "number of incidents of serving intoxicated patrons." Collinearity diagnostics were run on all independent variables going into this model and variance inflation factors were examined in order to access the level of multicollinearity among these variables. All of the variables included in the first OLS model demonstrated VIFs of below 3.0, indicating that multicollinearity was not an issue. As indicated, three variables included in the first OLS model demonstrated significant unique effects on incidents of serving intoxicated patrons. These variables are aversive environmental stimuli ($p < .01$), dancing ($p < .05$), and number of secondary servers of alcohol ($p < .01$). Examining the slopes for these variables reveals that for every one-unit increase in the number of secondary servers of alcohol, the number of incidents of serving intoxicated patrons is predicted to increase by 30.216. This finding supports the primary hypothesis guiding this study that increased numbers of secondary servers working in barrooms leads to increased alcohol service to obviously intoxicated patrons.

Table 3 also reveals that for very one-unit increase in aversive environmental stimuli, the number of incidents of serving intoxicated patrons is predicted to increase by 47.444. In addition, when there is dancing, the number of incidents of serving intoxicated patrons is predicted to increase by 33.089. Examining the standardized beta coefficients for these variables reveals that number of secondary servers of alcohol is the strongest predictor of incidents of serving intoxicated patrons (Beta = .396), followed by aversive environmental stimuli (Beta = .394). The Adjusted R^2 reveals that the variables included in this OLS model explain approximately 72.9% of the variation in the dependent variable incidents of serving intoxicated patrons.

Table 3. OLS regression model 1: Results for "number of secondary servers of alcohol" on "number of incidents of serving intoxicated patrons"

Variable	B	S.E.	Beta	T	P
(Constant)	-9.278	27.443		-.338	.736
Time	9.152	14.513	.038	.631	.529
Bar type	19.064	17.963	.065	1.061	.290
ID check	19.820	16.725	.073	1.185	.238
Aversive environmental stimuli	17.444	7.757	.394	6.116	.000
Dancing	33.089	16.433	.129	2.014	.046
Bouncers and doormen drinking alcoholic beverages	26.964	17.145	.087	1.573	.118
Bouncers and doormen not present	17.367	13.572	.065	1.280	.203
Cover charge	12.561	18.562	.041	.677	.500
Drink specials	-8.864	13.169	-.036	-.673	.502
Food	1.330	11.619	.006	.114	.909
Drinking in rounds	12.459	12.457	.052	1.000	.319
Servers of alcohol (any) drinking alcoholic beverages	17.272	13.891	.070	1.243	.216
Number of secondary servers of alcohol	30.216	4.497	.396	6.719	.000
R^2 = .753 Adjusted R^2 = .729					

Again, due to the significant and positive correlation between number of secondary servers and number of traditional bartenders, these variables could not be included in the same OLS regression model. Table 4 presents the results for the second OLS model examining the relative influence of "number of traditional bartenders" on "number of incidents of serving intoxicated patrons."

Collinearity diagnostics were run on all independent variables going into this model and it was determined that multicollinearity was not an issue. As indicated, three variables included in the second OLS model demonstrated significant unique effects on incidents of serving intoxicated patrons. These variables are aversive environmental stimuli ($p < .01$), bouncers and doormen drinking alcoholic beverages ($p < .05$), and number of traditional bartenders ($p < .01$). Examining the slopes for these variables reveals that for every one-unit increase in the number of traditional bartenders, the number of incidents of serving intoxicated patrons is predicted to increase by 15.510.

Table 4. OLS Regression model 2: Results for "number of traditional bartenders" on "number of incidents of serving intoxicated patrons"

Variable	B	S.E.	Beta	T	P
(Constant)	1.674	33.659		.050	.960
Time	.853	16.354	.004	.052	.958
Bar type	-5.605	19.789	-.019	-.283	.777
ID check	37.352	18.551	.138	2.013	.046
Aversive environmental stimuli	53.027	8.700	.440	6.095	.000
Dancing	22.261	18.600	.087	1.197	.233
Bouncers and doormen drinking alcoholic beverages	45.325	19.004	.146	2.385	.018
Bouncers and doormen not present	25.871	15.348	.096	1.686	.094
Cover Charge	24.514	20.793	.080	1.179	.241
Drink specials	-6.765	15.416	-.027	-.439	.661
Food	5.460	13.097	.023	.417	.677
Drinking in rounds	13.523	14.148	.056	.956	.341
Servers of alcohol (any) drinking alcoholic beverages	8.395	15.559	.034	.540	.590
Number of traditional bartenders	15.510	5.791	.185	2.678	.008
$R^2 = .687$ Adjusted $R^2 = .656$					

Table 4 also reveals that for very one-unit increase in aversive environmental stimuli, the number of incidents of serving intoxicated patrons is predicted to increase by 53.027. Furthermore, when bouncers and doormen are present and drinking alcoholic beverages, the number of incidents of serving intoxicated patrons is predicted to increase by 45.325. Examining the standardized beta coefficients for these variables reveals that aversive environmental stimuli is the strongest predictor of incidents of serving intoxicated patrons (Beta = .440), followed by number of traditional bartenders (Beta = .185). The Adjusted R^2 reveals that the variables included in this OLS model explain approximately 65.6% of the variation in the dependent variable incidents of serving intoxicated patrons, less than that explained by the variables included in the first OLS model (72.9%).

Table 5 presents the results for the third and final OLS model examining the relative influence of "total number of servers of alcohol" on "number of incidents of serving intoxicated patrons." Once again, collinearity diagnostics were run on all independent variables going into this model and again it was determined that multicollinearity was not an issue. As indicated, two variables included in the third OLS model demonstrated significant unique effects on incidents of serving intoxicated patrons. These variables are aversive environmental stimuli (p < .01) and total number of servers of alcohol (p < .01). Examining the slopes for these variables reveals that for every one-unit increase in the total number of servers of alcohol, the number of incidents of serving intoxicated patrons is predicted to increase by 17.646. Furthermore, for very one-unit increase in aversive environmental stimuli, the number of incidents of serving intoxicated patrons is predicted to increase by 47.335.

Table 5. OLS Regression model 3: Results for "total number of servers of alcohol" on "number of incidents of serving intoxicated patrons"

Variable	B	S.E.	Beta	T	P
(Constant)	-35.860	30.331		-1.182	.239
Time	10.699	15.052	.045	.711	.478
Bar type	17.401	18.621	.059	.934	.352
ID check	24.006	17.179	.089	1.397	.165
Aversive environmental stimuli	47.335	8.028	.393	5.897	.000
Dancing	24.675	16.929	.096	1.458	.147
Bouncers and doormen drinking alcoholic beverages	31.450	17.604	.101	1.787	.076
Bouncers and doormen not present	23.885	13.980	.089	1.708	.090
Cover Charge	14.543	19.128	.047	.760	.448
Drink specials	-17.485	13.976	-.070	-1.251	.213
Food	.352	12.012	.001	.029	.977
Drinking in rounds	8.780	12.923	.036	.679	.498
Servers of alcohol (any) drinking alcoholic beverages	15.320	14.304	.062	1.071	.286
Total number of servers of alcohol	17.646	3.002	.400	5.878	.000
$R^2 = .738$ Adjusted $R^2 = .712$					

Examining the standardized beta coefficients for the variables included in Table 5 reveals that total number of servers of alcohol is the strongest predictor of incidents of serving intoxicated patrons (Beta = .400), followed by aversive environmental stimuli (Beta = .393). The Adjusted R^2 reveals that the variables included in this OLS model explain approximately 71.2% of the variation in the dependent variable incidents of serving intoxicated patrons, which is still less than that explained by the variables included in the first OLS model (72.9%).

CONCLUSION

A comparison of Adjusted R-Squares for the OLS models presented in the results section reveals that the grouping of variables contained in the first OLS model (See Table 3) accounted for the greatest amount of variation in the dependent variable, number of incidents of serving intoxicated patrons. Again, variables in this model, which includes number of secondary servers of alcohol, explain approximately 72.9% of the variation in the dependent variable incidents of serving intoxicated patrons. Furthermore, number of secondary servers of alcohol was the strongest predictor of incidents of serving intoxicated patrons in this model (Beta = .396), which supports the primary hypothesis guiding this study that increased numbers of secondary servers working in barrooms leads to increased alcohol service to obviously intoxicated patrons.

Before discussing secondary servers of alcohol and their impact on irresponsible alcohol service and associated problems of alcohol-related harm, it is important to mention the other variables that demonstrated significant unique effects on incidents of serving intoxicated patrons in the multivariate analyses. As mentioned, the factor "aversive environmental stimuli" was also a significant predictor of alcohol service to intoxicated patrons in each of the OLS models (See Tables 3-5). Furthermore, it was the second strongest predictor of alcohol service to intoxicated patrons in the first OLS model (Beta = .394), which again contained the variable number of secondary servers of alcohol. This finding is in keeping with past research that suggests that variables such as excessive heat, crowding, and smoke may lead patrons to drink more heavily and become more intoxicated in order to relieve their discomfort (Fox and Sobol, 2000; Graham, et al., 1980; Homel et al., 1992; Homel and Clark, 1994; Macintyre and Homel, 1997; Quigley, Leonard, and Collins, 2003; Roberts, 1998; Tomsen, 1997; Tomsen, Homel, and Thommeny, 1991).

While the presence of aversive environmental stimuli may be pervasive and problematic in high risk drinking settings, minor modifications of the barroom landscape may reduce their effect on alcohol service to intoxicated patrons, as well as associated problems of alcohol-related harm occurring in and around licensed drinking establishments. For example, problems associated with excessive heat may be avoided by installing air conditioning units or ceiling fans. Similarly, problems with excessive smoke may be addressed by installing "smoke eaters" or other air filtration systems. Homel, Carvolth, Hauritz, McIlwain, and Teague (2004) state that strategies aimed at improving the overall level of comfort within bars are critical to reducing problems with alcohol-related harm. A major component of Graham, Osgood, Zibrowski, Purcell, Gliksman, Leonard, et al.'s (2004) "Safer Bars" initiative in Toronto, Canada was helping owners and managers identify ways to reduce environmental irritants. These researchers suggest that environmental changes designed to reduce or prevent problem behaviors in bars should be easier to market to owners and managers than interventions that focus primarily on tightening controls on alcohol sales.

The variables number of traditional bartenders and total number of servers of alcohol also demonstrated significant unique effects on the dependent variable number of incidents of serving intoxicated patrons (See Tables 4 and 5). Increased numbers of serving staff likely results in increased alcohol sales in most barrooms, as patrons have greater access to alcoholic beverages. This may be especially true in large, packed to capacity bars in which inadequate numbers of serving staff could substantially hinder alcohol sales. It would make sense, therefore, that increased numbers of servers would lead to increased alcohol service to intoxicated bar patrons, as they, like their sober counterparts, would also have greater access to alcoholic beverages. One would also expect increased numbers of servers working in barrooms to make monitoring patrons' alcohol consumption more difficult, as patrons may wander from bar to bar ordering drinks from different serving staff. Related to this, having many servers spread throughout licensed drinking establishments might also make communication between servers more difficult. For example, it would be near impossible for bar staff working in large barrooms with multiple rooms and floors to warn each other about a patron's aggressive drinking or early signs of intoxication, which is important information for those wishing to serve responsibly. According to Roberts (1998), secondary servers of alcohol exacerbate problems with staff communication and patron monitoring, which contributes to increased alcohol service to obviously intoxicated patrons. In the words of a male bartender interviewed in this study:

> I remember this one night I had a guy coming up for a beer about once an hour. Well, after serving him about his fifth beer, a bar-back comes up to me and says, "hey man, be careful how much you serve that guy." Now I'm thinking to myself, there is no way this guy is drunk yet. As it turned out he had been buying shots off of one of our girls (tub-girls) out on the dance floor all night. This can make it tough on us up front who are trying to monitor each person's drinking (Roberts, 1998, p. 99).

In addition to making it more difficult for bar staff to server responsibly, secondary servers reduce the effort it takes to purchase alcoholic beverages. What separates secondary servers from traditional bartenders, however, is that they cater primarily to obviously intoxicated patrons who are either unable or unwilling to wait in long lines at traditional bar stations. According to Roberts (1998), secondary servers are employed for the sole purpose of increasing the flow of alcohol throughout licensed drinking establishments. While several owners and managers interviewed in Roberts' (1998) study of Jersey Shore barrooms reported hiring secondary servers to make things "more convenient" for bar patrons, others were very frank about their desire to sell more alcohol and make more money, regardless of the cost. Again, owners and managers in this study also reported only hiring females for these positions in hopes of increasing alcohol sales to young, college-aged males. Homel and Clark (1994) also identified a desire to maintain and increase profitability as the primary motivations for most of the observed barroom practices in their study of licensed premises in Sydney, Australia. Reiling and Nusbaumer (2006) suggest that the economic motives of bar owners and managers significantly influence the attitudes and practices of servers, as well as the service of alcohol to obviously intoxicated bar patrons, stating:

> Indeed, what the current analysis might be suggesting is that owners who see greater economic benefit that cost in continuing to serve may be more likely to retain servers whose definitions of intoxication are compatible with increased sales to patrons and the willingness to accommodate patrons' continued consumption, even if beyond intoxication (p. 663).

Because of the overriding concern for profit in most barrooms, it would be unlikely for owners and managers to willingly limit or reduce the number of servers they employ, including, and maybe especially, secondary servers of alcohol, as fewer servers would likely result in reduced alcohol sales. Again, Graham et al. (2004) state that interventions that focus primarily on tightening controls on alcohol sales are typically hard sells to bar owners and managers.

RBS programs that train bar staff to serve alcohol responsibly may also be a hard sell, as promoting responsible alcohol service, like limiting the number of servers working in bars, would negatively affect alcohol sales. Research also suggest that servers themselves may not be very receptive to these programs, or responsible beverage service in general, as refusal of alcohol service to already intoxicated bar patrons may lead to loss of gratuities (McKnight, 1991), or some cases, physical altercations with individuals who are unhappy about being "cut off" (Felson et al., 1986). While several evaluations of these programs have shown positive changes in responsible alcohol service (Geller et al., 1987; Gliksman et al., 1993; McKnight and Streff, 1994; Russ and Geller, 1987; Toomey et al., 2001; Wallin et al., 2002), others have shown little increase in refusal of alcohol to intoxicated, or pseudo-intoxicated, bar patrons (McKnight, 1991; Lang et al., 1998; Rydon et al., 1996; Toomey et al., 1999).

Regardless of their potential for reducing irresponsible alcohol and associate problems with alcohol-related harm, RBS programs will not have the desired effect in establishments whose management and staff does not "truly" embrace responsible alcohol service. After all, some bars may participate in such programs just to "look" like they are doing something, possibly for insurance purposes or protection from potential lawsuits. Furthermore, Reiling and Nusbaumer (2006) suggest that one should not assume that all servers lack the ability to identity intoxication. As mentioned, some may simply be choosing to do so due to lack of incentives not to. Furthermore, these researchers suggest that focusing solely on the behaviors of servers puts the onus of responsibility on them rather than on unscrupulous bar owners and managers.

Finally, in considering RBS training as a solution to irresponsible alcohol service, findings from the present study suggest that even servers who are encouraged by barroom management to serve responsibly, and who have acquired such skills through participation in RBS training, may experience difficulty doing so in establishments that employ secondary servers of alcohol. Furthermore, as already mentioned, secondary servers interviewed in Roberts' (1998) study of Jersey Shore barrooms reported being exempt from RBS training, as owners and managers were said to view them not as fully functional servers of alcohol, but rather as "support staff" for traditional bartenders. In order for RBS programs to be effective, they must involve all servers of alcohol, not just traditional bartenders. After all, it makes little sense to expose only select members of a serving staff to RBS training in hopes of reducing irresponsible alcohol service, as bar patrons may simply seek out untrained servers who are less capable of serving responsibly. Furthermore, by not requiring that secondary servers participate in RBS training, owners and managers may inadvertently be sending a message to these staff members that they are somehow less accountable for their actions, which may contribute to their willingness to sell alcohol to intoxicated bar patrons. Again, this assumes that some servers sell alcohol to obviously intoxicated bar patrons not because of an inability to identify signs of intoxication, but rather because of lack of incentives not to. The inclusion of secondary servers in RBS training might also necessitate a complete overhaul of these programs, as they have been and continue to be designed with traditional bartenders in mind, not free-roaming secondary servers, such as shot-girls and cocktail waitresses.

Left to their own devises, it is unlikely that bar owners, managers, or staff members would do much to address irresponsible alcohol service and associated problems of alcohol-related harm occurring in and around these establishments. Knowing this, researchers have suggested the need for greater external regulation of barrooms by law enforcement agencies and alcohol beverage control (ABC) offices. According McKnight and Streff (1994), "...simple enforcement of existing laws and regulations prohibiting service of alcohol to already intoxicated patrons of bars and restaurants represents what appears to be a potentially cost-beneficial way of reducing accidental injury and death" (p. 87). Unfortunately, findings from the present study support claims that there is a gross lack of enforcement of existing liquor laws in many licensed drinking establishments (McKnight, 1991; Nusbaumer and Reiling, 2003; Toomey et al., 1999; Toomey et al., 2004).

In response to weak internal and external regulation of barrooms, a growing number of researchers have proposed and implemented community-based initiatives that seek to bring together all relevant "stakeholders," including bar owners, community members, and government regulators, in coordinated efforts to address problems in and around licensed premises. Stockwell (2001) stresses the importance of community support and involvement in interventions targeting barrooms, stating, "Even with a well-drafted liquor act with ample harm minimization provisions backed up by a well-organized system of regulation may be inadequate if the host community is hostile or otherwise unsupportive" (p. 264). Ross Homel and colleagues' "Surfers Paradise Safety Action Project" implemented in Australia (See Carvolth, Homel, Hauritz, Wortley, Clark, and McIlwain, 1996; Homel and Clark, 1994; Homel, Hauritz, Wortley, McIlwain, and Carvolth, 1997; Macintyre and Homel, 1997) and Kathryn Graham and colleagues' "Safer Bars" program implemented in Canada (See Chandler Coutts, Graham, Braun, and Wells, 2000; Graham, 2000; Graham, Jelley, and Purcell, 2005) provide two examples of community-based initiatives that were successful in facilitating both internal and external regulation of bars and bringing about substantial reductions in irresponsible alcohol service and associated problems of alcohol-related harm. Again, for these initiatives to be successful, researchers such as Reiling and Nusbaumer (2006) suggest that they must seek to address owners' economic incentive to allow the overserving of bar patrons by increasing the economic cost of the consequences for doing so.

The present study was not without limitations or weaknesses. One specific limitation was the use of only one observer during 98 of the 148 observation periods. During observation periods with two observers, any discrepancies in individual coding were discussed and decisions on how to code items for the third and final observation guide were agreed upon. This type of cross validation was not possible during those observation periods with a single observer. However, as mentioned, observers in the present study maintained a high degree of inter-rater reliability throughout the present study. The consistency of observer responses to items contained in the observation guide was likely the result of the observer training and pilot-testing of the data collection instrument that preceded the study. When possible, however, future research should utilize multiple observers, not just to ensure that the individual coding of observation guides remains consistent, but also to better examine the many situational variables present in the barroom environment.

Due to the homogeneity of barrooms (i.e., mostly watering holes) and patrons (i.e., primarily young and white) in the present study, the findings cannot be generalized to all types of drinking establishments or all populations of bar patrons. Whether predictors of alcohol service to obviously intoxicated patrons identified in the present study hold up in barrooms catering primarily to non-white or older bar patrons is a question that future research should attempt to address. Future research might also examine whether situational variables found to be good predictors of alcohol service to obviously intoxicated patrons in the present study hold up in large samples of sports bars, dance clubs, or band bars. The present study provides only limited evidence that they do.

A final limitation of the present study is that it did not assess differences in serving practices among different types of secondary servers of alcohol. Instead, it examined the collective serving practices of four distinct types of secondary servers: shot-girls, tub-girls, cocktail waitresses, and service bar attendants. Future research is needed that examines whether certain types of secondary servers contribute more to irresponsible alcohol service in barrooms than others. Furthermore, it might also be interesting to do a gender-based analysis of servers and serving responses to obviously intoxicated bar patrons. For example, it is unclear if female servers, whether they be traditional bartenders or secondary servers, are any more or less likely to serve alcohol to obviously intoxicated bar patrons than are male servers. Additionally, there is a need for continued studies of serving practices in barrooms throughout the United States, as most barroom research in general has been conducted in locations throughout Canada, Australia, and the UK. While research examining predictors of barroom aggression has been ongoing ever since Graham et al.'s (1980) groundbreaking study of licensed premises in Vancouver, Canada, the present study represents one of only a few studies to examine predictors of alcohol service to obviously intoxicated bar patrons. The identification of situational variables that predict alcohol service to intoxicated barroom patrons is critical to the developed of effective strategies for reducing irresponsible alcohol service in bars, as well as associated problems with alcohol-related harm occurring in and around licensed drinking establishments.

ACKNOWLEDGMENTS

I gratefully acknowledge the Rutgers University School of Criminal Justice and the First Securities Service Corporation for providing funding for this study. The opinions expressed in this article are those of the author and do not necessarily reflect the views or policies of the funding sources. I am also forever grateful to Drs Ronald V. Clarke, Marcus Felson, Michael Maxfield, and Helene Raskin White for their insights, guidance, and feedback during this project. I would also like to acknowledge the second observer in this study, Kimberly Lutter, who served as my second pair of ears and eyes during the data collection. Finally, I would like to thank Phyllis Schultz for her kind and continuous support and assistance.

REFERENCES

Andreasson, S., Lindewald, B., and Rehnman, C. (2000). Over-serving patrons in licensed premises in Stockholm. *Addiction, 95,* 359-363.

Carvolth, R., Homel, R., Hauritz, M., Wortley, R., Clark, J., and McIlwain, G. (1996). Swilling in Surfers: Responsible hospitality practice. *Community Quarterly: Community Development in Action, 38,* 22-28.

Chandler Coutts, M., Graham, K., Braun, K., and Wells, S. (2000). Results of a pilot program for training bar staff in preventing aggression. *Journal of Drug Education, 30,* 171-191.

Donnelly, N, and Briscoe, S. (2003). Signs of intoxication and server intervention among 18 – 39-year-olds drinking at licensed premises in New South Wales, Australia. *Addiction, 98,* 1287-1295.

Felson, R. B., Baccaglini, W., and Gmelch, G. (1986). Bar-room brawls: Aggression and violence in Irish and American bars. In A.Campbell and J. Gibbs (Eds.), *Violent transactions: The limits of personality* (pp. 153-166). Oxford, UK: Basil Blackwell.

Forster, J.L., McGovern, P.G., Wagenaar, A.C., Wolfson, M., Perry, C.L., and Anstine, P.S. (1994). The ability of young people to purchase alcohol without age identification in northeastern Minnesota, USA. *Addiction, 89,* 699-705.

Forster, J.L., Murray, D.M., Wolfson, M., and Wagenaar, A.C. (1995). Commercial availability of alcohol to young people: Results of alcohol purchase attempts. *Preventive Medicine, 24,* 342-347.

Fox, J.G., and Sobol, J.J. (2000). Drinking patterns, social interaction, and barroom behavior: A routine activities approach. *Deviant Behavior: An Interdisciplinary Journal, 21,* 429-450.

Geller, E.S., Russ, N.W., and Delphos, W.A. (1987). Does server intervention training make a difference? *Alcohol Health and Research World, 11,* 64-69.

Gliksman, L., McKenzie, D., Single, E., Douglas, R., Brunet, S., and Moffatt, K. (1993). The role of alcohol providers in prevention: An evaluation of a server intervention programme. *Addiction, 88,* 1195-1203.

Graham, K. (1980). Theories of intoxicated aggression. *Canadian Journal of Behavioral Science, 12,* 141-158.

Graham, K. (2000). Preventive interventions for on-premise drinking: A promising but underresearched area of prevention. *Contemporary Drug Problems, 27,* 593-668.

Graham, K., Jelley, J., and Purcell, J. (2005). Training bar staff in preventing and managing aggression in licensed premises. *Journal of Substance Use, 10,* 48-61.

Graham, K., La Rocque, L., Yetman, R., Ross, T.J., and Guistra, E. (1980). Aggression and barroom environments. *Journal of Studies on Alcohol, 41,* 277-292.

Graham, K., Leonard, K.E., Room, R., Wild, T.C., Pihl, R.O., Bois, C., and Single, E. (1998). Current directions in research on understanding and preventing intoxicated aggression. *Addiction, 93,* 659-676.

Graham, K., Osgood, D.W., Zibrowski, E., Purcell, J., Gliksman, L., Leonard, K., et al. (2004). The effect of the *Safer Bars* programme on physical aggression in bars: results of a randomized control trial. *Drug and Alcohol Review, 23,* 31-41.

Graham, K., Schmidt, G., Gillis, K. (1996). Circumstances when drinking leads to aggression: An overview if research findings. *Contemporary Drug Problems, 23,* 493-557.

Graham, K., West, P., and Wells, S. (2000). Evaluating theories of alcohol-related aggression using observations of young adult bars. *Addiction, 95,* 847-863.

Homel, R. Carvolth, R., Hauritz, M., McIlwain, G., and Teague, R. (2004). Making licensed venues safer for patrons: What environmental factors should be the focus of interventions? *Drug and Alcohol Review, 23,* 19-29.

Homel, R., Hauritz, M., Wortley, R., McIlwain, G., and Carvolth, R. (1997). Preventing alcohol-related crime through community action: The Surfers Paradise Safety Action Project. *Crime Prevention Studies, 7,* 35-90.

Homel, R., and Clark, J. (1994). The prediction and prevention of violence in pubs and clubs. *Crime Prevention Studies, 3,* 1-46.

Homel, R., Tomsen, S., and Thommeny, J. (1992). Public drinking and violence: Not just an alcohol problem. *The Journal of Drug Issues, 22,* 679-697.

Lang, E., Stockwell, T., Rydon, P., and Beel, A. (1998). Can training bar staff in responsible serving practices reduce alcohol-related harm? *Drug and Alcohol Review, 17,* 39-50.

Lang, E., Stockwell, T., Rydon, P., and Lockwood, A. (1995). Drinking settings and problems of intoxication. *Addiction Research, 3,* 141-149.

Macintyre, S., and Homel, R. (1997). Danger on the dance floor: A study of interior design, crowding and aggression in nightclubs. In R. Homel (Ed.), *Policing for prevention: Reducing crime, public intoxication and injury, Crime Prevention Studies* (Vol. 7, pp.91-113). Monsey, New York: Criminal Justice Press.

McKnight, A.J. (1991). Factors influencing the effectiveness of server-intervention education. *Journal of Studies on Alcohol, 52,* 389-397.

McKnight, A.J., and Streff, F.M. (1994). The effect of enforcement upon service of alcohol to intoxicated patrons of bars and restaurants. *Accident Analysis and Prevention, 26,* 79-88.

Nusbaumer, M.R., and Reiling, D.M. (2002). Environmental influences on alcohol consumption practices of alcoholic beverage servers. *The American Journal of Drug and Alcohol Abuse, 28,* 733-742.

Nusbaumer, M.R., and Reiling, D.M. (2003). Where problems and policy intersect: Servers, problem encounters and targeted policy. *Drugs: Education, prevention and policy, 10,* 21-29.

Quigley, B.M., Leonard, K.E., and Collins, R.L. (2003). Characteristics of violent bars and bar patrons. *Journal of Studies on Alcohol, 64,* 765-772.

Reiling, D.M., and Nusbaumer, M.R. (2006). When problem servers pour in problematic places: Alcoholic beverage servers' willingness to serve patrons beyond intoxication. *Substance Use and Misuse, 41,* 653-668.

Roberts, J.C. (1998). *Alcohol-related aggression in the barroom environment: A study of drinking establishments at the Jersey shore,* Unpublished master's thesis, Rutgers University School of Criminal Justice, Newark, New Jersey.

Russ, N.W., and Geller, E.S. (1987). Training bar personnel to prevent drunken driving: A field evaluation. *American Journal of Public Health, 77,* 952-954.

Rydon, P., Stockwell, T., Lang, E., and Beel, A. (1996). Pseudo-drunk-patron evaluation of bar-staff compliance with Western Australian liquor law. *Australian and New Zealand Journal of Public Health, 20,* 290-295.

Stockwell, T. (2001). Responsible alcohol service: Lessons from evaluations of server training and policing initiatives. *Drug and Alcohol Review, 20,* 257-265.

Stockwell, T., Lang, E., and Rydon, P. (1993). High risk drinking settings: The association of serving and promotional practices with harmful drinking. *Addiction, 88,* 1519-1526.

Tomsen, S. (1997). A top night: Social protest, masculinity and the culture of drinking violence. *British Journal of Criminology, 37,* 90-102.

Tomsen, S., Homel, R., and Thommeny, J. (1991). The causes of public violence: Situational "versus" other factors in drinking related assaults. In D. Chappell, P. Grabosky, and H. Strang (Eds.), *Australian violence: Contemporary perspectives* (pp. 177-194). Canberra: Australian Institute of Criminology.

Toomey, T.L., Wagenaar, A.C., Erickson, D.J., Fletcher, L.A., Patrek, W., and Lenk, K.M. (2004). Illegal alcohol sales to obviously intoxicated patrons at licensed establishments. *Alcoholism: Clinical and Experimental Research, 28,* 769-774.

Toomey, T.L., Wagenaar, A.C., Gehan, J.P., Kilian, G., Murray, D.M., and Perry, C.L. (2001). Project ARM: Alcohol risk management to prevent sales to underage and intoxicated patrons. *Health Education and Behavior, 28,* 186-199.

Toomey, T.L., Wagenaar, A.C., Kilian, G., Fitch, O., Rothstein, C., and Fletcher, L. (1999). Alcohol sales to pseudo-intoxicated bar patrons. *Public Health Reports, 114,* 337-342.

Wallin, E., Gripenberg, J., and Andreasson, S. (2002). Too drunk for a beer? A study of overserving in Stockholm. *Addiction, 97,* 901-907.

Wolfson, M., Toomey, T.L., Forster, J.L., Wagenaar, A.C., McGovern, P.G., and Perry, C.L. (1996). Characteristics, policies, and practices of alcohol outlets and sales to youth. *Journal of Studies on Alcohol, 57,* 670-674.

In: Crime and Law Enforcement Issues   ISBN 978-1-61122-877-9
Editor: James E. Hirsch   © 2011 Nova Science Publishers, Inc.

Chapter 9

ACADEMY TRAINING TO RETIREMENT: PERMEATING LEADERSHIP IN POLICE ORGANIZATIONS

*Patrick J. Hughes** and Samuel Morgan*
Central Pennsylvania College

ABSTRACT

Many police organizations across the United States promote leadership training to those individuals that are first line supervisor positions. Many departments, however, do not have a true command structure in place. This in turn introduces the basic patrol officer to many leadership situations. Recent research has shown those not of rank do not receive leadership training. One specific issue is with increasing the patrol officers leadership abilities or behavior for situations that are faced often. Other research uncovers issues relating to the lack of leadership training for not only aspiring first line supervisors but basic patrol as well. First line supervisors have been traditionally viewed as managers rather than leaders. This meta-analysis offers insight to the improvement of police leadership training beginning with the basic police academy curriculum. By doing so, it may improve the overall organizational leadership, but also aid in succession planning as well.

* E-mail: PatrickHughes@centralpenn.edu

Keywords: Leadership, Police leadership, basic academy training, succession planning.

INTRODUCTION

Police organizations and their design appear to be like no other organizations. Usually they are closely compared to that of the military. According to Toch (2008), when describing police organizations he refers to them as "hyper-bureaucratic military organizational attributes-those of formal rank, formal hierarchy, and a chain of unquestioned and unquestioning command" (2008, p. 62). Only until a few years the term "police management" was used to describe what police believed to be leadership. It was perceived that this "police management" displayed what is currently known as leadership. This concept was designated for only those who held a title. Members of these police organizations believe strongly in the maintaining of this design. The top down design of communication, coupled with the centralization of decision-making, is what many in the field believe sets them apart. However, more recent years have shown that managers are not necessarily leaders. Rather, people placed into managerial roles should possess leadership skills, behaviors and knowledge. By employing such a process it could improve an officer's connection with his/her department. It would also aid in succession planning when promoting future leaders within the department.

So do basic patrol officers hold a police leadership position and what is done to measure their leadership behavior and skills? Should these individuals receive basic leadership training given the many situations they encounter from a patrol standpoint? Why do humans naturally follow certain people within given situations? And is this leadership? Police research for the past few decades have dealt with topics, such as leadership styles of those already in positions of authority (Dentsen, 2003; Kuykendall and Unsinger, 1982; and Schwarzwald et al, 2001). Others focused on studying leadership as it pertains to gaining organizational commitment (Eisenberger et al, 1990, Maertz et al, 2007; and Rhoades and Eisenberger; 2002). There has been little research studying the basic academy curriculum and how it can impact organizational leadership and commitment. Police corruption is being seen more frequently, especially from those in chiefs' and front line supervisory positions. There appears to be a need to research and create changes to both the design of these agencies, as well as the training and education available to these "Street level" leaders. There are studies that support and discuss these very concepts.

This article will explore the current lack of leadership training to the basic patrol officer. It will further discuss leadership education and its availability and applicability to basic patrol officers starting from academy training. The last portion draws a connection between leadership education and training from the basic academy could ultimately increase leadership throughout the entire department increasing effective succession planning.

THE PARAMILITARY DESIGN

When focusing specifically on organizational design, police organizations are very structured. Their chart is well defined as well as the roles that accompany those titles. Communication inside these agencies is very top down. It has been debated that this design is needed because the severe situations these men and women encounter. To further that, the liability that accompanies those situations is also great. These organizations and their design do lack wanted items by the officers. Among these are better communication networks, more participation, better decision-making, and better ethical leadership. It is through these officers requesting change that organizational commitment may increase. Jermier and Berkes (1979) write "participative role clarification improved organizational commitment."(p.17). Inside of a militaristic designed organization the levels of rank in management and their importance are often over simplified. Many times they are seen as mere conduit of communication having no real influence on those they manage. It is further argued by Jermier and Berkes (1979) that "obedience socialization and military command supervision across the hierarchal levels appears to distort the nature of police work." (p. 17). Police organizations face change and a changing environment at a faster than normal pace. If this were the case, then the structure must be flexible enough to handle such situations. It must also have the flowing communication and leadership structure firmly embedded into its design. Looking at most police structures the ranks would transcend from Chief, Deputy Chief, Captain, Lieutenant, Sergeant, Corporal, and patrol officer. These levels are seen more in a larger metropolitan or county level department. This is mainly due to the amount of officers employed by the agency. However, in some states, such as Pennsylvania, department size does not allow for such rank design making the levels of sergeant and patrol officer more open to leadership situations. In the most recent (2009) statistics released by the Municipal Police Officers Education and Training Commission of Pennsylvania, there are 1,135 total local departments across the state (Young, 2009). The report further notes among those departments there are

Number of Police Departments by size and the total number of officers:

	# of PDs	# of Officers
1-5 Officers	292	887
6-10 Officers	296	2374
11-30 Officers	447	7522 (Young, 2009, p. 1)

After seeing such statistics it would appear that most departments have a very limited or so command structure at all. It ultimately is then the patrol officer who is thrust situationally into the leadership role. The term "police situational leadership" will be suggested later. In the 1979 study by Jermier and Berkes it is said the "quasi military model makes no provision for the situational effects of a leaders behavior." (p. 17). Miller, Watson, and Webb (2009) echo this by suggesting:

> Although many agencies appear to rely on military arrangements in terms of structure, rank, and hierarchies, this model may not effectively serve police leaders and their respective organizations. Replacing the military model of leadership development with behavioral competency development may be more effectual in leadership and agency performance. (p. 51)

Many in the police arena believe that police organizations differ greatly from their counterparts in the private arena. In a Miller et al study (2009) they compared the scores of police leaders on the California Personality Inventory (CPI) with those from the business world. They found "results indicate very similar scores."(p. 58). Is there truly a difference in how leadership is applied between the policing and business worlds? Some in the police world will argue at their basic cores the two arenas differ in followers, motivation, wanted leadership styles. When the word "entrepreneur" is spoken, many people associate it with the world of business. In a 2008 study by Robert Smith, he introduces the concept of "Entrepreneurial policing" (p. 210). The basis behind such a term is to show that the leadership concepts in policing do not differ greatly from that of business. He suggests:

Entrepreneurial policing is an open style of management linked to, but transcending, individual leadership styles because it can be practiced by everyone within the police service irrespective of rank. This link between the rubrics of entrepreneurship and leadership is vital because for a practical theory of entrepreneurial policing to develop, policing requires the active participation of future generations of police leaders. (2008, p. 212)

This concept not only intertwines the business world with policing, but it also is an example that leadership should be seen at all levels within the police organization. To further support this Smith connects entrepreneurship and policing by reporting it "is action-orientated cognitive human ability, which guides policing as an everyday practice and paradoxically links managerialism and conformity to risk-taking behaviour." (p. 212). Whereas Smith's style is the most recently introduced, other studies (Huberts, Kaptein and Lasthuizen, 2007, Jermier and Berkes, 1979, Krimmel, and Lindenmuth, 2001, Murphy, 2007, and Toch, 2008) have reported other perceived leadership styles versus the most sought and practiced by officers. The styles reported were gathered from the perceptions of officers. Some common themes emerged from these studies. The reported findings in Krimmel and Lindenmuth (2001) found the Machiavellian and bureaucratic styles (p. 484). Jermier and Berkes (1979) attached task to the style utilized. Among the tasks "directive" (p. 4) was perceived, however, "support and "participation were positively related to job satisfaction and organizational commitment" (p.13). Other research such as Huberts et al, (2007) studied how perceived leadership styles effect officer integrity violations. The three styles identified were "openness", "role model", and "strictness" (p. 596). They also concluded "All three aspects of leadership, role modeling, strictness and openness, have a significant effect on the frequency with which corruption occurs." (p. 596). In a 2007 study completed by Murphy he found the most effective perceived style "admired" by officers to be "transformational leadership" (p. 176). Research conducted in 2008 by Toch focused on officers as the "change agents" (p. 60) in police organizations. He argues, "police departments could be well advised to encourage participatory involvement as a vehicle for organizational reform." (p. 61).

As seen above, many studies have researched and identified styles. The patrol officer themselves should be trained and educated in theses styles as well. It appears through employing these styles officers may have stronger organizational commitment. By supervisors and officers engaging in these styles it may strengthen integrity and ethical behavior of the organization. It appears by strengthen leadership among every officer within the department, would of great benefit for many police organizations and their followers. If police organizations need more flexibility and incorporate leadership at all ranks, what then should change, and who should be involved in that change? Further questions that need to be researched further would be; are the basic police academy curriculums teaching cadets these styles, and if not how can that process be improved to do so? Given the many situations officers face on patrol should they receive situational leadership training making them more effective?

BASIC POLICE ACADEMY TRAINING

In this section the questions previously mentioned in the last section will be discussed. For the purpose of this research, the term "police situational leadership" first needs to be defined. "Police situational leadership" is the art of having fellow officers following your plan on how to handle a given situation without a supervisor on-scene. Situational leadership theory as defined by Northouse (2006) as "different situations demand different kinds of leadership… to be an effective leader requires that a person adapt his or her style to the demands of different situations" (p. 91). It is no great secret that in the world of police patrol, officers face an infinite amount of situations. How then do officers deploy for a situation, but no leadership to carry it out quickly.

Police academies nation-wide are not providing the tools to police cadets on how to recognize and develop leadership qualities in themselves or fellow officers. When discussing basic police academy training the word standardization is often associated. All 50 states have created, by legislation, Police Officer Standards and Training commissions (P.O.S.T). It is these commissions that create, implement, and deliver the training they agree is necessary for an officer to succeed upon graduation. Walker and Katz (2002) claimed "this formal training includes both technical skills, such as self defense and use of weapons, as well as knowledge, such as criminal and constitutional law and community policing" (ctd, White, 2008, p. 31). After researching the basic police academy training curriculums for all 50 P.O.S.T.'s nationwide, it was found only four provide initial leadership training module to police cadets. All other academies provide leadership courses to veteran officers usually of rank only. In research conducted by Lowry (1997) and most currently Miller, Watson, and Webb (2009) leadership training was the focus. In the Miller et al study, promotional candidates in Texas attending leadership training in were given the California Psychological Inventory (p. 1). Researchers gave both a pretest and posttest. Researchers here confirm " results indicate that the CPI-260 can be utilized to assess change through training and that, in this case, the training seemed effective at helping the law enforcement executives develop their leadership skills, awareness, and abilities." (Miller, et al, 2009, p.58). In the current processes many candidates never attend, nor are given the opportunity to attend, any of the leadership training prior to testing. Some attributing factors may be; cost, shift coverage, availability of training, or simply not viewed as needed. By taking this a step further to basic police academy training leadership development can begin to be fostered in the cadet.

Smith (2009) said it correctly that "Leadership is a behavioural quality which has to be demonstrated in everyday contexts."(p.221). By further investing time into creating a better leadership training into the basic police academy curriculum's, law enforcement agencies would be improving their organizational design and internal leadership. Ultimately, they would be permeating leadership into every officer of the department. This would be especially beneficial for those smaller departments discussed earlier. It would also be a positive step into planning for the future for many agencies. The concept of succession planning is not often considered of in law enforcement organizations.

PLANNING FOR THE FUTURE

The last question to be investigated would be how do police organizations plan and train future leaders of their departments? The training issue has already been discussed briefly. Many departments do not invest time or money into sending officers to leadership trainings. This could be at a federal, state, or local level. On a federal level the FBI maintains The Leadership Development Institute. Some states may also have some type of leadership seminars or classes. For example, Pennsylvania, through the Penn State Justice and Safety Institute, offers leadership development courses. They offer nine courses in all. (Penn State Justice and Safety Institute) Of these courses seven require the officer must be a rank of lieutenant or higher, one course requires the officer is in the promotional process or promoted, and one course has nothing noted about who may attend. This concept in offering leadership training does not appear to be in line with the concept of succession planning. Instead of supplying training to those choosing or aspiring to be leaders, the training occurs after the officer is chosen from a list of eligible candidates. By educating in that manner it appears to be "placing the cart before the horse." As mentioned earlier officers are seeking certain styles from those that lead them. Rowe (2006) suggests "the quality of police leadership could be improved by more effective methods to identify officers in the middle rankings posts who had the potential to become chief officers" (p.759). He supports that succession planning can increase overall police leadership and it can be done through training all officers. His research sought to "modernise the police workforce, enhancing training and career progression to improve leadership and management skills at all levels of the service." (Rowe, 2006. p.759). This very point seems to contradict the requirements to attend police leadership trainings as well as to those it is offered.

Another issue in succession planning might be that not enough individuals want to be involved. This could be for various reasons such as, satisfaction with the current assignment, monetary loss, lack of support of motivation, poor test taking ability, disconnect with current administration values. In the 2005 study by Murphy officers perceived their promotional process as "not picking the best police officers" and "the testing and selection method" (p. 256). Whatever the reason may be this does not suggest that there is a lack of those that can lead given the right tools and education. Sometimes as stated in 2001 study by Whetstone officers have the "perception that promotions are not based on merit and reflect a hidden administrative agenda."(p.153). However, in the same study "black test takers indicate leadership as a prominent concern."(Whetstone, 2001, p.152). While this is a positive sign of those focusing on leadership, this very notion needs to be permeated through all in the organization. Through proper succession planning this can be possible. According to Murphy (2005), Kesner and Sebora (1994) they agreed on "the importance of creating a seamless continuity in leadership development and succession planning." (p. 254). By law enforcement changing the admission and availability of currently offered leadership training, simultaneously with the basic police academy curriculum, police organizations can begin to assure leadership beginning the moment the officer's graduate from basic training.

CONCLUSION

The purpose of this paper is to open a dialogue on the concept of increasing police leadership to improve succession planning. It attempted to show connectivity of the research of many. Research has shown that the current design of police organizations does not support change easily. However, research also suggests change is wanted by officers. They state how future leaders are chosen, as well the style they wish them to exhibit needs to be improved. Without the systematic approach to recognize new leaders and having a system in place to cultivate their interests or demonstrative talent in this field we will continue to down this path of inaction to the point of no return. The partnership of police recruit training in leadership traits and awareness, coupled with departments having programming and personnel development tracks in place will encourage and stretch new officers to look within themselves for development. In the end this leaves the agency stronger and on firm footing for the future. Police academies' nation-wide are not providing the tools to police cadets on how to recognize and develop leadership qualities in themselves or fellow officers. This critical area of patrol response needs to be addressed at the academy level as patrol officers need to have the tools to develop as their time on the job increases. Without the tools to recognize these traits, police organizations are wasting a vast resource of truly outstanding leaders.

Further research could be warranted, specifically focusing on the leadership trainings offered from states. It also can be built into the organizations overall succession planning of police organizations improving their overall leadership throughout the organization. In this day and age where police corruption is increasing, especially among administration, these changes seemed warranted. Future research could focus solely of succession planning and if in fact it is successful for police agencies who utilize it. As Ian Blair (2003) states about policing in the 21st century " 'our job now is to go out and garner learning from wherever it exists and increase the richness of our leadership culture . . . Police leadership is not essentially different' from all other forms of leadership." (ctd, Ginger, 2003, p. 112).

REFERENCES

Densten, I. L. (2003). Senior police leadership: does rank matter? *Policing*, *26*(3), 400-418.

Eisenberger, R., and Fasolo, R. (1990). Perceived organizational support and employee diligence, commitment, and innovation. *Journal of Applied Psychology*, *75*(1), 51-60.

Ginger, J. D. (2003). Book Review: Police Leadership in the Twenty-First Century: Philosophy, Doctrine, And Developments (R. Adlam and P.

Villiers, Eds.). *International Journal of Police Science and Management,* 6(2), 112-114. Retrieved May 28, 2009, from Academic Search Premier.

Huberts, L., Kaptein, M., and Lasthuizen, K. (2007). A study of the impact of three leadership styles on integrity violations committed by police officers. *Policing: An International Journal of Police Strategies and Management,* 30(4), 587-607.

Jermier, J. M., and Berkes, L. J. (1979). Leader Behavior in a Police Command Bureaucracy: A Closer Look at the Quasi-Military Model. *Administrative Science Quarterly,* 24(1), 1-23. Retrieved June 15, 2009, from http://www.jstor.org/stable/2989873.

Krimmel, J. T., and Lindenmuth, P. (2001). Police Chief Performance and Leadership Styles. *Police Quarterly,* 4(4), 469-484.

Kuykendall, J., and Unsinger, P. C. (1982). The leadership style of police managers. *Journal of Criminal Justice,* 10(4), 311-321.

Lowry, P. E. (1997). Journal of Social Behavior and Personality. *The Assessment Center Process: New Directions,* 12(5), 53-62. Retrieved May 21, 2009, from Academic Search Premier.

Maertz, C. P., Griffeth, R. W., Campbell, N. S., and Allen, D. G. (2007). The effects of perceived organizational support and perceived supervisor support on employee turnover. *The Journal Organizational Behavior,* 28, 1059-1075.

Miller, H. A., Watkins, R. J., and Webb, D. (2009). The use of psychological testing to evaluate law enforcement leadership competencies and development. *Police Practice and Research,* 10(1), 49-60.

Murphy, S. A. (2007). The role of emotions and transformational leadership on police culture: an autoethnographic account. *International Journal of Police Science and Management,* 10(2), 165-178. Retrieved May 26, 2009, from Academic Search Premier.

Murphy, S. A. (2006). Executive development and succession planning: qualitative evidence. *International Journal of Police Science and Management,* 8(4), 253-265. Retrieved May 21, 2009, from Academic Search Premier.

Northouse, P. G. (2006). *Leadership Theory and Practice* (4th ed.). Minneapolis: Sage Publications, Inc.

Penn State Justice and Safety Institute. (n.d.). Retrieved July 01, 2009, from http://jasi.outreach.psu.edu/#index.php?lawenf/Programs.

Rhoades, L., and Eisenberger, R. (2002). Perceived organizational support: A review of the literature. *Journal of Applied Psychology,* 87(4), 698-714.

Rowe, M. (2006). Following the leader: front-line narratives on police leadership. *Policing, 29*(4), 757-767. Retrieved May 21, 2009, from Academic Search Premier.

Schwarzland, J., Koslowsky, M., and Agassi, V. (2001). Captain's leadership type and police officers' compliance to power bases. *European Journal of Work and Organizational Psychology, 10*(3), 273-290.

Smith, R. (2009). Entrepreneurship, Police Leadership, and the. *Journal of Investigative Psychology and Offender Profiling, 5*, 209-225. *Wiley InterScience.* Retrieved May 28, 2009, from www.interscience.wiley.com

Toch, H. (2008). Police officers as change agents in police reform. *Policing and Society, 18*(1), 60-71.

Whetstone, T. S. (2001). Copping out: Why police officers decline to participate in the sergeant's promotional process. *American Journal of Criminal Justice: AJCJ, 25*(2), 147-159. Retrieved May 21, 2009, from Criminal Justice Periodicals.

White, M. D. (2008). Identifying Good Cops Early: Predicting Performance in the Academy. *Police Quarterly, 11*(1), 27-49.

Young, E. B. (2009, September). Police Officers Renew Certifications (R. Grubesky, Ed.). *Municpal Police Officers Education and Training Commission Newsletter, 32*, 1.

INDEX

D

F

G